FORD RANCHERO
MUSCLE PORTFOLIO
1957-1979

Compiled by R M Clarke

ISBN 1 85520 4614

BROOKLANDS BOOKS LTD.
P.O. BOX 146, COBHAM,
SURREY, KT11 1LG. UK

Printed in Hong Kong

Brooklands Books

MOTORING

BROOKLANDS ROAD TEST SERIES

Abarth Gold Portfolio 1950-1971
AC Ace & Aceca 1953-1983
Alfa Romeo Giulietta Gold Portfolio 1954-1965
Alfa Romeo Giulia Coupés 1963-1976
Alfa Romeo Giulia Coupés Gold Port. 1963-1976
Alfa Romeo Spider 1966-1990
Alfa Romeo Spider Gold Portfolio 1966-1991
Alfa Romeo Alfasud 1972-1984
Alfa Romeo Alfetta Gold Portfolio 1972-1987
Alfa Romeo Alfetta GTV6 1980-1986
Allard Gold Portfolio 1937-1959
Alvis Gold Portfolio 1919-1967
AMX & Javelin Muscle Portfolio 1968-1974
Armstrong Siddeley Gold Portfolio 1945-1960
Aston Martin Gold Portfolio 1948-1971
Aston Martin Gold Portfolio 1972-1985
Aston Martin Gold Portfolio 1985-1995
Audi Quattro Gold Portfolio 1980-1991
Austin A30 & A35 1951-1962
Austin Healey 100 & 100/6 Gold Portfolio 1952-1959
Austin Healey 3000 Gold Portfolio 1959-1967
Austin Healey Sprite Gold Portfolio 1958-1971
BMW 6 & 8 Cyl. Cars Limited Edition 1935-1960
BMW 1600 Collection No.1 1966-1981
BMW 2002 Gold Portfolio 1968-1976
BMW 6 Cylinder Coupés & Saloons Gold P. 1969-1976
BMW 316, 318, 320 (4 cyl.) Gold Port. 1975-1990
BMW 320, 323, 325 (6 cyl.) Gold Port. 1977-1990
BMW M Series Gold Portfolio 1976-1997
BMW 5 Series Gold Portfolio 1981-1987
BMW 6 Series Gold Portfolio 1976-1989
BMW Z3 & Z3M Limited Edition
Bricklin Gold Portfolio 1974-1975
Bristol Cars Gold Portfolio 1946-1992
Buick Automobiles 1947-1960
Buick Muscle Cars 1965-1970
Cadillac Allanté 1986-1993
Cadillac Automobiles 1949-1959
Cadillac Automobiles 1960-1969
Checker Limited Edition
Chevrolet 1955-1957
Impala & SS Muscle Portfolio 1958-1972
Corvair Performance Portfolio 1959-1969
El Camino & SS Muscle Portfolio 1959-1987
Chevy II & Nova SS Muscle Portfolio 1962-1974
Chevelle & SS Muscle Portfolio 1964-1972
Caprice Limited Edition 1965-1976
Chevrolet Muscle Cars 1966-1971
Chevy Blazer 1969-1981
Camaro Muscle Portfolio 1967-1973
Chevrolet Camaro & Z-28 1973-1981
High Performance Camaros 1982-1988
Chevrolet Corvette Gold Portfolio 1953-1962
Chevrolet Corvette Sting Ray Gold Port. 1963-1967
Chevrolet Corvette Gold Portfolio 1968-1977
High Performance Corvettes 1983-1989
Chrysler 300 Gold Portfolio 1955-1970
Imperial Limited Edition 1955-1970
Valiant 1960-1962
Citroen Traction Avant Gold Portfolio 1934-1957
Citroen 2CV Gold Portfolio 1948-1989
Citroen DS & ID 1955-1975
Citroen DS & ID Gold Portfolio 1955-1975
Citroen SM 1970-1975
Cobras & Replicas 1962-1983
Shelby Cobra Gold Portfolio 1962-1969
Cobras & Cobra Replicas Gold Portfolio 1962-1989
Crosley & Crosley Specials Limited Edition
Cunningham Automobiles 1951-1955
Daimler SP250 Sports & V-8 250 Saloon Gold P. 1959-1969
Datsun Roadsters 1962-1971
Datsun 240Z & 260Z Gold Portfolio 1970-1978
Datsun 280Z & ZX 1975-1983
DeLorean Gold Portfolio 1977-1995
De Soto Limited Edition 1952-1960
Charger Muscle Portfolio 1966-1974
Dodge Muscle Cars 1967-1970
Dodge Viper Performance Portfolio 1990-1998
ERA Gold Portfolio 1934-1994
Excalibur Collection No.1 1952-1981
Facel Vega 1954-1964
Ferrari Limited Edition 1947-1957
Ferrari Limited Edition 1958-1963
Ferrari Dino 1965-1974
Ferrari Dino 308 & Mondial Gold Portfolio 1974-1985
Ferrari 328 348 Mondial Gold Portfolio 1986-1994
Fiat 500 Gold Portfolio 1936-1972
Fiat 600 & 850 Gold Portfolio 1955-1972
Fiat Pininfarina 124 & 2000 Spider 1968-1985
Fiat X1/9 Gold Portfolio 1973-1989
Fiat Abarth Performance Portfolio 1972-1987
Ford Consul, Zephyr, Zodiac Mk. I & II 1950-1962
Ford Zephyr, Zodiac, Executive Mk. III & IV 1962-1971
Ford Cortina 1600E & GT 1967-1970
High Performance Capris Gold Portfolio 1969-1987
Capri Muscle Portfolio 1974-1987
High Performance Fiestas 1979-1991
High Performance Escorts Mk. I 1968-1974
High Performance Escorts Mk. II 1975-1980
High Performance Escorts 1980-1985
High Performance Escorts 1985-1990
High Perf. Sierras & Merkurs Gold Portfolio 1983-1990
Ford Automobiles 1949-1959
Ford Fairlane Performance Portfolio 1955-1970
Ford Ranchero Muscle Portfolio 1957-1979
Edsel Limited Edition 1957-1960
Falcon Performance Portfolio 1960-1970
Ford Galaxie & LTD Limited Edition 1960-1973
Ford Thunderbird 1955-1957
Ford Thunderbird 1958-1963
Ford GT40 Gold Portfolio 1964-1987
Ford Torino Limited Edition 1968-1974
Ford Bronco 4x4 Performance Portfolio 1966-1977
Ford Bronco 1978-1988
Goggomobil Limited Edition
Holden 1948-1962
Honda CRX 1983-1987
Hudson Limited Edition 1946-1957
International Scout Gold Portfolio 1961-1980
Isetta Gold Portfolio 1953-1964
ISO & Bizzarrini Gold Portfolio 1962-1974
Jaguar and SS Gold Portfolio 1931-1951
Jaguar C-Type & D-Type Gold Portfolio 1951-1960
Jaguar XK120, 140, 150 Gold Portfolio 1948-1960
Jaguar Mk. VII, VIII, IX, X, 420 Gold Port. 1950-1970
Jaguar Mk. 1 & Mk. 2 Gold Portfolio 1959-1969
Jaguar E-Type Gold Portfolio 1961-1971
Jaguar E-Type V-12 1971-1975
Jaguar S-Type & 420 Limited Edition
Jaguar XJ12, XJ5.3, V12 Gold Portfolio 1972-1990
Jaguar XJ6 Series I & II Gold Portfolio 1968-1979
Jaguar XJ6 Series III Perf. Portfolio 1979-1986
Jaguar XJ6 Gold Portfolio 1986-1994
Jaguar XJS Gold Portfolio 1975-1988
Jaguar XJS Gold Portfolio 1988-1995
Jaguar XK8 Limited Edition
Jeep CJ5 & CJ6 1960-1976
Jensen Interceptor Gold Portfolio 1966-1986
Kaiser - Frazer Limited Edition 1946-1955
Lagonda Gold Portfolio 1919-1964
Lancia Aurelia & Flaminia Gold Portfolio 1950-1970
Lancia Fulvia Gold Portfolio 1963-1976
Lancia Beta Gold Portfolio 1972-1984
Lancia Delta Gold Portfolio 1979-1994
Lancia Stratos 1972-1985
Land Rover Series I 1948-1958
Land Rover Series II & IIa 1958-1971
Land Rover Series III 4x4 Perf. Portfolio 1971-1985
Land Rover 90 110 Defender Gold Portfolio 1983-1994
Land Rover Discovery 1989-1994
Land Rover Story Part One 1948-1971
Fifty Years of Selling Land Rover
Lincoln Gold Portfolio 1949-1960
Lincoln Continental 1961-1969
Lincoln Continental 1969-1976
Lotus Sports Racers Gold Portfolio 1953-1965
Lotus Seven Gold Portfolio 1957-1973
Lotus Caterham Seven Gold Portfolio 1974-1995
Lotus Elan Gold Portfolio 1962-1974
Lotus Elan Collection No. 2 1963-1972
Lotus Elan & SE 1989-1992
Lotus Europa Gold Portfolio 1966-1975
Lotus Elite & Eclat 1974-1982
Marcos Coupés & Spyders Gold Portfolio 1960-1997
Maserati 1965-1970
Matra Limited Edition 1965-1983
Mazda Miata MX-5 Performance Portfolio 1989-1996
Mazda RX-7 Gold Portfolio 1978-1991
McLaren F1 Sportscar Limited Edition
Mercedes 190 & 300 SL 1954-1963
Mercedes G-Wagen 1981-1994
Mercedes S & 600 1965-1972
Mercedes S Class 1972-1979
Mercedes 230 • 250 • 280SL Gold Portfolio 1963-1971
Mercedes SLs & SLCs Gold Portfolio 1971-1989
Mercedes SLs Performance Portfolio 1989-1994
Mercury Limited Edition 1947-59
Mercury Comet & Cyclone Limited Edition 1960-1970
Mercury Muscle Cars 1966-1971
Cougar Limited Edition 1967-1973
Messerschmitt Gold Portfolio 1954-1964
MG Gold Portfolio 1929-1939
MG TA & TC Gold Portfolio 1936-1949
MG TD & TF Gold Portfolio 1949-1955
MGA & Twin Cam Gold Portfolio 1955-1962
MG Midget Gold Portfolio 1961-1979
MGB Roadsters 1962-1980
MGB MGC & V8 Gold Portfolio 1962-1980
MGB GT 1965-1980
MGC & MGB GT V8 Limited Edition
MG Y-Type & Magnette ZA/ZB Limited Edition
MGF Limited Edition
Mini Gold Portfolio 1959-1969
Mini Gold Portfolio 1969-1980
Mini Gold Portfolio 1981-1997
High Performance Minis Gold Portfolio 1960-1973
Mini Cooper Gold Portfolio 1961-1971
Mini Moke Gold Portfolio 1964-1994
Morgan Three-Wheeler Gold Portfolio 1910-1952
Morgan Plus 4 & Four 4 Gold Portfolio 1936-1967
Morgan Cars Gold Portfolio 1968-1989
Morris Minor Collection No. 1 1948-1980
Shelby Mustang Muscle Portfolio 1965-1970
High Performance Mustang IIs 1974-1978
High Performance Mustangs 1982-1988
Mustang 5.0L Muscle Portfolio. 1982-1993
Nash & Nash-Healey Limited Edition 1949-1957
Nash-Austin Metropolitan Gold Portfolio 1954-1962
Oldsmobile Automobiles 1955-1963
Oldsmobile Muscle Portfolio 1964-1971
Cutlass & 4-4-2 Muscle Portfolio 1964-1974
Oldsmobile Toronado 1966-1978
Opel GT Gold Portfolio 1968-1973
Opel Manta Limited Edition 1970-1975
Packard Gold Portfolio 1946-1958
Pantera Gold Portfolio 1970-1989
Panther Gold Portfolio 1972-1990
Barracuda Muscle Portfolio 1964-1974
Pontiac Tempest & GTO 1961-1965
GTO Muscle Portfolio 1964-1974
Firebird & Trans-Am Muscle Portfolio 1967-1972
Firebird & Trans-Am Muscle Portfolio 1973-1981
High Performance Firebirds 1982-1988
Pontiac Limited Edition 1949-60
Pontiac Fiero 1984-1988
Porsche 356 Gold Portfolio 1953-1965
Porsche 912 Limited Edition
Porsche 911 1965-1969
Porsche 911 1970-1972
Porsche 911 1973-1977
Porsche 911 SC & Turbo Gold Portfolio 1978-1983
Porsche 911 Carrera & Turbo Gold Port. 1984-1989
Porsche 911 Gold Portfolio 1990-1997
Porsche 924 Gold Portfolio 1975-1988
Porsche 928 Performance Portfolio 1977-1994
Porsche 944 Gold Portfolio 1981-1991
Porsche 968 Limited Edition
Porsche Boxster Limited Edition
Range Rover Gold Portfolio 1970-1985
Range Rover Gold Portfolio 1986-1995
Reliant Scimitar 1964-1986
Renault Alpine Gold Portfolio 1958-1994
Riley Gold Portfolio 1924-1939
R.R. Silver Cloud & Bentley 'S' Series Gold P. 1955-1965
Rolls Royce Silver Shadow Gold Portfolio 1965-1980
Rolls Royce & Bentley Gold Portfolio 1980-1989
Rolls Royce & Bentley Limited Edition 1990-1997
Rover P4 1949-1959
Rover 3 & 3.5 Litre Gold Portfolio 1958-1973
Rover 2000 & 2200 1963-1977
Rover 3500 & Vitesse 1976-1986
Saab Sonett Collection No.1 1966-1974
Saab Turbo 1976-1983
Studebaker Gold Portfolio 1947-1966
Studebaker Hawks & Larks 1956-1963
Suzuki SJ Gold Portfolio 1971-1997
Vitara, Sidekick & Geo Tracker Perf. Port. 1988-1997
Avanti 1962-1990
Sunbeam Tiger & Alpine Gold Portfolio 1959-1967
Toyota Land Cruiser Gold Portfolio 1956-1987
Toyota Land Cruiser 1988-1997
Toyota MR2 Gold Portfolio 1984-1997
Triumph Dolomite Sprint Limited Edition
Triumph TR2 & TR3 Gold Portfolio 1952-1961
Triumph TR4, TR5, TR250 1961-1968
Triumph TR6 Gold Portfolio 1969-1976
Triumph TR7 & TR8 Gold Portfolio 1975-1982
Triumph Herald 1959-1971
Triumph Vitesse 1962-1971
Triumph Spitfire Gold Portfolio 1962-1980
Triumph 2000, 2.5, 2500 1963-1977
Triumph GT6 Gold Portfolio 1966-1974
Triumph Stag Gold Portfolio 1970-1977
TVR Gold Portfolio 1959-1986
TVR Performance Portfolio 1986-1994
VW Beetle Gold Portfolio 1935-1967
VW Beetle Gold Portfolio 1968-1991
VW Beetle Collection No.1 1970-1982
VW Karmann Ghia 1955-1982
VW Bus, Camper, Van 1954-1967
VW Bus, Camper, Van 1968-1979
VW Bus, Camper, Van 1979-1989
VW Scirocco 1974-1981
VW Golf GTI 1976-1986
Volvo PV444 & PV544 1945-1965
Volvo Amazon-120 Gold Portfolio 1956-1970
Volvo 1800 Gold Portfolio 1960-1973
Volvo 140 & 160 Series Gold Portfolio 1966-1975
Forty Years of Selling Volvo
Westfield Limited Edition

BROOKLANDS *ROAD & TRACK* SERIES

Road & Track on Alfa Romeo 1964-1970
Road & Track on Alfa Romeo 1971-1976
Road & Track on Alfa Romeo 1977-1989
Road & Track on Aston Martin 1962-1990
R & T on Auburn Cord and Duesenburg 1952-84
Road & Track on Audi & Auto Union 1952-1980
Road & Track on Audi & Auto Union 1980-1986
Road & Track on Austin Healey 1953-1970
Road & Track on BMW Cars 1966-1974
Road & Track on BMW Cars 1975-1978
Road & Track on BMW Cars 1979-1983
R & T on Cobra, Shelby & Ford GT40 1962-1992
Road & Track on Corvette 1953-1967
Road & Track on Corvette 1968-1982
Road & Track on Corvette 1982-1986
Road & Track on Corvette 1986-1990
Road & Track on Ferrari 1975-1981
Road & Track on Ferrari 1981-1984
Road & Track on Ferrari 1984-1988
Road & Track on Fiat Sports Cars 1968-1987
Road & Track on Jaguar 1950-1960
Road & Track on Jaguar 1961-1968
Road & Track on Jaguar 1968-1974
Road & Track on Jaguar 1974-1982
Road & Track on Jaguar 1983-1989
Road & Track on Lamborghini 1964-1985
Road & Track on Lotus 1972-1983
R & T on Mazda RX-7 & MX-5 Miata 1986-1991
Road & Track on Mercedes 1952-1962
Road & Track on Mercedes 1963-1970
Road & Track on Mercedes 1971-1979
Road & Track on Mercedes 1980-1987
Road & Track on MG Sports Cars 1949-1961
Road & Track on MG Sports Cars 1962-1980
R & T on Nissan 300-ZX & Turbo 1984-1989
Road & Track on Pontiac 1960-1983
Road & Track on Porsche 1951-1967
Road & Track on Porsche 1968-1971
Road & Track on Porsche 1972-1975
Road & Track on Porsche 1975-1978
Road & Track on Porsche 1979-1982
Road & Track on Porsche 1985-1988
R & T on Rolls Royce & Bentley 1950-1965
R & T on Rolls Royce & Bentley 1966-1984
Road & Track on Saab 1972-1992
R & T on Toyota Sports & GT Cars 1966-1984
R & T on Triumph Sports Cars 1953-1967
R & T on Triumph Sports Cars 1967-1974
R & T on Triumph Sports Cars 1974-1982
Road & Track on Volkswagen 1951-1968
Road & Track on Volkswagen 1968-1978
Road & Track on Volkswagen 1978-1985
Road & Track on Volvo 1957-1974
Road & Track on Volvo 1977-1994
R & T - Henry Manney at Large & Abroad
R & T - Peter Egan's "Side Glances"
R & T - Peter Egan "At Large"

BROOKLANDS *CAR AND DRIVER* SERIES

Car and Driver on BMW 1955-1977
Car and Driver on Corvette 1978-1982
Car and Driver on Corvette 1983-1988
C and D on Datsun Z 1600 & 2000 1966-1984
Car and Driver on Ferrari 1955-1962
Car and Driver on Ferrari 1963-1975
Car and Driver on Ferrari 1976-1983
Car and Driver on Mopar 1956-1967
Car and Driver on Mopar 1968-1975
Car and Driver on Mustang 1964-1972
Car and Driver on Pontiac 1961-1975
Car and Driver on Porsche 1955-1962
Car and Driver on Porsche 1963-1970
Car and Driver on Porsche 1970-1976
Car and Driver on Porsche 1977-1981
Car and Driver on Porsche 1982-1986
Car and Driver on Volvo 1955-1986

RACING

Le Mans - The Bentley & Alfa Years - 1923-1939
Le Mans - The Jaguar Years - 1949-1957
Le Mans - The Ferrari Years - 1958-1965
Le Mans - The Ford & Matra Years - 1966-1974
Le Mans - The Porsche Years - 1975-1982
Mille Miglia - The Alfa & Ferrari Years - 1927-1951
Mille Miglia - The Ferrari & Mercedes Years - 1952-57

A COMPREHENSIVE GUIDE

BMW 2002

BROOKLANDS *PRACTICAL CLASSICS* SERIES

PC on Austin A40 Restoration
PC on Land Rover Restoration
PC on Metalworking in Restoration
PC on Midget/Sprite Restoration
PC on MGB Restoration
PC on Sunbeam Rapier Restoration
PC on Triumph Herald/Vitesse

BROOKLANDS *HOT ROD* 'MUSCLECAR & HI-PO ENGINES' SERIES

Chevy 265 & 283
Chevy 302 & 327
Chevy 348 & 409
Chevy 350 & 400
Chevy 396 & 427
Chevy 454 thru 512
Chrysler Hemi
Chrysler 273, 318, 340 & 360
Chrysler 361, 383, 400, 413, 426, 440
Ford 289, 302, Boss 302 & 351W
Ford 351C & Boss 351
Ford Big Block

BROOKLANDS RESTORATION SERIES

Auto Restoration Tips & Techniques
Basic Bodywork Tips & Techniques
BMW 2002 Restoration Guide
Classic Camaro Restoration
Chevrolet High Performance Tips & Techniques
Chevy Engine Swapping Tips & Techniques
Chevy-GMC Pickup Repair
Chrysler Engine Swapping Tips & Techniques
Engine Swapping Tips & Techniques
Ford Pickup Repair
Land Rover Restoration Tips & Techniques
MG 'T' Series Restoration Guide
MGA Restoration Guide
Mustang Restoration Tips & Techniques

MOTORCYCLING

BROOKLANDS ROAD TEST SERIES

AJS & Matchless Gold Portfolio 1945-1966
BMW Motorcycles Gold Portfolio 1950-1971
BMW Motorcycles Gold Portfolio 1971-1976
BSA Singles Gold Portfolio 1945-1963
BSA Singles Gold Portfolio 1964-1974
BSA Twins A7 & A10 Gold Portfolio 1946-1962
BSA Twins A50 & A65 Gold Portfolio 1962-1973
BSA & Triumph Triples Gold Portfolio 1968-1976
Ducati Gold Portfolio 1960-1973
Ducati Gold Portfolio 1974-1978
Ducati Gold Portfolio 1978-1982
Honda CB750 Gold Portfolio 1969-1978
Laverda Gold Portfolio 1967-1977
Moto Guzzi Gold Portfolio 1949-1973
Norton Commando Gold Portfolio 1968-1977
Triumph Bonneville Gold Portfolio 1959-1983
Vincent Gold Portfolio 1945-1980

BROOKLANDS *CYCLE WORLD* SERIES

Cycle World on BMW 1974-1980
Cycle World on BMW 1981-1986
Cycle World on Ducati 1982-1991
Cycle World on Harley-Davidson 1962-1968
Cycle World on Harley-Davidson 1978-1983
Cycle World on Harley-Davidson 1983-1987
Cycle World on Harley-Davidson 1987-1990
Cycle World on Harley-Davidson 1990-1992
Cycle World on Honda 1962-1967
Cycle World on Honda 1968-1971
Cycle World on Honda 1971-1974
Cycle World on Husqvarna 1966-1976
Cycle World on Husqvarna 1977-1984
Cycle World on Kawasaki 1966-1971
Cycle World on Kawasaki Off-Road Bikes 1972-1979
Cycle World on Kawasaki Street Bikes 1972-1976
Cycle World on Norton 1962-1971
Cycle World on Suzuki 1962-1970
Cycle World on Suzuki Off-Road Bikes 1971-1976
Cycle World on Suzuki Street Bikes 1971-1976
Cycle World on Triumph 1967-1972
Cycle World on Yamaha 1962-1969
Cycle World on Yamaha Off-Road Bikes 1970-1974
Cycle World on Yamaha Street Bikes 1970-1974

MILITARY

BROOKLANDS MILITARY VEHICLES SERIES

Allied Military Vehicles No.2 1941-1946
Complete WW2 Military Jeep Manual
Dodge Military Vehicles No.1 1940-1945
Hail To The Jeep
Military & Civilian Amphibians 1940-1990
Off Road Jeeps: Civilian & Military 1944-1971
US Military Vehicles 1941-1945
US Army Military Vehicles WW2-TM9-2800
VW Kubelwagen Military Portfolio 1940-1990
WW2 Jeep Military Portfolio 1941-1945

12068

CONTENTS

ACKNOWLEDGEMENTS

This latest Brooklands book on the much-liked Ford Ranchero replaces our earlier and smaller volume which has now sold out. Demand for the title remained strong enough for us to dig a little more deeply into our archives this time around, and we came up with an extra 40 pages of material which was not in the original 100-page book. So here it all is, now upgraded to make one of our Muscle Portfolio volumes.

Like all the Brooklands books of its type, this one exists because of the kind co-operation of those leading magazines which originally published the copyright material it contains. We are therefore pleased to acknowledge the generosity of *Car Craft, Car Life, Car South Africa, Cars, Classic American, Custom Car UK, Ford High Performance, Hot Rod, Motor Life, Motor Trend, Pickups and Mini-Trucks, Popular Mechanics, PV4, Road Test* and *Special Interest Autos*.

Our thanks also go to Tony Beadle, the well known writer and American car enthusiast who who so graciously came to our aid with regard to supplying our front cover photograph.

R.M. Clarke

The Ranchero lasted a formidable 22 years in production, and in that period it captured the affections of thousands of buyers, some of them needing a straightforward utility but - particularly towards the end - many also seeking a sporty truck. The idea of the coupe-utility dated back to the pre-war era, and the Ranchero was introduced in 1957 to give Ford another weapon in the sales battle against Chevrolet. That year, it was a close-run thing: Ford out-produced Chevy but Chevy sold a tiny number of extra cars. Nevertheless, this time Chevy had been out-pointed, and it would be two years before the GM division came up with its El Camino to counter the Ford truck.

The Ranchero line switched sizes and platforms several times over the years. As introduced, it was based on the full-size Custom sedans with their 116-inch wheelbase (and more specifically on the Ranch Wagon derivative). However, disappointing sales over the 1957-1959 period persuaded Ford to switch to the compact Falcon for the Ranchero's platform, and for the next few years the truck was on a wheelbase of 109.5 inches. Sales immediately rose. The vogue for compacts waned, however, and by 1967 the Ranchero was wearing the front-end sheet metal of the big Fairlane to give it an intermediate image and to allow it to compete with Chevy's strong-selling El Camino.

Over the next decade, the Ranchero became progressively more sporty to suit the tastes of the truck market, taking on elements of the Torino and, from 1977, the front-end sheet metal of the LTD II. However, the market was already changing. Sport-utilities were the big sellers, alongside small pick-ups, and the Ranchero was neither. So the line made its last appearance in 1979.

Options were the name of the game for the Ranchero, and it was possible to create an exciting and glamourous piece of machinery from the Ford extras list. Many of the Rancheros from the 22-year period are as practical today as ever, and increasing numbers are finding enthusiastic owners from a different generation. Owners and would-be owners will find some fascinating material about their favourite trucks between the covers of this book.

James Taylor

FORD RANCHERO PICKUP IS IDEAL CROSS BETWEEN NORMAL PICKUP AND STATION WAGON, HAS LOOKS, COMFORT AND GOOD UTILITY

RANCHERO ROAD TEST

FOR THE person who has always wanted a pickup but is balked by the looks or riding qualities inherent in normal pickup trucks, Ford has come to the rescue. And what a job they have done.

Call it what you will; a passenger car with a pickup bed, a pickup built like a passenger car, or a station wagon with the back portion of the top removed, which it actually is, the Ranchero is both useful and decorative.

Combining the looks and comfort of a passenger car with the ruggedness and utility of a pickup has necessitated some compromises, but not as many as might be expected.

THREE ENGINES are available in the Ranchero; the economical 144 hp six, a 190 hp V-8, and the 212 hp Thunderbird V-8 for owners who are interested in performance.

The rated load carrying capacity of the Ranchero is 1190 lbs., according to Ford advertising. and the maximum gross vehicle weight is 4600 lbs. While testing the Ranchero we weighed it at a certified public scale and the total weight, with one-half tank of gas, was 3640 lbs.

Fore and aft weight distribution (still with one-half tank of gas) came to 2100 lbs. on the front wheels and 1560 on the rear, giving a discrepancy (from the total weight) of 20 lbs., which we were informed by the scale operator happens quite often when weighing cars or trucks one end at a time.

As mentioned earlier, the Ranchero is basically a station wagon with the rear portion of the top removed and actually has the station wagon sub flooring under the pickup bed. For the custom enthusiast, and there are many pickups sold to customers who wish to customize rather than use the truck for work, the spare tire could be moved from its present location behind the passenger's seat, to the location at the rear used by the station wagon. This would necessitate fabricating some means of quicker access to the compartment, which is now covered by a bolt-down panel. Hinging the panel is one solution, and several other methods could undoubtedly be figured out by each owner.

For those not interested in hauling a load of any great size, moving the spare tire to the rear would help balance the Ranchero a little better as it now has 57.3 per cent of the weight on the front wheels. Ford has undoubtedly balanced it this way purposely, as the addition of a load

in the bed would distribute the weight more evenly between the front and rear axles. Moving the spare from the passenger compartment would also double the "lockable" luggage space in the cab. At the present time, the luggage space consists of the area behind the driver's seat, next to the spare tire. Much luggage could of course be carried in the bed but has no provision for locking.

The model tested was the Custom Ranchero with the Thunderbird 212 hp V-8 engine, Fordomatic transmission, power steering, and a radio. No other extras were installed, but any extra available for Ford passenger cars can be obtained on the two Ranchero models.

Rancheros can be distinguished from Custom Rancheros by the absence of side trim and bright metal around the top of the lbody and rear of cab. Two engines are available in the Ranchero; the 144 hp six, or the 190 hp V-8. Custom Ranchero models can be powered by either the 144 hp six or the 212 hp Thunderbird V-8.

Both Ranchero models are on the 116 inch wheelbase chassis and have the same springs as the Ford station wagons. These are somewhat stiffer than the normal passenger car springs but the ride is affected so little as to be almost unnoticeable.

Actually, the stiffer springs add a measure of safety to the car, in addition to increasing its load-carrying capacity, by reducing the body lean on curves and eliminating much of the pitching action shown by normal passenger cars on certain types of roads.

CONTINUED ON PAGE 7

LUGGAGE SPACE inside cab and behind seats is limited; it also houses the spare tire. The area, however, is easily accessible. Although base price of the Ranchero has not yet been reported, it'll probably be around $2,000, maybe more.

Pretty PICKUP From FORD

REMEMBER when a pickup truck was just that—a truck? Recent years have seen pickups take on new glamour, however, and Ford's new Ranchero represents the production ultimate in that direction.

The Ranchero looks, rides and handles more like a passenger car but has all the practical, workhorse features of a normal pickup.

It's 16 inches lower and 18 inches longer than a 1956 Ford pickup. From front bumper to midpoint, the Ranchero is a dead ringer for a 1957 Ford passenger car. From midpoint back, it is a highly styled pickup truck—but with more load space and a lower loading height than conventional half-ton pickups.

The Ranchero is the first truck in the industry to have side body trim with two-tone color scheme just like its companion car lines. A gold anodized aluminum trim strip is offered as an option and interiors are finished in the same style as Ford's 1957 station wagons.

The vehicle's payload capacity is nearly three-quarters of a ton. Instead of a pickup box mounted on the rear of the cab as in conventional truck design, the Ranchero's entire body is welded together into an integral structure. (This does not mean unit body-frame construction is used, however, because there is a separate frame.) This, together with a double steel floor, gives it extra strength and rigidity.

The new pickups come in two models.

FIRST OF ITS KIND is the Ranchero, a hybrid passenger car and pickup. The development may be quite logical in the utility field, since the glorification of station wagons is causing some luxury versions to lose their dual-purpose characteristics in deference to looks.

6

The regular Ranchero has less ornate trim and uses Ford's 272-cubic-inch, 190-hp V-8. Custom Rancheros have Fairlane passenger car side trim and use the 212-hp V-8 with displacement of 292 cubic inches. (Either model can be had with Ford's 144-hp Six also.) Standard, overdrive or Fordomatic transmissions are available.

The Ranchero chassis is similar to that used by Ford passenger cars and is the first Ford truck to use ball-joint front suspension.

Actually the pickup is cobbled from Ford Ranchwagon components. It has the same wheelbase, 116 inches. Overall height is 58.7 inches and length is 203.5 inches.

No price had been announced, but Rancheros are expected to cost more than regular Ford pickups and less than station wagons.

Appearance of the Ranchero is indicative of increasing interest in pickup trucks which began a few years back.

Customizing enthusiasts "discovered" pickups and began using them as a basis for their art more frequently—which has undoubtedly been a big factor in sparking the trend to more attractive trucks of this type.

Chevrolet was the first to attempt to market a distinctive pickup, the Cameo Carrier, and its success was a factor in Ford's development of the Ranchero. There will be more of these "pretty pickups" in the future, too. ●

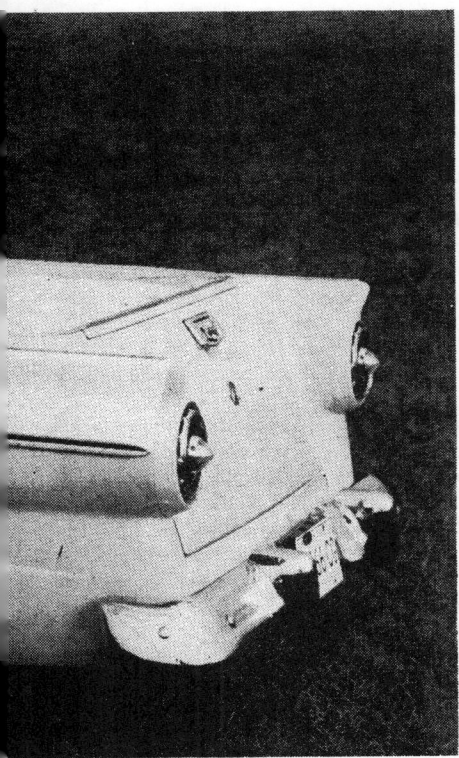

CARGO SPACE in the Ranchero is not quite as large in area as a standard pickup, but the maximum payload is rated at 1,000 lbs., making the Ranchero a useful vehicle for most purposes for which a pickup is designed. And, it is a much more comfortable vehicle to drive.

CONTINUED FROM PAGE 5

Handling characteristics of the Ranchero are, generally speaking, very good. However, I found it possible to get over-confident of the car's cornering ability due to the steering ease afforded by the power steering unit. This is not meant to be a criticism of Ford only, but of power steering-equipped cars in general. With power steering it is so effortless to hold the wheel in what you assume to be the correct amount of turn for a fast curve, that you tend to forget the centrifugal force being exerted on almost 4,000 lbs of mass. Even though you can hold the wheel, with only one finger, in the correct position for the most violent turns, the law of physics is still working on the car in spite of power steering. It would be very easy to drift right off the road, with the wheels still in the correct attitude to take the turn under other conditions.

Acceleration of the Ranchero was good, and compares quite closely to the Ford sedan tested by MOTOR LIFE (reported in the January issue). The averages of two-way acceleration runs were: 0-30 mph in 3.5 seconds, 0-45 in 6.2 and 0-60 in 11.3.

These times undoubtedly could have been improved with some additional weight on the rear wheels, as a considerable amount of wheelspin was induced, even when starting with the selector lever in drive range. Rapid starts with the selector in low range was useless due to wheelspin, so it was not used in the acceleration tests.

A gas mileage check over 525 miles of combined town and country driving gave 14.6 mpg which is not at all bad by present day standards. Obviously the mileage could be improved, if so desired, by buying the Ranchero with the smaller V-8 engine or the six, and using a standard three speed transmission with overdrive in place of the Fordomatic. The rear end ratio in the Ranchero tested was 3.56-to-1 which is standard on models equipped with automatic transmissions.

Fourteen inch wheels are used on the Ranchero models, just as on the passenger cars in the Ford line for 57. Ford's regular pickups are equipped with 15 inch wheels.

Visibility from the driver's seat is excellent (better by far than any known station wagon or passenger car with the exception of a convertible with the top down) and is probably surpassed only by the standard pickup in which the seats are much higher off the ground.

Taking everything into consideration, the Ranchero was a pleasure to drive in either city traffic or highway cruising. Freeway or dirt roads made little difference to the ball joint front suspension which, by the way, is probably the only truck in the world with ball joint front suspension.

The attention attracted by the Ranchero wherever it was driven suggested that it would be an excellent attention-getter for small commercial firms. Any company that needs a pick-up could do much worse than advertise its name on the side of a Ranchero. ●

RANCHERO TEST DATA

Test Car: Custom Ranchero
Basic Price: $2224.44
Engine: 292 cubic inch ohv V-8
Carburetion: Single two throat
Compression Ratio: 9.1 to 1
Horsepower: 212 @ 4500 rpm
Torque: 297 @ 2700 rpm
Dimensions: 116 inch wheelbase, tread 59 inch front—56.4 inch rear, overall length 203.5 inches (211.3 inches with tailgate down) Height (with maximum load) 58.7 inches
Weight as tested: 3640 lbs.
Transmission: Fordomatic three-speed automatic
Acceleration: 0 to 30—3.5 sec., 0 to 45— 6.2 sec., 0 to 60—11.3 sec. (average figures)
Speedometer Correction: Actual 30, 45 and 60 is 32, 50 and 66 on the speedometer
Gas Mileage: 14.6 mpg

BARREN WASTELAND just 10 years ago, sunny clime, 3000-foot altitude, and promotional push make Apple Valley an embryo city.

Ford's new all-purpose Ranchero

EVEN IF your luggage is not as desirable as these Halliburton aluminum cases, you'll have to stow them behind the driver's seat and elsewhere in the cab each time you park, to prevent theft. Space behind the passenger's seat is occupied by the spare tire and tools. See page 51 for a custom idea.

"A CUSTOM PICKUP? . . . A real beauty! . . . A station wagon with the top off . . . A passenger car with a pickup bed . . . I *like* that! . . ." These are just some of the early and spontaneous reactions I've had to the Ford Ranchero I've been driving through city streets, over freeways, open highways, mountain grades, and desert roads for the past week.

Of course, it's too early to tell just how it's going to go over, and somewhat foolish to speculate. Nevertheless, I'll go on record with a prognostication that the Ranchero will be copied in principle by other manufacturers—it's too good to pass up.

Actually, the Ranchero could be called anything you like and you'd be partly right: it's a truck, in that it has a pickup bed and is distributed through Ford's Truck Division; it's a ". . . wagon with the top off . . ." in that the 116-inch chassis is the same as that for the station wagon (including the stiffer springs); it's a ". . . car with a pickup bed . . ." for the entire front section, including the interior, is basically the same as a Ford car, with minor modifications such as the tire stowage behind the passenger's seat.

With a choice of three engines in the Ranchero, you can do just about any job that needs doing: economy hauling and economy transportation is best with the 144-hp, ohv six; if you like the sound and the fury of a V8 you can get the 190-hp engine that goes with Customline Fords; if you want more go— up to 110 mph, acceleration to 60 mph from standstill in about 11.5 seconds, overall fuel economy in the 15-17 mpg range— you can order your Ranchero with the 212-hp "Thunderbird" engine.

In city driving, you'll have better vision than in most cars, though not as good as in ordinary pickups because of the advantage the latter have in their greater height. With the back of the cab close to you, and the large rear window to see out of, it's almost as if you could touch everything behind you. You can back into tight spots by gauging yourself through use of the flush-side side rails. The rest of your driving can be made as convenient as your pocketbook will allow: no shifting with Fordomatic, parking ease with power steering, less braking effort with power brakes, no window cranking with power windows, no seat pushing with power seats.

Over the road you can cruise as quickly and as easily as in any "car." Bad dips on desert roads that come up unexpectedly won't make the Ranchero misbehave. When encountering sudden bends in the road or when driving continuously through winding, hilly country, you won't have to back off for fear of

8

leaving the road; its attitude in turns, including the small amount of body lean, is remarkably good. It seems a shame, though, that it takes almost five turns lock to lock; less turns would mean less work and a more positive feel.

On the way back from Apple Valley Inn, where I guested for the weekend, I stopped at Jim Davies' Wood Yard for some firewood and a trial of the Ranchero with a load. Up to just slightly over the side rails made about ⅓-cord, or some 700 pounds of extra weight. From the wood yard I drove over roads where the asphalt was chewed out in big bitefuls, over dirt washboards that would shake out any loose fillings, and over other roads that were reminiscent of a roller coaster.

On all these roads the Ranchero's behavior was better than when it was unloaded. With the added weight over the rear wheels it hugged the road closer and took some of the float out of the ride. Over washboard it stayed in line; empty at speeds above 30 mph the rear end would begin to come around.

While I was at the Apple Valley Inn soaking in sunshine and shooting pictures, a couple was drawn over by the newness of the Ranchero. After a fairly thorough once-over and a few questions, the husband stated his desire to trade in his year-old car on the Ranchero, while his wife was not so easily convinced. "Who," she asked, "do you expect will buy this type of car?" My reply was that it should appeal, for example, to couples living in areas like the high desert region of Apple Valley. For many such pioneering couples the need for a full-sized sedan doesn't exist, but the necessity for a more practical-type vehicle does. The Ranchero gives the room and "personal" feel of a Thunderbird, the comfort of a sedan, and the load-carrying capacity of a small pickup. It also seems to me that with the addition of a few clever accessories (a metal tarpaulin to cover the bed, stake sides to allow the carrying of a bulkier load, a camper unit, and better use of water space), the Ranchero will reach out to an ever-larger market.

driving around **with walt woron**

ONE WAY to hide luggage and other items from prying eyes and the weather might be a tarpaulin, such as this slick one on John Fahy's moderately customized Ranchero.

THE TRUCK bed measures 6.0 by 4.5 by 1.2 feet, giving a volume of 32.4 cubic feet. Here it's loaded with ⅓-cord of firewood.

PHOTOS BY BOB D'OLIVO

SUB-FRAME OF RANCHERO is same as wagon, but is hidden by bolted-down floor. Wagon's wheel well (above) could serve as optional or permanent spare tire location by hinging floor. Tools could be stored in compartment astride driveshaft (left), with access from cab interior through doors over existing cutouts.

Photo Story by Eric Rickman

FORDILLAC...1957-58

Ever popular practice of stuffing a Cadillac engine in a Ford chassis continues, but the

Dropping the big displacement overhead valve V8's into chassis' formerly occupied by flathead engines has been going on for quite some time now and it has become commonplace in nearly all parts of the U.S. Another type of engine swapping is also taking place though and we predict that it, too, will reach major proportions before long. The latest practice is to buy a new car in the low price field and then substitute an engine from one of the higher horsepower models. A good example is the '57 Ford Ranchero on these pages. The car was taken to Wally Baynes' garage in Los Angeles, where custom engine installations are a specialty, and a 365-cubic-inch '56 Cadillac engine was fitted in place of the 292-inch Ford V8.

Late Ford chassis' are particularly troublesome when it comes to engine swapping since they have a large tubular crossmember and steering linkage that passes directly beneath the engine. Ford engines have their oil sump ahead of this crossmember and most of the larger displacement V8's have their sump at the rear of the engine, so the main point of interference was at

this member. Late Cad V8's have a windshield wiper motor vacuum boost pump on the bottom of the oil pump in conjunction with the fuel pump. Wally's first move was to eliminate the vacuum pump from the bottom of the oil pump which permitted him to cut a 1½-inch section from the sump portion of the pan. This gave a shallower sump which combined with a one-inch higher engine position than the Ford engine to give adequate steering linkage clearance. With the Cad oil capacity lessened, the sump portion of a Ford pan was grafted to the fore part of the Cad pan ahead of the troublesome crossmember and the oil pump pickup lengthened to reach the new sump ahead of the member.

Another point of interference to be solved was the starter motor versus the crossmember. The standard '56 starter motor hit the member but a '57 Cad motor was slightly shorter and fit fine except for mounting screws. The threaded starter mounting holes were drilled through the '55 Cad bell housing so that the motor could be secured from the rear side of the housing with

10

Late model Cadillac engines do not have the end of the crankshaft bored to accept a pilot bearing, so it was necessary to machine a pilot bearing adaptor to fit the end of the crank.

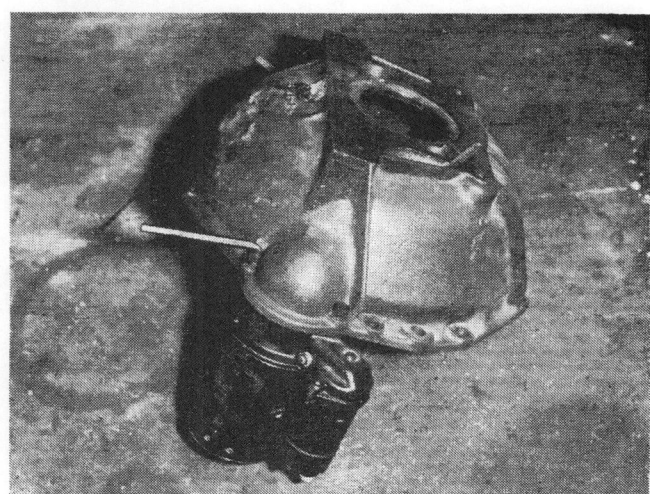

Late Cad starter motor is shorter than the early versions but cap screws enter from the rear of the bell housing. Threaded holes in housing were drilled out and Allen head screws used.

One of the hardest parts of the engine swap was to section the Cad oil pan, then add a Ford pan sump to the front portion. Oil pickup tube from pump was extended to new pan sump.

A vane type vacuum booster pump for the windshield wiper motor bolts to the bottom of the Cad oil pump. By removing this pump, it was possible to section pan for better clearance.

VERSION

method has been revised to keep pace with the times.

Allen head cap screws.

The transmission used with the Cad engine was a reworked '53 Cad Hydra-Matic built by Transmission Specialists, Los Angeles, but any 1954-55 Cad or Chevy truck Hydra-Matic can be used without modifications. The Cad or Chevy truck units are required since they have main drive and torus member shafts that are shorter than the pre-'54 H-M's. The '54 or '55 Cad flywheel can be bolted to the crankshaft or a 1954-56 standard H-M Olds flywheel can also be used by elongating one hole to match the Cad crank flange. 1956 and later Cad engines do not have provisions for a pilot bushing in the flywheel so Wally made up a steel adaptor which presses into the rear of the crank and uses a standard H-M pilot bushing. The depth of the adaptor makes it necessary to grind ¼ inch from the nose of the pilot shaft.

Ford front mount brackets on the tubular crossmember were cut off with an acetylene torch and a new pair of front mounts

Stock Ford motor mount brackets were trimmed from tubular crossmember and new ones fabricated from ¼-inch steel plate. New brackets match Cad insulators and are welded in place.

Ford center crossmember supports the rear of the engine-transmission unit. Bracket to match the Hydra-Matic trans had to be extended. New bracket was fabricated from ¼-inch steel plate.

A section of the Ford floor pan had to be cut away to give adequate clearance to the Hydra-Matic valve body and control levers. Aluminum was shaped to fit, then screwed into place.

FORDILLAC

fabricated from ¼-inch steel plate. With the Cad engine positioned in the chassis, the fabricated mounts were tack welded to the frame rails, then securely arc welded after the engine had been removed. Cadillac front engine brackets and insulators were used. At the rear, ³⁄₁₆ steel plate was used to fabricate a longer bracket on the Ford center crossmember beneath the Hydra-Matic to support the rear of the engine through the H-M insulator. The Ford hand brake lever pivot was also relocated slightly.

Stock Cad exhaust manifolds were used and cleared the chassis easily except at one point. The right manifold flange which couples to the exhaust head pipe required a small indentation in the firewall for clearance. All exhaust pipe routing was open and easy to hook up.

The Ford driveshaft was shortened approximately 2½ inches, and a Cadillac driveshaft flange was grafted onto the Ford shaft

so that it would match with the Hydra-Matic tailshaft.

The Cad generator bracket was discarded and another one made to fasten beneath a pair of head bolts on the left side so that fender panel clearance would be adequate. A Studebaker low profile air cleaner was modified to match the Cad carburetor, and the Ford fan fit the Cad water pump shaft without modifications. The Ford radiator was also untouched.

As expected, the results are quite good. The stock Cad engine easily outshines the Ford not only in the performance category but also in smoothness of operation. Weight differences between the two engines with automatic transmissions are negligible and the Ford engine brought enough money on the swapper's market to defray a large part of the cost of the Cad engine and swap job. Looking for power, economy and dependability in that '57 or '58 Ford? The swap pictured on these pages will apply to cars of both years and we guarantee you'll like the results.

Early type Hydra-Matics (pre-'56) are preferable to late models since they are more positive. The Cad unit is better to use than Olds or other units since it has rear mount on tailshaft.

Completed engine swap viewed from the bottom side shows how the H-M transmission is mounted to Ford crossmember. Note also that hand brake pivot has been reworked to new bracket.

Ford radiator was left in stock position and did not have to be altered to match the Cad hose sizes. Ford fan bolts to the Cad water pump without alteration, has good clearance.

Another bottom side shot shows how the reworked Cadillac oil pan fits through the dropped tube crossmember. Steering linkage was also critical point. Cad exhaust manifolds are used.

Completed installation required no cutting on the chassis or body and therefore is not noticeable from the exterior. Studebaker air cleaner with offset oil bath was used to give hood clearance since Cad engine was set about one inch higher in chassis.

RANCHERO
VERSUS
EL CAMINO

Chevrolet's answer to the Ranchero is the El Camino, which combines passenger car comfort with pickup truck usefulness.

Ford's success in the fancy pickup field is challenged by Chevrolet's new El Camino. Here's how they compare.

BY RAY BROCK, HRM TECHNICAL EDITOR

When we tested the 1957 Ford Ranchero a couple of years ago, we were quite enthused and predicted that it would be a very successful addition to the ever increasing number of body styles placed on the market. We also predicted that other manufacturers would be quick to follow suit. Actually, we expected Chevrolet and possibly Plymouth to introduce comparable models in 1958, but it wasn't until this year that Chevy made the move and of course Plymouth still has not decided to do so.

Chevrolet's answer to the Ranchero is called the El Camino and, like the Ranchero, is made with the same basic formula. This formula calls for a two-door station wagon chassis and body minus the top above the belt line of the car from just behind the front seat. It is not quite that simple but will give you an idea of how both Ford and Chevy convert passenger car styling to ½-ton pickup usefulness. These luxury model pickups cannot compete with the regular pickups for price or ground clearance but they can carry as much load if needed and certainly are much more comfortable for family travel. They are well suited for the job they were designed to fulfill and that is to be a dual-purpose vehicle.

SIZE AND WEIGHT

EL CAMINO—Chevrolet wheelbase for 1959 is 119 inches, 1.5 inches more than '58. Tread has been widened 1.5 inches in the front to 60.3 inches and one-half inch at the rear to 59.3 inches for '59. Maximum car width is just a fraction under 80 inches, overall length is nearly 211 inches and the El Camino is 58.75 inches high unloaded. The weight of the El Camino we tested was a hefty 3880 pounds with a full load of fuel (17 gallons), 2080 on the front wheels and 1800 on the rear for a 53.6-46.4% ratio, remarkably well balanced for a pickup job when empty. Remember not too long ago when Chevies weighed well under 3500 pounds? Don't let anybody tell you that you're not getting more for your money in the modern automobile.

RANCHERO—Ford has added another two inches to their wheelbase for '59 to give a total of 118 inches. Tread width is unchanged with the front wheels spread 59 inches apart and the rear only 56.4 inches. Although Ford uses an all-new body for 1959, they didn't go for the extra width like Chevrolet so the Ranchero body is only 72.6 inches wide at the doors compared to 79 inches for the El Camino. Maximum Ford width at the bumper tips is 76.6 inches. Car length is 208 inches, nearly 3 inches less than Chevy, and unloaded height is 58 inches. The Ranchero we tested had more weight adding extras than the El Camino but still weighed 40 pounds less. Total weight was 3840 pounds, 2190 on the front wheels and 1650 on the rear wheels for a weight ratio of 57-43%.

INTERIOR

EL CAMINO—There is only one model made in this body style so some trim features are extra cost options. Such items as right side sun visor, arm rests, foam seats, padded dash and cigarette lighter can be fitted but the El Camino does not have them as standard equipment. One thing that has always griped us about Chevy is the lack of an accessory position on the ignition switch—they don't have it this year either. Also, the El Camino does not have a door switch to operate the interior light as standard equipment. Interior trim is attractive but not flashy with wear resistant plastic material on seats and panels. All El Camino interiors are the same color—gray. Instruments are grouped in front of the driver for easy reading and vision is good in all directions with the rear window as well as front of the wrap-around variety. Seat width is 66 inches across the hips and 60.5 inches at shoulder height. The spare tire fastens to the body behind the right seat back half with storage room behind the left seat back.

RANCHERO VERSUS EL CAMINO

With tailgates open, the two beds are the same length. With tailgate closed, Ranchero has the longer bed and the El Camino has the wider bed. Note different rear windows.

RANCHERO—Only one model is available for 1959, the Custom model. The Deluxe of '57 and '58 has been dropped. Custom trim includes two sun visors, arm rests, foam seats and cigarette lighter and fancy interiors like those used in Country Sedan Ranch Wagons. Several interior color combinations are available for Rancheros to match the nearly two-dozen exterior color choices. Seat width is 60.4 inches with 56.7 inches shoulder room. The spare tire and jack for the Ranchero are also behind the right seat back with a token amount of storage space behind the left seat back. Instrument panel grouping is in front of the driver for easy checking and vision to all sides is good. Those drivers who prefer to glance over their shoulder before changing lanes instead of trusting the rear view mirror will find that

the Ranchero has a wider door post than the El Camino so slightly less vision at that point but it would be impossible for a car to "hide" in such a small blind spot.

BED CAPACITY

EL CAMINO—The narrowest part of the bed is 46 inches between the rear wheel wells and the maximum width across the top of the bed is 59.5 inches. Average depth is 14 inches. The length at the top of the bed with tailgate closed is 70 inches and at the bottom 76 inches. When opened, the tailgate aligns perfectly with the ribbed metal bottom of the El Camino so that a 91-inch bed is available for long loads. Both the bed bottom and the inner side of the tailgate are covered with durable ribbed sheet steel. The front of the bed is also the back of the cab and has no protection against shifting loads buckling the metal. The Ranchero has a triangular metal brace across the front of the bed which would protect the cab should brakes be quickly applied and a heavy box slide forward. A possible problem might also show up on the El Camino if the tailgate is left down when traveling over rocky roads. The sculptured metal on the rear of the tailgate which flares into the thin rear fender fins hangs so low behind the rear bumper that the paint will probably be susceptible to rock and sand blasting.

Standard rear coil springs for the El Camino have a design height which places the body at a completely level attitude without any load in the bed. With a 700 pound test load added squarely over the wheels, the El Camino settled very noticeably and "bottomed" against the frame snubbers on the smallest dips. Optional heavy-duty rear springs are available but

Ranchero interior trims are the same as those used in the Ford station wagons with a variety of color schemes to match exterior paint. Seat belts and padded dash are among extra options.

Gray colored interior is used for all El Camino models. Floor shift lever is for Corvette four-speed transmission. Although seat is lower than Ford, passengers become used to it quickly.

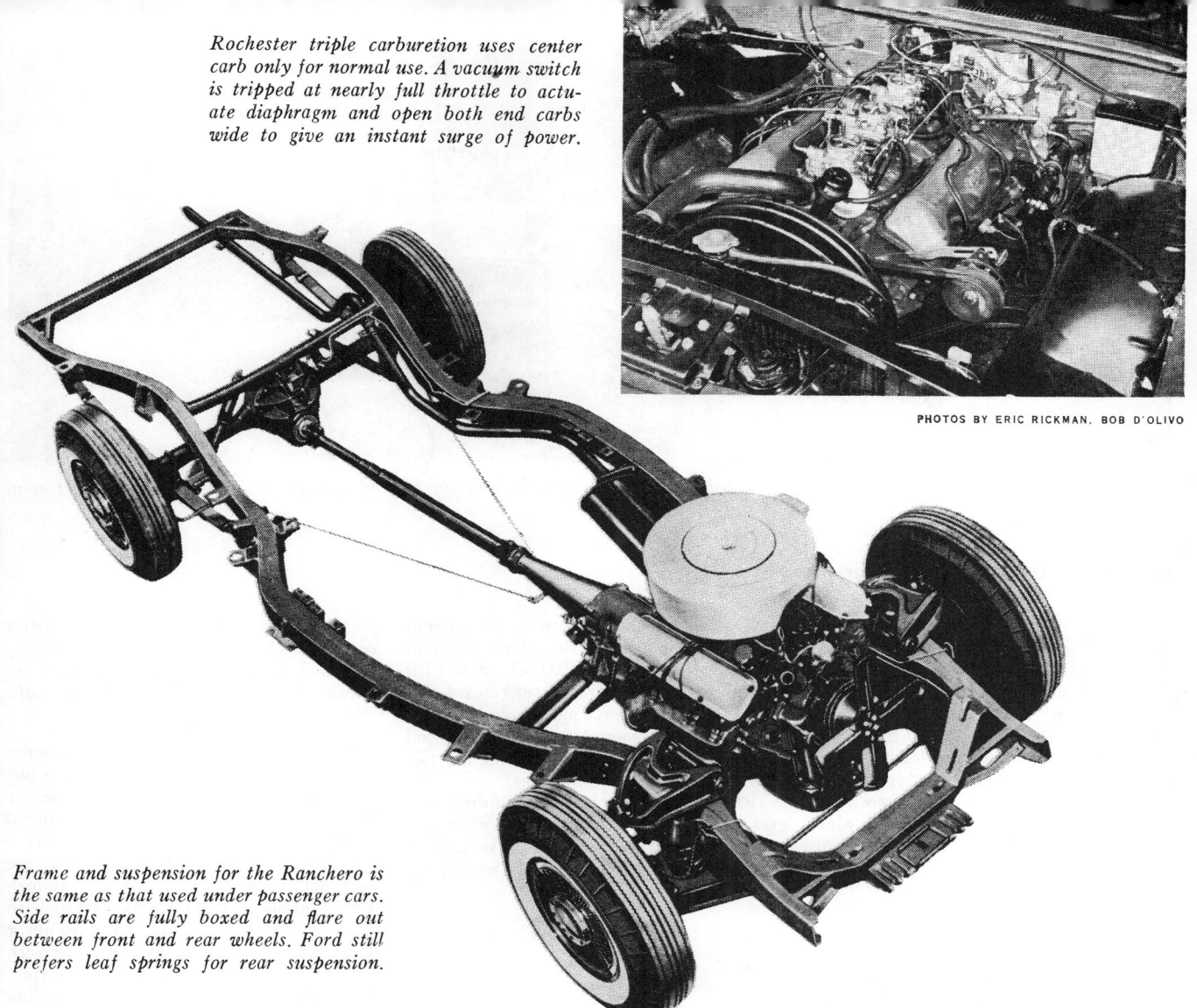

Rochester triple carburetion uses center carb only for normal use. A vacuum switch is tripped at nearly full throttle to actuate diaphragm and open both end carbs wide to give an instant surge of power.

Frame and suspension for the Ranchero is the same as that used under passenger cars. Side rails are fully boxed and flare out between front and rear wheels. Ford still prefers leaf springs for rear suspension.

must be ordered specially. These will naturally cause the empty El Camino to have a noticeable "rake" with the rear of the body higher than the front. Heavy-duty shock absorbers are not listed but would definitely be needed if heavy loads are anticipated because the stock shocks are just adequate even without a load.

RANCHERO — Due to the narrower rear tread of the Ford, distance between the wheel wells is only 42 inches and the widest measurement across the top of the bed is 55.5 inches, both 4 inches less than the El Camino. Bed depth averages 14.5 inches. The Ranchero is longer with tailgate closed than the El Camino, measuring 76 inches at the top edge and 83 inches along the floor. The tailgate does not open on the same level as the bed, instead coming to rest about one inch higher than the bed. With the tailgate down, floor length is the same as Chevy, 91 inches, but the floor isn't level due to the higher tailgate. The smooth surface on the Ranchero tailgate is well protected by the rear bumper so won't

be susceptible to rocks as is the El Camino.

Rear springs for the Ranchero are the same as those used on Ford station wagons so cause the Ranchero to have a pronounced "rake" without a load. A 700 pound test load directly over the rear axle was just enough to level the body and still provide ample wheel travel so that average dips did not "bottom" the car. Shocks also have stiffer valving and effectively dampen the motion of the loaded Ranchero, something which the El Camino shocks did not do. The Ranchero is designed for a payload of 1100 pounds and should carry the weight easily with the stock springs and shocks.

FRAME AND SUSPENSION

EL CAMINO—Since the passenger car is used as a basis for building the El Camino, all under-body components are identical to those used on other 1959 Chevies. The frame is the same type as that introduced in 1958, an "X" type frame with box section side rails spreading out both fore and aft of the narrow

tubular center section. The front suspension is the same as '58 with unequal length control arms and coil springs between the lower control arms and the frame side rails. Shock absorbers mount inside the coil springs and a link type stabilizing bar fastens between the lower control arms.

A few changes have been made in Chevy's rear suspension for 1959. The horseshoe shaped upper control arm used in '58 to eliminate sidesway, cancel braking forces and control torque forces has been discarded. In its place, a short upper control arm hooks between a frame bracket and the rear axle housing to counteract braking and torque forces in much the same way as the horseshoe control arm did last year. A cross-chassis anti-sway bar from the left frame rail to a bracket on the right side of the axle housing controls sidesway. Lower control arms are the same for '59 as last year, pivoting from frame brackets ahead of the rear axle, with a coil spring between each control arm and

Ranchero suspension didn't allow excessive body lean on sharp corners but weight shifted enough to let inside rear wheel spin.

RANCHERO VERSUS EL CAMINO

the side frame rail just ahead of the rear axle housing. Shock absorbers are angularly mounted between frame and axle housing brackets.

RANCHERO—The same is true of the Ranchero as the El Camino; all chassis components used are identical to those used by other '59 Ford passenger cars. The frame is of the ladder type construction with fully boxed side rails which flare out toward the sides of the body for increased foot room in the passenger

Ford's biggest engine for 1959 has 352-inch displacement, machined wedge combustion chamber and a single four-barrel carburetor. 332-inch engine is same except for stroke.

section. The front suspension is independent with unequal length control arms to maintain constant front wheel tread, with coil springs between the lower control arm and frame rail on each side. Tubular shock absorbers are mounted inside the coil springs and a link type stabilizing bar ties the front suspension together.

Rear springing is by semi-elliptical leaf springs mounted parallel to the center line of the car. The rear axle housing is clamped to the springs well forward of the midway

point so that the shorter, stiffer front section will resist torque and braking forces. Tubular shocks are bracketed between the axle and side frame rails.

ENGINES

EL CAMINO—Chevrolet's six cylinder engine is standard for the El Camino but we doubt if many people will settle for this when there are so many optional powerplants available. The 235-inch six is rated at 135 horsepower and that's all we need say about it. The popular 283-inch V8 is optional in many forms starting with 8.5:1 compression, a two-barrel carburetor and a rating of 185 hp at 4600 rpm with 275 foot/pounds of torque at 2400 rpm. The same engine with 9.5:1 compression and a four-barrel carburetor is rated 230 hp at 4800 rpm and 300 foot/pounds of torque at 3000 rpm. With 10.5:1 compression, and fuel injection, the horsepower jumps to 250 at 5000 and the torque is 305 at 3800 rpm. Tops in the 283-inch engine line is one with 10.5:1 compression, fuel injection and a hot camshaft that delivers 290 hp at 6200 rpm and 290 foot/pounds of torque at 4400 rpm.

In the 348-inch displacement version, the lowest horsepower rating is 250 at 4400 rpm with 355 foot/pounds of torque at 2800 rpm. This engine has 9.5:1 compression and a four-barrel carburetor. With Rochester's triple carburetor option, the same engine is rated 280 hp at 4800 rpm and 355 foot/pounds of torque at 3200. With 11:1 compression, a special camshaft and a single four-barrel carburetor, power jumps to 300 at 5600 rpm and the torque is rated 350 at 3600 rpm. Tops in the 348-inch line is the same engine, 11:1 compression, special cam, but with the Rochester triple carburetion. This one is rated 315 horsepower at 5600 rpm and 356 foot/pounds of torque at 3600 rpm. This fierce sounding combination happens to be the one with which our test car was fitted.

Wide El Camino body provided lots of lean with its soft springing but still manages to negotiate curves as well as Ranchero.

RANCHERO—The standard engine is the 223-inch six cylinder version rated at 145 horsepower. Optional V8's start at 292 cubic inches with 8.8:1 compression, a two-barrel carburetor and a power rating of 200 hp at 4400 with 285 foot/pounds of torque at 2200 rpm. Next on the list is a 332-inch V8 of different design, having 8.9:1 compression, a two-barrel carburetor and 225 horses at 4400 rpm. The torque is 325 foot/pounds at 2200 rpm. The final optional engine for the '59 Ford line is a 352-inch V8 with 9.6:1 compression, a four-barrel carburetor, 300 hp at 4600 rpm and 380 foot/pounds of torque at 2800 rpm.

This last engine is the same as the top horsepower model offered in 1958 but with lower compression and a few other minor changes. With the drop in compression from 10.2:1 last year, a different cam design and a modified ignition advance curve, the engine is probably a little stronger than it was in 1958 although still rated the same. This is the engine used in our Ranchero test car.

TRANSMISSIONS—AXLE RATIOS

EL CAMINO — A three-speed column shift transmission is standard for the El Camino. Gear ratios are 2.47:1 in first, 1.53:1 in second, direct in third and 2.80:1 in reverse. The high ratio three-speed used with the 348-inch engine in '58 is no longer offered, all engines use the above transmission and an overdrive is available for the six or 283 V8's. For those who are willing to pay the extra price, the Corvette full synchromesh four-speed transmission is available. It has the same floor shift pattern used in the Corvette, with ratios of 2.20 in first, 1.66 in second, 1.31 in third, direct in fourth and 2.26 in reverse. This is actually a side-shift transmission with the shift lever bracketed on the tail-shaft and a linkage hookup but action is com-

pletely positive either up-shifting or down-shifting.

Automatic transmissions are available —two of them, Powerglide and the Turboglide. The Powerglide is a two-speed planetary gear transmission with a torque converter and the Turboglide is a similar type but with a variable pitch stator like that found in the Buick Dynaflow. The automatic transmissions are not available when the special camshafts are used.

Rear axle ratios used with the 283-inch V8 and six cylinder engines are 3.55 with the standard transmission, 4.11 with overdrive and 3.36 with automatics. For the 348-inch V8. the standard transmission axle ratio is 3.36 and the ratio for automatic transmissions is 3.08.

RANCHERO — Ford's three-speed transmission is standard equipment for all Rancheros with all but the 352-inch engine using the same transmission. Ratios are 2.40 in first, 1.49 in second, direct in third and 2.86 in reverse. For the big displacement V8, a stronger transmission is used with ratios of 2.37 in first, 1.51 in second, direct in third and 2.81 in reverse. Overdrive is optional with either unit. the smaller transmission having a 30% overdrive while the larger transmission has a 28% overdrive.

Ford also has a pair of optional automatic transmissions. Fordomatic and Cruise-O-Matic. The Fordomatic is changed for '59 with only two forward speeds instead of three as in the past. The Cruise-O-Matic has three forward speeds and is a refined version of the previous Fordomatic.

Axle ratios are many. Starting with the six cylinder engine, they include a 3.56 for standard transmission, 3.70 for overdrive and 3.56 for Fordomatic. Ratios are the same for the 292-inch V8 except that a 3.10 is used with Fordomatic. With the 332-inch V8, the standard

TOP—Optional in all model Chevrolets for the first time, the close-ratio Corvette four-speed transmission has shift lever mounted on the tailshaft housing with linkage to side-shift arms. Shifts are positive. BELOW—View of '59 Chev rear suspension reveals new upper control arm (A), an additional crossmember (B), the cross-chassis anti-sway bar (C), larger brakes (D) and resonator mufflers to quiet duals.

transmission ratio is 3.56, 3.70 for over-drive and 2.91 for both Fordomatic and Cruise-O-Matic. With the 352-inch V8, standard transmissions use a 3.56 ratio, 3.70 for overdrive, 2.91 with Fordomatic and 2.69 with Cruise-O-Matic.

STEERING—BRAKES

EL CAMINO — Chevrolet changed their steering around last year, placing the gear box and linkage in front of the wheels and for some reason we've yet to figure out, they ended up with a car that required super-human strength to maneuver into a tight parking place. This year, they increased the steering gear ratio so that the car is once more easy to drive. The only trouble now is that the 28:1 overall ratio is about the slowest in the automotive industry and the six-plus turns of the wheel from lock-to-lock is too much. The optional power steering ratio of 24:1 is much better and we definitely recommend power steering to get the more suitable ratio.

Chevy brakes have 30 more square inches of lining area for '59 with a total of 199.5 square inches. Drum diameter remains the same, 11 inches, but front drums are .75 inch wider (2.75 inches) and the rear drums are .25 inch wider (2 inches). Both front and rear drums have a cooling flange on the open end which projects past the backing plate to help dissipate heat into the air flow beneath the car. During high speed and acceleration tests with the El Camino, the brakes responded perfectly without signs of fade or erratic stops. No attempt was made to completely fade the brakes but it is evident that they will take plenty of abuse before refusing to stop.

RANCHERO — Ford's gear ratio for the conventional steering doesn't appear to be much better than the El Camino, with an overall ratio of 27:1 listed on their specification sheet, but we suspect that the ratios listed don't tell the whole story because the Ranchero will cut a curb-to-curb turning diameter from 40.6 feet versus 40.2 for the El Camino, yet has a full turn less from lock-to-lock. The power steering option for Rancheros has a ratio of 25:1, just slightly slower than the El Camino.

Brakes for the Ranchero are the same as those used on station wagons which gives an extra 11 inches of lining area over passenger cars for a total of 191.44 square inches. Drums are 11-inch front and rear, 2.25-inch lining width on the front and 2 inches on the rear. Like the El Camino they operated perfectly during our testing session and showed good holding ability after several quick stops between acceleration runs.

RIDE AND HANDLING

EL CAMINO — Springing for the El Camino is about right without a load in the bed so will deliver a soft, easy ride over average roads. When empty, the shock absorbers are strong enough to effectively control the roll and bounce over secondary roads. With a heavy load in the bed and stock rear springs and shocks, you might as well make up your mind to take it easy because the bounce and rebound over any type of bump is too severe to permit fast speeds.

When empty, the El Camino will handle very well although the slow ratio of the standard steering will keep a driver plenty busy on a twisting mountain road. The soft springing will allow the El Camino to lean in an alarming manner on corners but after reaching a heeled-over position, the El Camino will get a good grip on the road and go through the corners with good control and feel. Expected over-steer without a load over the rear wheels fails to materialize on the tightest corners as long as the rear wheels are driving.

RANCHERO — Stiffer springs on the Ranchero give a slightly more rigid feel to the ride department than does the El Camino but the Ranchero is well suited to carry a heavy load and impart a (Continued on page 80)

secure feeling to the driver. Without a load, the heavier suspension keeps the Ranchero on a fairly even keel through tight corners. Cornering ability of the Ranchero is to the best of our judgment about even with that of the El Camino we tested although the Ford is far less spectacular in the body lean department.

PERFORMANCE

EL CAMINO — With the 315 horse-power and four-speed Corvette transmission, our test car was a tiger — after it was rolling. The 3.36 rear axle ratio coupled with the high ratios of the Corvette transmission (2.20 in first) fails to set any new records at the start, but once under way you quickly realize that you're accelerating. The gear ratios are so closely spaced that you only spend a few seconds in each one before jumping up another step in the ladder. Shifts up or down through the gears are made as fast as you can move the hand and clutch foot. From 0-30 mph in first, an average of 3.6 seconds is needed; from 0-60 mph in first and second, 8.7 seconds; 30-60 mph simulated passing time, 5.0 seconds; 50-80 mph simulated passing in second and third, 7.5 seconds; standing ¼ mile, 16.0 seconds; and speed at the end of the quarter, 90 mph.

At the Santa Ana, California, drag strip, the 3.36 gear was too much and the El Camino was only mediocre up to about 40 mph. Above 40, acceleration was strong with a shift to second at about 55 mph and a shift into third just over 80 mph. We only got into third gear just before the ¼-mile timing lights so didn't make high speed shifts into fourth. Estimated shift point for fourth would be between 100 and 105 mph. No top speed runs were made but estimated top speed would probably be near 130 mph for the car we tested. With a gear ratio of about 4.55 to 1 and the optional Positraction differential, this car would break 100 mph in the quarter and come close to 14 seconds flat. There sure would be a lot of engine noise for street use with such a gear ratio, however.

We experienced some difficulty with the triple carburetion during the early part of our test but soon solved this problem. The secondary carburetors were being tripped open at just over half throttle on the center carburetor and the engine would stutter momentarily under the large fuel/air charge. Reversely, same would happen when the secondary carburetors closed too late, suddenly stopping the major portion of fuel/air charge. By adjusting the lever actuating the secondary system so that it did not open the end carburetors until the center carburetor was more nearly wide open, the hesitation was eliminated on

"Reggie found out it was going to be LeMans start."

"Ready for the stockers now, Charlie?"

acceleration and also when the throttle was being closed.

Although the 315 hp engine and the Corvette transmission made an interesting combination for our test, we don't believe that too many Chevrolet customers would be justified in paying the price for the four-speed gearbox. The ratios are too high for the 3.36 axle ratio to permit smooth starts and a lower ratio of 3.90 or 4.10 would give excessive engine rpm's at highway speeds. With the big powerful engine, we usually eliminated either second or third or both from the shift pattern in city traffic. Guess the age for automatic transmission has caught up with us for everyday driving.

RANCHERO — Performance-wise, its hard to make a comparison between the Ranchero we tested and the El Camino just described because they were so differently equipped. Although the Ranchero had Ford's healthiest engine for 1959, it certainly does not produce as much brute horsepower as the Chevy of nearly equal displacement, but more compression, carburetion, cam timing and rpm's: The Ranchero was equipped with Cruise-O-Matic transmission and a 2.69 rear axle ratio. When judged for acceleration against the average passenger car, our test car didn't fare too badly, negotiating 0-30 mph in 4.4 seconds; 0-60 mph in 9.9 seconds; 30-60 mph in 6 seconds; 50-80 mph in 8.5 seconds; ¼ mile standing start in 17.2 seconds; and a speed of 84 mph at the end of the ¼-mile. No bomb, but it is a pretty peppy automobile for the average driver.

CONCLUSION

The combination of passenger car and pickup not only makes an attractive automobile but is the logical answer for the fellow who has to combine business transportation with pleasure transportation. Ford has proven the popularity of the Ranchero and of course for every Ford lover in the country, there is at least one Chevy lover. So, it is probably safe to say that before long, the streets and highways of the U.S. will be liberally sprinkled with these two models.

Readers interested in additional information on the El Camino will receive a free illustrated color brochure by simply sending name and address to Chevrolet Motor Division, General Motors Corporation, Detroit 2, Michigan. Ask for El Camino literature.

The same special service is offered those interested in added information about the Ranchero. For a free informative color folder, send name and address to Ford Division, Truck Advertising Department, Box 658, Dearborn, Michigan. Ask for Ranchero literature.

RANCHEROS

'57 Ranchero has chopped top, DeSoto front bumper with full pan molded into front fender, round corners on hood, exhaust pipes extend up beyond rear wheel wells.

'57 Ranchero features a '55 Plymouth grille, accessory clip chrome pieces over headlights, double '58 Ford taillights, Plymouth hubcaps. Custom has high-polish paint.

'58 Ranchero has two-tone paint impressions done in gold and candy red. It has laker pipes, Dodge Lancer hubcaps, chromed handrails along side of rear bed compartment.

RANCHERO ROAD TEST

Smart design,

Handling characteristics smack more of the pickup truck. With only about 1615 lbs. of a total of 3870 (unladen) on the rear wheels, the Ranchero is definitely noseheavy and this shows up in its behavior on the road.

Rear wheels chatter and bounce on rough surfaces and the rear end thus tends to drift when cornering at even moderate speeds on poor roads. This is not so noticeable on smooth pavement but the light feeling of the rear end is still there. With enough weight in the bed to give better front-rear weight balance, the Ranchero is superior to most of the standard Ford passenger cars, however.

(It should be noted, too, that the Ranchero tested was equipped with the heaviest engine-transmission combination offered. With a lighter V-8 or the ohv-6 and manual or two-speed automatic transmission the forward weight bias would be less pronounced and handling correspondingly improved.)

Performance of the test Ranchero was surprisingly good; especially since it had a 2.69 rear axle and such a small percentage of total weight on the driving wheels. Standing starts were made by revving the engine to about 2000 rpm (more than that caused wheelspin) with brakes on and transmission in low range. Manual shifts to second permitted turning higher rpm in low than if the transmission was permitted to shift automatically and resulted in optimum acceleration.

Fuel economy was quite good considering the size of the engine and the weight of the vehicle, along with the

---

PIONEER of the plush pickups, Ford's Ranchero is now in its third year of existence and has established that there is a market—if a limited one—for this type of vehicle.

The Ranchero continues to be, as it has from the start, a combination of passenger car, station wagon and pickup truck. It is built on a station wagon chassis, has a sedan-like cab interior or passenger compartment and carries a long and roomy truck bed at rear.

Styling of Rancheros has been very pleasing since their introduction in the 1957 model year and the 1959 version is no exception. There is nothing cobbled or makeshift about the de luxe pickup's appearance; the design is well integrated and attractive—even more so than companion passenger cars, to some eyes!

These good looks and sedan-type comfort are obviously the two biggest assets the Ranchero has, aside from its utility value as a light hauler.

Ride is a bit firmer than that of Ford sedans, but much softer and smoother than in conventional pickups. In fact, with seating position and seat design so closely resembling standard passenger cars, it is possible to forget you are riding in a truck until you look back and see the pickup bed.

PERFORMANCE of the Ford Ranchero was surprisingly good. Fuel economy was quite satisfactory considering size of engine and weight of the vehicle.

sedan-type comfort are Ranchero's big assets

fact that it was driven rather hard with no particular attempt made to get maximum miles per gallon.

Quality was about on a par with standard 1959 Ford passenger cars. There were a few flaws—rough edges on the horn ring and mismatching of the stainless pickup bed trim molding with that of the tailgate molding, for example. In general, however, detail finish was substantially better than that of most conventional pickup trucks.

The interior was fully as attractive as that seen in most passenger cars.

The two-section seat back is hinged, like that in Ford's two-door station wagon, and folds forward to provide access to a storage compartment behind the seat. The spare tire is mounted at right and there is space for several suitcases in the left side. There are also small storage wells under the seats. The seats themselves and the seating positions are very close to those in two-door station wagons.

All-round vision is at least equal to 1959 Ford cars and the instrument panel is reasonably well laid out. It's easy to read all instruments without taking your eyes off the road for more than a split-second.

In judging the Ranchero as purely a utility vehicle, it is obvious that it is not capable of handling many of the more rugged hauling duties for which more prosaic half-ton pickups are used.

The Ranchero has much softer springs, for one thing—though this could be remedied to some extent by use of Air Lift inflatable rubber bags. Its six-inch minimum ground clearance is also a bit

RANCHERO is designed more for those who need or want a pickup-type vehicle for light hauling duty only, and want passenger car riding comfort and attractive styling, too.

on the low side for hauling on really rough surfaces.

Since the bed has rounded corners and uses a station wagon tailgate, the rear opening for loading material into the bed is not full-width. In addition, rear wheel housings extend into the bed quite a way so that the full width of the bed can't be utilized over its entire length.

Nor would the extremely low numerical rear axle ratio in the test Ranchero be the best choice for really heavy hauling, although the engine is powerful enough to compensate for that in most cases where this vehicle would be practical.

There is little doubt, however, that few buyers will choose a Ranchero primarily for utility purposes. Standard pickups will fill those needs for much less money.

The Ranchero is designed for those who need or want a pickup-type vehicle for light hauling duty only, and want passenger car riding comfort and attractive styling too.

It is the ideal solution for those who need a pickup in their work and can't afford a second family car. (The big advantage Rancheros have over station wagons in this respect is lower price— some $250 or more less than comparably equipped wagons in most cases.)

Rancheros also have great appeal for gentlemen farmers, outdoor hobbyists

and as tow cars for competition machines.

Limits of the market for plush pickups will be probed further this year because of introduction of Chevrolet's El Camino, but it looks very much like these vehicles are attractive to enough buyers to insure them a permanent future. ●

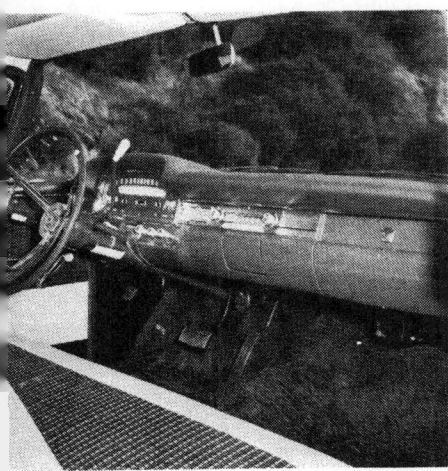

INSTRUMENT PANEL is well laid out and vision is equal to '59 Ford cars. Interior was as attractive as that of passenger cars.

Test Data

Test Car: 1959 Ford Ranchero
Body Type: pickup
Basic Price: $2287
Engine: ohv V-8
Carburetion: single four-barrel
Displacement: 352 cubic inches
Bore & Stroke: 4.0 x 3.5 inches
Compression Ratio: 9.6-to-1
Horsepower: 300 @ 4600 rpm
Horsepower per cubic inch: .85
Torque: 380 lbs.-ft @ 2800 rpm
Test Weight: 3780 lbs. without driver
Weight Distribution: 57% on front wheels
Power-Weight Ratio: 12.6 lbs. per hp
Transmission: Cruise-O-Matic three-speed automatic with torque converter
Rear Axle Ratio: 2.69-to-1
Steering: 5 turns lock-to-lock
Dimensions: overall length 208 inches, width 76.6, height 57.8, wheelbase 118, tread 59 front and 56.4 rear
Tires: 8.00x14
Gas Mileage: 13.2 city, 15.5 highway
Speedometer Error: Indicated 30, 45 and 60 mph are actual 27, 40 and 54 respectively
Acceleration: 0-30 mph in 4.4 seconds, 0-45 in 6.5 and 0-60 mph in 9.9 seconds

Cabs of El Camino, above, and Ranchero, below, offer comfort, plush appointments.

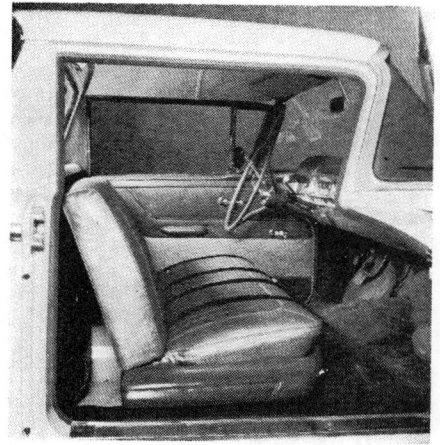

by Bill Callahan Detroit Editor

WHEN FOMOCO'S HIGHLY STYLIZED, high-performance Ranchero pickup proved a popular choice among truck purchasers it was a foregone conclusion that Chevrolet would not be far behind. Chevy's answer for 1959 is the El Camino—a name inscribed in glamorous script on a practical pickup that sports all the high styling of the Chevy passenger car line.

MOTOR TREND was interested to know just how this new unit by Chevy stacked up with the Ford offering in the same category. Red underwear weather that ensconced itself over the lower peninsula of Michigan, coating roadways with snow and ice, particularly in the by-lanes where this type of vehicle should prove most acceptable, precluded any bonafide road test. However, we were able to check out a driver reaction to both units.

THE EL CAMINO came from Chevrolet Engineering at the GM Tech Center. It was powered by a 283-cubic-inch V8 with a compression ratio of 9.5 to 1 which with a four-barrel carburetor develops 230 hp at 4800 rpm and 300 pounds-feet of torque at 3000 rpm. The odometer read 1529.5 which meant the job could be driven at speed without worry. The transmission was a single range Powerglide, and rear end ratio 3.36 to 1. No power steering or power brakes.

THE RANCHERO came from Ford Engineering in Dearborn. It was powered by a 352-cubic-inch V8 with a compression ratio of 9.6 to 1. Equipped with a four-barrel carburetor it developed 300 hp at 4600 rpm and 380 pounds-feet of torque at 2800 rpm. Transmission was a dual-range Cruise-O-Matic and the rear axle ratio 2.69 to 1. Power steering and power brakes were used. Both trucks were rolling on 8.00 x 14 tires.

FIRST TEST STEP was to check speedometer accuracy. The Ranchero was badly off. At true 30 the speedo read 34, at true 45 it read 53, at true 50 it showed 58 and at true 60 it read 69. The El Camino was much more consistent, reading 32 at true 30, 47 at true 45, 52 at true 50 and 62 at true 60.

WEIGHING PERFORMANCE against these corrected readings the two cars checked out surprisingly close. The El Camino was considerably more agile in the zero to 60 runs, turning in low average of 9.3 seconds against the Ranchero's 10.9. In the zero to 45 range, the El Camino averaged 6.6 seconds, the Ranchero 7.2. In both cases the averages were based on the best four out of eight or more runs.

IN PASSING SPEEDS the El Camino also is a little quicker in the 30 to 45 mph range, requiring only 3.9 seconds against the Ranchero's 4.1. From 45 to 60 mph the El Camino needed only

From rear both pickups resemble passenger cars. El Camino provides 33 cubic feet of storage and Ranchero has 27 feet.

Front views are exactly as sedans. Ride, acceleration, braking and handling are very much unlike conventional trucks.

3.9 seconds against the Ranchero's 4.2. The Ranchero, however, topped the El Camino in the step-up from 50 to 80 mph requiring only 11.2 seconds against the El Camino's 12.1. This was due to the fact that the El Camino dropped out of the accelerating gear at about 63 mph while the Ranchero remained in kick-down gear up to 68 mph.

DRIVER REACTION is that both the El Camino and Ranchero handle like anything but trucks. While the El Camino leans quite a bit on hard cornering and has far too slow a steering ratio, it is stable and does follow the direction of the wheels. The Ranchero, with slightly faster steering is also a little flatter on sharp curves, but the inside rear wheel does lift under severe cornering conditions. Braking and steering, both power assisted on the Ranchero, naturally were easier than on the El Camino tested, which had no power assists for these functions. Stopping the El Camino without power brakes is no problem, but the steering is so slow that this might revive the "necker's knob" to assist in parking.

SETTING UP REAR SPRINGING for combined "touring-trucks" such as these two cars, which might run empty or overladen as much as 50 per cent, is a real problem for the engineer. Solution: a happy medium. The El Camino with its coil spring rear suspension gives a softer ride on washboard roads than the Ranchero with variable rate leaf springs. However, it had a lot more bounce and a rougher ride on really bumpy cross-country, off-pavement driving. Both cars were run unladen and would most certainly be quite different with their recommended maximum loads. With the type of springing and unladen weight distribution they have, bottoming could be expected if load recommendations were exceeded.

CAB INTERIORS are as plush as the passenger car models—with attractive upholstery, comfortable seats and conveniently located controls. Visibility is good in both. In this department again comparisons are close and the choice would be largely a matter of buyer

Chevrolet's El Camino sports high styling of passenger car line, yet provides space for 1030-pound load. It should prove hot competitor to Ford's Ranchero during 1959.

taste. Noise level in the Ranchero cab is considerably higher than in the El Camino but unless one looks into the rear view mirror, the illusion of driving a passenger car is complete. Here again the choice rests between whether you like quiet, quick performance, or a nice gutteral getaway.

CARRYING CAPACITIES are about the same in the weight department but vary in volume of space. The Ranchero on a 118-inch wheelbase provides about 27 cubic feet of space in its seven-foot body with tailgate raised. Payload is put at 1100 pounds. The El Camino wheelbase is 119 inches, with body length at the floor 76.3 inches and 70.6 inches at the top with tailgate closed

(which provides 33 cubic feet of space). Payload is placed at 1030 pounds. The El Camino is lower with a tailgate height of 25.3 inches against the Ranchero's 27 inches. Both pickups are available with either six- or eight-cylinder engines.

FALCON RANCHERO

TEST DATA

TEST CAR: Ford Falcon
BODY TYPE: Ranchero
BASIC PRICE: $1862
ENGINE: ohv six
DISPLACEMENT: 144 cubic inches
BORE & STROKE: 3.5 x 2.5
COMPRESSION RATIO: 8.7-to-1
CARBURETION: single barrel
HORSEPOWER: 90 @ 4200 rpm
TORQUE: 138 lbs.-ft. @ 2000 rpm
TRANSMISSION: two-speed automatic
REAR AXLE RATIO: 3.56
GAS MILEAGE: 22/26 mpg.
ACCELERATION: 0-30 mph, 6 seconds; 0-45 mph in 11 seconds and 0-60 mph in 18.2 seconds
SPEEDOMETER ERROR: Indicated 30, 45 and 60 mph are actual 28.9, 43.7 and 57.1 mph respectively
POWER-WEIGHT RATIO: 27.7 lbs. per horsepower
HORSEPOWER PER CUBIC INCH: .63

Ford revives a familiar name in a new size

BORROWING the name "Ranchero" from the passenger car-like truck that was dropped from the 1960 model line-up and lifting the chassis, engine/drive line and front sheet metal from the highly successful Falcon compact, Ford Division of Ford Motor company now comes forth with the new Falcon Ranchero—a luxurious little pickup that offers economy with a limited degree of operational potential.

Worthy of a truck classification by virtue of an advertised 800-lb. payload, the new vehicle delivers the same type of low maintenance and high gasoline mileage that has endeared the conventional Falcon sedans and station wagons to so many new owners.

This test vehicle, a Ranchero with automatic two-speed transmission, delivered over 23 mpg in extremely cold weather and over an assortment of icy highways. Equipped with a 3.89 rear axle ratio, the new pickup demonstrated the same type of performance that the passenger car version has shown; i.e., 0-to-60 mph in 18.1 seconds.

Basically, the Ranchero is a Falcon station wagon—cut off at the back of the front seat and fitted with a normal pickup box in place of a rear seat and trunk area.

The cargo compartment measures 71.6 inches in length, 14.6 inches in height and 55.6 inches in width, combining to allow a floor area of 25.1 square feet and a box volume of 31.6 cubic feet.

The truck's engine/drive line components are direct pick-ups from the normal Falcon. Developing 90 hp at 4200 rpm with a torque output of 138 lbs.-ft. at 2000 rpm, the six-cylinder ohv engine is a duplicate of the passenger car unit. The chassis components designed for the Falcon station wagon, namely a larger rear end housing, a 3.89 axle ratio, stiffer shocks and spring rates and larger brakes at the rear, are used on the Ranchero, contributing to the vehicle's cargo-hauling potential—with a resultant loss in riding quality.

The vehicle handles much the same as the passenger car version. The ride is stiffer, the handling identical. These observations were made without a load, of course. If the full 800 lb. cargo rating were loaded aboard, the handling, economy and general performance would naturally be affected.

The cab compartment is a duplicate of the regular Falcon station wagon layout. Bench seats are used along with the dash assembly and steering wheel. The spare tire is housed behind the driver's seat back and the 14-gallon fuel tank is placed behind the passenger's seat below the level of the cushion. A filler neck for the tank is on the outside, to the rear of right door panel.

The test vehicle indicated that careful attention is being given to Falcon quality control. In general, the unit's entire appearance could be summed up as an excellent example of studied styling and a very pleasing approach to a truck for light hauling.

However, with a curb weight of 2,497 lbs. and a payload of 800 lbs. plus a passenger load of, say, 200 lbs. the unit would, without doubt, be straining a great deal to deliver any sort of desirable performance. On the other hand, when the unit's limitations are explained and demonstrated to the truck customer who requires a light, economical pickup for *light* hauling, the vehicle should respond satisfactorily for such a person.

In short, if hauling an occasional load of sand, bale of hay or box of tools is a part of someone's work-a-day routine, the new Falcon Ranchero should answer the need. But, remember, it isn't a heavyweight and it mustn't be treated like one. ●

FALCON RANCHERO

Falcon Ranchero survived months of testing with heavy loads over rough terrain.

THE FALCON RANCHERO, an economy-size pickup truck with the styling and comfort of a sedan, has been unveiled by the Ford Motor Co. Copying many features from the compact Falcon sedan, the new Ranchero has unitized body; six-cylinder, ohv, 90-hp, 144.3-cubic-inch engine; three-speed manual gearbox (two-speed automatic optional); plus 800 pounds of payload capacity on a 109.5-inch wheelbase. Underbody brackets and panels are zinc-coated for anti-rust protection, and special attention has been given to provide reliable operation under rugged conditions, yet total curb weight is only 2435½ pounds. Box (71.6 inches long) provides 31.6 cubic feet of space.

Angled swivel on passenger seatback allows easy access to spare and tools.

First of the compact car pickup trucks from an American manufacturer, Falcon Ranchero's rugged suspension and 90-hp engine easily haul king-size camper.

27

After a rough day of pounding a commercial rig through Tacoma traffic, trucker Jerry Grout hurries home to pamper his....

PICKUP
WITH PRIVILEGES

Tacoma, Washington  Photos by Pete Sukalac

LEFT — An extremely fine grille shell was hand-formed by owner Jerry Grout's friend, Derald Christensen. Note canted and upswept fender line, '56 Ford truck headlights and smooth hood. Tube grille bars are tipped with lucite. Great care was taken to fill body seams to accent smooth appearance.

RIGHT — 23 year old Jerry Grout is a trucker by trade, also secretary of the Tacoma Capers Car Club. His '57 Ford Ranchero has the tailgate welded solid to body, rear fins lengthened 6 inches, fenders extended 4 inches to house the 8-inch tunneled taillights. A couple of '53 Stude splash pans were used to form the rear grille cavity, enhanced with a series of chrome drawer handles against a lighter color tone. License framework is molded into the rear deck panel. Car is lowered legal limit front and rear.

RIGHT — Modestly warmed '57 Ford mill is muscular enough with Isky F300 cam, Thompson pistons, a Tri-power manifold. 292-inch V8 turns Schiefer flywheel and pressure plate assembly.

FAR RIGHT — Completely reupholstered in white and turquoise vinyl, interior helps Jerry make out at car shows —each show a win. Note relocated aerial.

BELOW—Elegant even in stock form, the Ranchero gets real 'sneaky' looking with added lowness and length. With its heavy work capacity gone, this little truck is guaranteed a future soft life.

LUGGER WITH A

photos by Don Klumpp

Daryl Emery did just about everything to his customized Ford Ranchero, three of the major modifications being a Lincoln engine, a custom interior and a chopped top

Moorhead, Minnesota

LEFT — We might as well start at the front which is, in Emery's case, dominated by a 370 cubic inch, '57 Lincoln engine. Valves pop courtesy action of an Isky cam and pass gas to Jahns pistons via ported and polished heads. An Edmunds intake mounts dual quads, down below torque is passed along to the '61 Ford trans by Schiefer flywheel.

BELOW—The tailgate area has received extensive revamping, now sports Edsel taillights. Tailgate itself has corners rounded, and all the hardware removed.

LOWERED LID

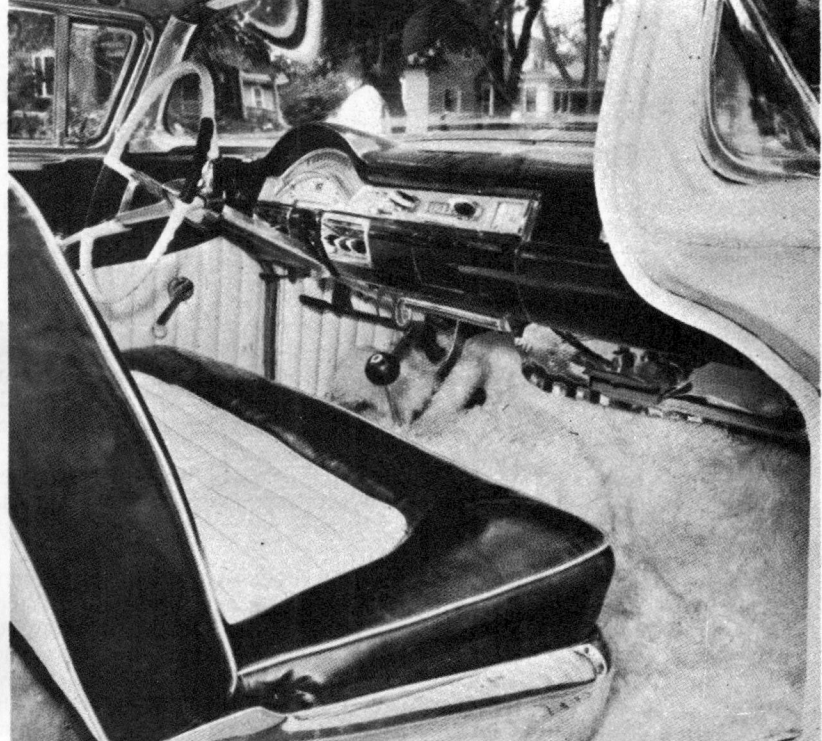

From any angle, this '58 Ranchero is distinctive. Scoops were built into the natural lines of each fender, Studebaker front gravel pans used to form the cavity for Corvette grille. The minor chop doesn't detract from interior done in Naugahyde with big, furry rugs that help keep out cold winter winds. A construction worker, Daryl Emery belongs to Swanks club, likes customs and boats.

Hauling Ranchero

Equally at home toting hay to the north pasture or kids to the country club dance, Ford's racy Ranchero is one of the most versatile, useful sets of wheels around

by Bob McVay, Technical Editor

A **PRESTIGE PICKUP** with classy styling and passenger-car comfort — that's Ford's Falcon Ranchero. For all-around usefulness, this machine showed us some very good thinking.

With three adults in the roomy cab and a couple of lightweight motorcycles in the pickup bed, the Ranchero proved the perfect vehicle for a day at the races or a weekend in the wide-open spaces. Power steering and automatic transmission (Ford's smooth three-speed unit) were concessions appreciated by the fair sex, while the 289-inch, ohv V-8 with a two-barrel carb gave the man of the family his share of the good things in automobiles — power with economy.

Our Ranchero, with three people and a motorcycle aboard, recorded 20 mpg on the freeway at 65 mph. Without the third passenger and the load, it was capable of 0-60 mph in 10.6 seconds and breezed through the quarter-mile in 18.2 seconds, with a terminal speed of 77 mph. Top speed was an honest

99 mph at 3800 rpm, where the two-barrel carb did restrict things a bit. Since Ford offers the four-barrel, 225-hp version, and with Shelby-American offering all sorts of speed equipment for the 289-incher, it's possible to get just about as much power as owners are willing to pay for.

Standard axle with the 200-hp V-8 and Cruise-O-Matic is a 2.80 ratio — a good combination for performance and economy. For towing or mountain use, the 3.50 ratio would be more desirable, especially if you anticipate much heavy load carrying.

It's a comfortable car to ride in. The Ranchero did show considerable under-steer when hustled through corners at above-average speeds, though. This was accompanied by a normal amount of body lean, which encouraged us to leave sports-car cornering to sports cars.

Since it's essentially a Falcon, the entire array of Falcon options can be ordered and fitted to the Ranchero. But because it lends itself so beautifully to

the outdoorsman, let's look a little closer at the sportier options. The two-barrel V-8 engine costs $157 extra, with the four-barrel option going for $211. Bucket seats cost $84.80, but they have to be ordered with the deluxe trim package — an additional $84.80. An all-synchromesh four-speed, floorshift transmission is $188, and the center console costs $51.50 more.

Falcon towing options include heavy-duty radiator, rear springs, load-leveling shocks, brake linings, battery, and 42-amp alternator. A limited-slip differential is also available, as is a frame-mounted, load-equalizing trailer hitch.

Set up as a sporty, fun car or a utilitarian, light-duty pickup, the Ranchero makes a perfect second car for the sport-loving family. The six-cylinder, 105-hp standard engine, three-speed manual shift combination starts as low as $2088. This pickup is equally at home in front of the country club or hauling an 800-pound payload. The Ranchero's as useful as it is classy. /MT

(ABOVE) *An adequate performer, "289" proved smooth, quiet, economical. A 200-inch, seven-main, 120-hp Six is also offered.*

(LEFT) *An excellent go-to-the-races machine, Ranchero carries three people, two lightweight motorcycles, plus picnic gear.*

PHOTOS BY DARRYL NORENBERG

Understeer was strong in nose-heavy Ranchero. Exuberant cornering techniques made body lean; car plowed right off track.

Spacious, comfortable interior has full carpeting and room for two-suiter and companion case behind three-passenger split seat.

FALCON RANCHERO

2-door, 3-passenger pickup

OPTIONS ON TEST CAR: "289" V-8, Cruise-O-Matic transmission, power steering, heater/defroster, radio, 2-tone paint, padded dash, trim package, whitewalls, 2-speed wipers.

BASE PRICE: $2245.84
PRICE AS TESTED: $2794.84 (plus tax and license)
ODOMETER READING AT START OF TEST: 4124 miles
RECOMMENDED ENGINE RED LINE: 5200 rpm

PERFORMANCE

ACCELERATION (2 aboard)
0-30 mph.................................... 3.5 secs.
0-45 mph.................................... 6.5
0.60 mph....................................10.6

PASSING TIMES AND DISTANCES
40-60 mph...............................5.8 secs., 423 ft.
50-70 mph...............................6.1 secs., 537 ft.
Standing start ¼-mile — 18.2 secs. and 77 mph
Speeds in gears @ shift points
   1st ....40 mph @ 4000 rpm   3rd .....99 mph @ 3800 mph
   2nd ...72 mph @ 4000 mph

Speedometer Error on Test Car
   Cars' speedometer reading 34 49 54 64 73 81
   Weston electric speedometer ...30 45 50 60 70 80
Observed mph per 1000 rpm in top gear ....22 mph
Stopping Distances—from 30 mph, 35.5 ft.; from 60 mph, 145.5 ft.

SPECIFICATIONS FROM MANUFACTURER

Engine
Ohv V-8
Bore: 4.005 ins.
Stroke: 2.87 ins.
Displacement: 289 cu. in.
Compression ratio: 9.3:1
Horsepower: 200 @ 4400 rpm
Horsepower per cubic inch: 0.66
Torque: 282 lbs.-ft. @ 2400 rpm
Carburetion: 1 2-bbl.
Ignition: 12-volt coil

Gearbox
3-speed automatic torque convertor; column shift

Driveshaft
1-piece, open-tube

Differential
Hypoid, semi-floating
Standard ratio: 2.80:1

Suspension
Front: Independent, SLA drag strut, with ball joints, tubular double-acting shocks mounted inside coil springs, link-type anti-roll bar.
Rear: Solid axle; 4-leaf semi-elliptical springs, tubular, double-acting shocks

Steering
Recirculating ball and nut,

with linkage-type power assist
Turning diameter: 38.8 ft.
Turns lock to lock: 3.73

Wheels and Tires
5-lug, steel disc wheels with 5-inch-wide rims
6.95 x 14 rayon tubeless whitewall tires

Brakes
Hydraulic, duo-servo; composite cast-iron drums
Front: 10.0-in. dia. x 2.25 ins. wide
Rear: 10.0-in. dia. x 1.75 ins. wide
Effective lining area: 127.8 sq. ins.
Swept drum area. 251.3 sq. ins.

Body and Frame
Unitized, with reinforced side rails, crossmembers and rocker panels
Wheelbase: 109.5 ins.
Track: front, 55.6 ins.; rear, 56.0 ins.
Overall length: 181.6 ins.
Overall width: 71.6 ins.
Overall height: 55.2 ins.
Curb weight: 3000 lbs.

Back lit by the shimmering Pacific, Ranchero etches a stylish silhouette in lengthening shadows.

Town &

Longer, lower, more luxurious, more powerful and in short, just plain better — this year's Ranchero puts a lot of good things on the line

by Eric Dahlquist/*technical editor*   *photography:* Eric Rickman

hrm ROAD TEST

Although it is contradictory to the actual fact of an ever more specialized American culture, there still seems a strong current of sentiment, as well as a ready market for the multi-purpose creation; things which combine the best of two or more worlds: lawnmowers that have alter egos as snow blowers, a winning drag machine that is satisfactory for everyday use, a Harvard education and a Yale degree (to note a famous quip).

Nowhere is this more true than in the automotive industry, and the most striking example is the passenger car pickup. The vehicle which, if you are to accept the validity of our advertising age, carries hay and fodder to the flock in the daylight and then at the curtain of night whisks you in magnificence to the front door of the country club without the slightest chance of being thought uncouth. So, how about it? Is it all ballyhoo? Do the Rancheros and El Caminos deliver the goods in both contexts or are they merely compromises that have limited passenger as well as cargo capacity?

It's been a number of years since we've tested one of these svelte beasts of burden, the Camino in '64 and the Ranchero 'way back when it first came out in 1957, but we've never really been too far away from the subject since our Photo Editor, E. Rickman, has a late Camino and Editor Bob Greene has probably the cherriest '58 Ranchero in captivity. Our idea: sample both current offerings and see how they stacked up against what they profess to be; the Ranchero this month and Camino next.

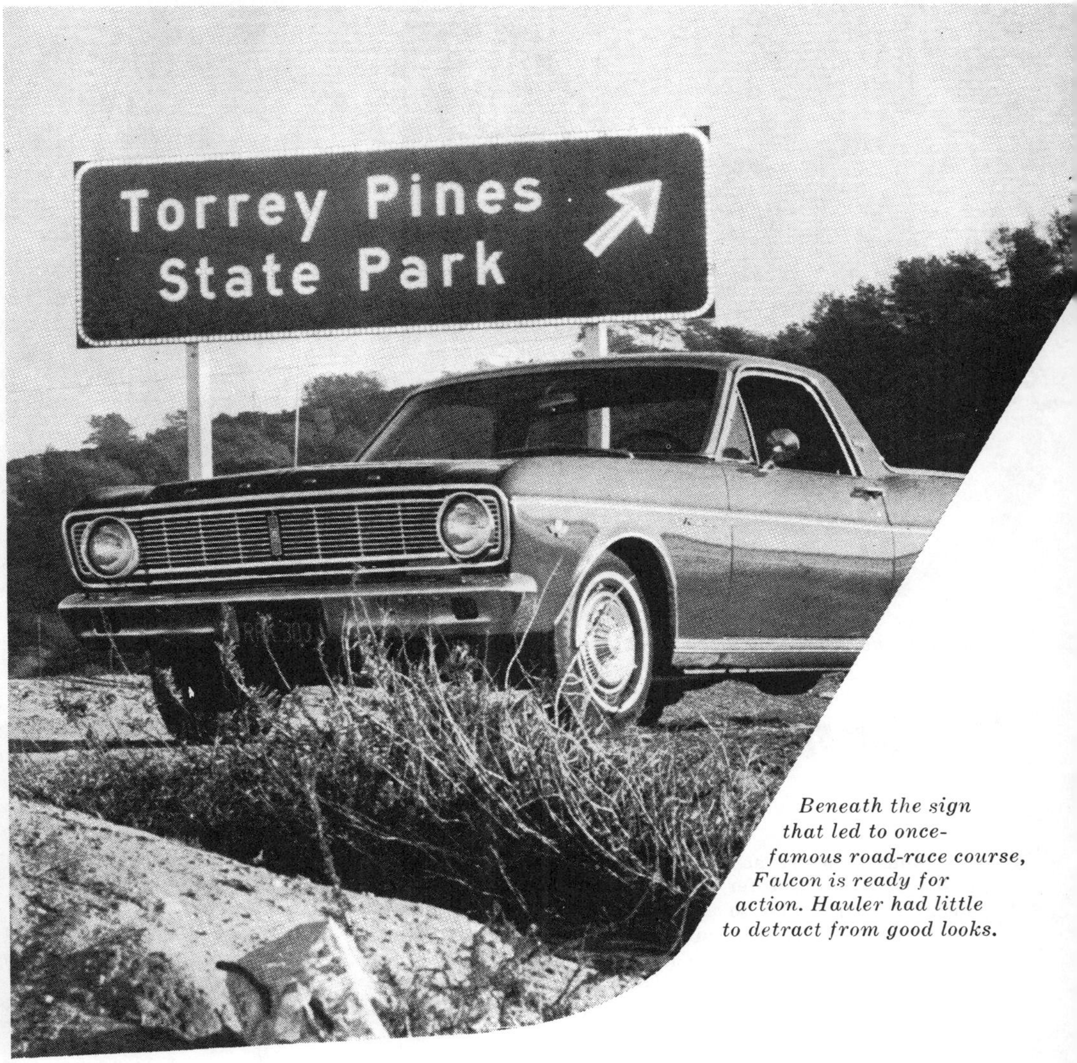

*Beneath the sign
that led to once-
famous road-race course,
Falcon is ready for
action. Hauler had little
to detract from good looks.*

Country Hauler

As with all American rolling stock of late, automobiles tend to reflect the economy which nourishes them, small in lean years, bigger when the "skies above are clear again." The Ranchero was conceived back in '57, carved out of the regular-sized Ford line, which is the only one they had at the time. And then in '60, when people looked with favor on smaller cars because they meant smaller gas bills, the pickup was transferred to the Falcon line, which meant it *Ford has cleverly combined Thunderbird roofline with long-hooded Mustang flavor. Wheel cutouts are generous, tire changes easy.* was less expensive but also less practical, because the carrying capacity was diminished. It still is in the Falcon line, but since that group now shares a common unit structure with the Fairlane, it's big again, larger inside and out, in fact, bigger than the '57 dimensions — in some aspects. Looking at it another way, the bed space is about 2 inches wider and deeper, and about 5 inches longer than the original Ranchero.

From the outside, the Falcon Ranchero bears not so much resemblance to its forebearer as to the El Camino, which is just about in the same league as far as dimensions go but offers a mite more engine flexibility. In fact, one passenger thought he was actually in an El Camino prototype, a misapprehension which ought to be food for thought at either or both styling camps.

This business about sharing basic Fairlane body structure tacitly implies several more bonuses than just a larger size which, in the Ranchero, incidentally, was .5-inch longer overall at 197.5 inches than the GT/A we tested last month. Try this for size. Almost all the suspension parts under the Falcon 289-V8, our test machine, were identical to those of its bigger brother, the Fairlane. This means that the pieces aren't necessarily more sturdy in proportion (because the Falcon is not that much smaller), but that some of those good Fairlane GT things would fit the Ranchero

You may bring home many bushels of seashells in the new Ranchero but surfboards or motorcycles or even a small boat would be more likely prospects. Rear window is recessed, allowing more bed space and shading—and a bit of a blind spot.

Town & Country Hauler

even though they're not specifically listed as options. Like the bigger brakes, stiffer springs, fatter anti-sway bar and quicker steering, just to enumerate a few fleeting surface reflections. And, as the Fairlane's unit construction was a stable platform on which to build, the Ranchero is especially solid because of that extra passenger compartment bulkhead stiffening up the entire structure. This particular idio-

syncrasy, capitalized to its maximum, would have allowed a door closing sound closely akin to the vault at the Chase Manhattan Bank. But, for some reason, the few cents worth of necessary insulation was conspicuously absent, and while not quite in the same steel-drum department as the Baja Marimba Band, it was less a statement than an echo. Since Ford has taken particular pains to place themselves in the low-volume sound chamber, it is hard to fathom the reason why the Ranchero had such a hollow ring. One possible reason may be that the extra bulkhead could make the structure a little too solid, causing the doors to oil-can when slammed. Well, maybe.

Other than this, our brick-red Ranchero was uncommonly

Test truck had stock suspension but heavy-duty kit is available for 1200-lb. loads. Five-leaf spring is wrapped in butyl rubber, completely isolating it from the rear axle. Engine was proven 289 cubic-incher that delivered good gas mileage but felt a little strangled on the upper end. Thermactor emission control was first we've come in contact with in tests.

Interior appointments were far above average in both balance and quality. Bucket seats were good compromise between adequate support and softness. Beneath fiberboard panel that finished bulkhead neatly, space was provided for tire, parcels.

free from assembly-line faults. All the trim ended where it should have and was properly fastened and aligned. Even the thin, twin white stripes which ran down the midsection gave a sense of individual detailing.

Once quartered in one of the bucket seats, the "in-group" is treated to the bossest of boss sights, an all-black interior that runs from the doors, paneled in vinyl, to waves of rolling deep-pile carpeting that just oozes luxury. Tasteful contrast is the gleaming instrument control group which consists totally of two round nacelles and, between the seats, the side-saddle Sports-Shift console. If you recall, last month our hackles were raised by the firmness of the buckets, and the radio which didn't bathe us in soft serenade. Now sup-

posedly, these items are similar from the Fairlane to the Falcon and vice versa. At least they look the same, but somehow the Ranchero's saddles were more enjoyable, as was the audio.

We didn't have the Ranchero nearly as long as we would have liked, especially after getting a taste of long stretches of open road. To say that the Falcon Engineering hawks have truly worked wonders in getting the car to float along at 60-70 mph without annoying chop or bounce or pitch fails in trying to relate how great the Ranchero's ride really is. Ford is anxious to have people get out and test drive their offerings and this is one of the prime reasons.

Only bits of tuning performed on Ranchero engine were checks to see that: contacts had right gap, butterflies opened all the way and positioning of accelerator pump arm in highest throttle arm hole. These things helped slightly. Front suspension is typical FoMoCo coil over A-arm arrangement that was good for ride but less than great for cornering. Options would help.

Town & Country Hauler

Lying like a distant cloud on the horizon was the anticipation that the soft springing and shocking required for the cushioned-carpet effect would not augur well for superior handling on humpy, twisting back roads. And it didn't, at least not to the Fairlane GT's level of accomplishment. Oh, it will get around a turn safely enough for average conditions, but with a weight bias front to rear of 53.4-46.6 (percent), and recommended tire pressure of 24-30 pounds front to rear, it means that you dash about with care, especially when the movements are quick because the body tends to lift just a little as the chassis gets set up. It's a forgiving machine, though, for although we lost it for just an instant in the rain on one occasion, it recovered in marvelous fashion. It would demand only a few pieces to improve the situation, such as a bigger anti-roll bar (the stock is .065-inch) and higher rate springs. Interestingly enough, the Ranchero offers a heavy-duty load package, stated to up total carrying capacity from 850 pounds to 1250 and, although we didn't learn exactly of what the heartier things consisted, it probably isn't too unlike the Fairlane GT options.

The last Ford we tested didn't have discs and really didn't need them, but that was with 314 square inches of swept drum area on a machine weighing 3600 pounds or so. Reduce the swept area to 282.6 inches and the area-to-weight ratio, while adequate, is not outstanding. We made our usual number of hard stops from 60 mph and found that the molded organic linings get the job done but not without fade. For our dough, the minimum anchors for the Ranchero should be identical to the Fairlane GT.

The Rancheros in '66 can be had with three choices of powerplants: a 120 hp 200 cubic inch six; a 200 hp 289 cubic inch V8 with 2-barrel carburetor; and the 4.005 x 2.87-inch bore and stroke 225 hp 289 we had in the test car. Engineering on the mills hasn't been altered greatly from 289's of the past, and the same type carburetor and distributor are retained. There is one thing that is new, however, the Thermactor exhaust control device. California has led the nation in its continuing fight against smog and the exhaust hydrocarbons which allegedly produce it, and they are the first to require a piece of equipment that helps the engine to burn its fuel more efficiently, thereby reducing the number of hydrocarbons reaching the clean air.

In effect, there is a tiny air injector pump (another belt-driven accessory) which forces fresh oxygen into the exhaust manifold where it re-ignites and burns away most of those hydrocarbons which somehow get away scot-free from the chambers. Besides increasing exhaust manifold temperature (no more custom headers), it also requires some slight modifications to the carburetor and ignition, like leaning the mixture and retarding the spark about 6 degrees.

The 289 has always been fairly snappy but our Ranchero just seemed to run out of breath on top end. When first encountering this condition, we checked the point and plug gap (.015 and .032 inches respectively) and the carburetor to see if the barrels were opening to their maximum. Everything was fine.

While the air cleaner was off, we moved the accelerator pump arm to its highest position, a trick on a Ford-produced carburetor that is the hot-tip. Although this helped slightly, it didn't unleash any lightning, as 0-60's in the low 10's reflected. We didn't take the Ranchero to the drags, but similarly equipped machines are turning high 17-second runs in the mid 70's.

Our engineering qualifications do not permit us to state that the Thermactor decreased performance but we noted with interest that our Fairlane GT had somehow been delivered without one.

Transmission choice in this Ranchero was the 3-speed Cruise-O-Matic with ratios of 2.46, 1.46 and 1.00. It has a neat feature that will especially be appreciated where King Winter holds court. You see, the selector could be left in D (green) and the box would mesh on its appointed rounds or, by putting the indicator in D (red), (one notch forward), the trans would take off in second gear, just right when coupled with the 3.00 rear end ratio for quick getaway in slip and slide scenes.

Another thing that we liked, and will no doubt find favor with everyone, is that the Ranchero, equipped with 4-barrel and all, weaned out surprisingly good gas mileage. On a 300-mile jaunt to Bruce Crower's in Chula Vista, California, 5 miles from the American/Mexican border, the Ford recorded a laudable 17.1 mpg at sustained 65-70 mph speeds. And around town, in both normal and express thoroughfares, this figure elevated to about 18 mpg flat, quite high as current U.S. models go.

And the price wasn't bad, either, listing out at some $3118.00 with power steering, brakes, radio, buckets and the other extra cost items. These two things, gas economy with reasonable performance and nonprohibitive sticker price, are two reasons why the new Falcon has a good year ahead. If it also incorporated bigger brakes and stiffer suspension, correcting those difficulties which dull the brilliance of its luster, who knows — there might be a Ford in almost everyone's future. ▪▪

Falcon Ranchero V-8

Ford's Fancy Funabout Is More than Mere Utility

SELDOM DO WE receive for testing a car that is so pleasant, and seldom does our testing become so enjoyable. This was the case with the 1966 Falcon Ranchero, which was a pleasant surprise from the beginning. It was a car we hadn't expected to get—hadn't even requested, as a matter of fact—but there it was, one of the first '66s to show up in our parking lot. Moreover, it was ours to play with for a good long time, with no pressure to return it for some other assignment.

Car Life sampled a Falcon some time ago, before the Mustang onslaught. It was a 289-cu. in. Sprint V-8 convertible, likewise a "fun" car, extremely pleasant despite those few drawbacks dictated by cost considerations. The Falcon, in the final analysis, is and has been a minimal cost answer to the transportation needs of the American public. From that point of view, it is difficult to fault the Falcon with any great conviction.

For the first time since 1960, the Falcon really is new this year. There was a major change in lower sheet metal in 1964, coinciding with the appearance of the Chevelle and B-O-P A-body intermediates, but the change then was only skin deep. Not only is there a full-blown new body this year, but a significant realignment of the full Falcon/Fairlane spectrum also occurred. The upshot of this change-about is a thoroughly upgraded Falcon of virtual Fairlane standards. As one product planner told a CL editor re-

Falcon Ranchero V-8

cently, "The level of quality which was sufficient for 1960 is no longer adequate in the mid-'60s."

Dimensional comparisons illustrate the change in Falcon/Fairlane relationships this year:

	'65 Falcon	'66 Falcon	'66 Ranchero	'65 Fairlane	'66 Fairlane
Wheelbase	109.5	110.9	113.0	116.0	116.0
Overall length	181.6	184.3	197.5	198.8	197.0
Width	71.6	73.5	74.7	73.8	74.0
Height	54.5	54.6	56.2	55.8	54.3
Tread, f/r	55/56	58/58	58/58	57/56	58/58
Curb weight, base car, lb.	2510	2677	2615	2975	2922
Std. engine	170/105	170/105	200/120	200/120	200/120
Max. engine	289/225	289/200	289/225	289/271	390/335
Base tire	6 6.00-13	6.50-13	7.35-14	6.95-14	6.95-14
V-8	6.45-14	6.95-14	7.75-14	7.35-14	7.75-14

To be completely accurate, another column should be added to the chart for the Comet. It fits immediately after the Ranchero and before the Fairlane, completing the progressive range of dimensions from prior Falcons to present Fairlanes. The Ranchero column does, in fact, contain figures which are representative of all three brands, because all share the same station wagon body, basis of the Ranchero pickup.

Such close alignment among the "light cars," as company spokesmen characterize them, might be expected to lead to a great deal of internecine cannibalism. But, as the GM divisions have proven with their A-body cars, there's enough action in that market segment to satisfy everybody and, additionally, it is growing. From early sales results, the Ford realignment bears this out. The Falcon may not be doing spectacular things, but Ford marketers didn't expect it to until spring. Other '66 cars were expected to take the early spotlight (which they did) and Mustang momentum was enough to initially obscure the arrival of the new Falcon. At introduction time, *Car Life* characterized the Falcon as the "sleeper" and it's just about time for awakening.

It seems almost odd, in view of the more utilitarian nature of the Ranchero, that it should so readily awaken attention wherever it is driven. It is, obviously, styled with restraint and a great deal of taste, but it really shouldn't attract all that attention. In fact, when passing an El Camino on the street, there's a little too much resemblance noticeable. Still, that's hardly unusual among light trucks, where often only huge tailgate nameplates serve to differentiate brands.

CLOSER COMPARISON to the El Camino reveals a mixed scorecard. Most obviously, the Chevrolet pickup can be ordered with a much larger engine—up to the 396 cu. in./360 bhp level. For another thing, it is minutely larger in most dimensions and a full 2 in. longer in wheelbase. The El Camino has had in the past the appearance, at least, of being somewhat more expensive than the Ranchero, though probably this no longer is true. Where the Ranchero chalks up points, however, is in being unitized. It is a much more solid vehicle on the road, without any particular sacrifice in riding comfort (unladen), and tips the scales at 300 lb. less in basic form.

The test Ranchero was the Custom model, identified initially by the twin-stripe paint highlight along the body midline and bright metal trim around wheel openings and along the rocker sill. Though equipped with the 4-barrel 225-bhp V-8 engine, it initially impressed our testers as having the 2-barrel, 200-bhp engine which tops the regular Falcon sedan option list. It was not until the engine was physically examined, once uncertainties cropped up in preparing the data panel, that the fact of the matter was discovered.

There were several explanations for this state of affairs. Most obvious was an extremely erroneous speedometer, which announced a more sluggish pace of performance than actually was the case. There was some hint of this when one driver, indicating 60 mph on the freeway, discovered he was moving faster than the rest of the traffic. Without the grim determination to continually rate and relate the Ranchero—which normally happens with a test car—this aspect was ignored until all the data were gathered.

Another item, psychologically at least, put a damper on performance: The Thermactor exhaust control device. Like a California Albatross strung by a fan belt to the engine's neck, it emitted an incessant, continually audible inhaling of air. Its purpose is ostensibly to complete fuel combustion in the exhaust manifold, but visions of radically disorganized air flows within the engine beclouded that knowledge. The moan of air being ingested sounded like nothing so much as a sick engine, hence the vehicle just didn't *seem* healthy to our drivers. Perhaps it was; auto engineers say that engine performance isn't inhibited by the exhaust devices, though their smiles may seem a bit weak when they say it. Maybe the engine just sounds that way and there is another explanation for significantly better performance in a non-Therm-actored '65 CL test car. That was a Mustang with an identical power train, but only 300 lb. lighter in weight (CL, April 1965), which achieved a 16.8 sec. quarter-mile with an 84 mph terminal velocity, an 8.5 sec. 0-60 and a 15.8 sec. 0-80. It, too, recorded a 15-18 mpg range in fuel consumption. Or there was the even closer parallel of the '65 Fairlane (CL, March '65) weighing 100 lb. more, but producing 25 bhp less with only a 2-barrel carburetor, which returned performance figures as good as the Ranchero's. But, perhaps there's some other explanation.

Be that as it may, the Ranchero was sprightly enough for the purposes to which it may be put. The overall pleasantness of the vehicle contributed greatly toward overcoming the Therm-actor distraction. While it is difficult to pinpoint the reason for the car's appeal, we suspect a large part of it was due to the 2-passenger nature of the cabin. Ford, despite corporate objections to 2-passenger vehicles, has produced one in the Ranchero. It isn't a sports car by any stretch of the imagination, but the cabin gives the impression of one. There is something about having the rear window just behind one's shoulders which imparts a closer kinship between driver and machine. Even the utilitarian nature of the Ranchero couldn't destroy this cozy relationship.

Bucket seats and console added to this illusion, permitting occupants to forget about that trailing cargo space (which really isn't all that commodious). Custom trim adds $136 to the cost of the vehicle and it is up to the individual buyer to determine whether such accommodations are worth the tariff. The buckets are quite flat, sitting somewhat higher than expected, and separated by the asymmetrically rounded console which is Ford fashion this year. The seats provide a minimum of lateral support although back support is adequate for long distance traveling.

THE SEATING POSITION was what has come to be regarded as typically

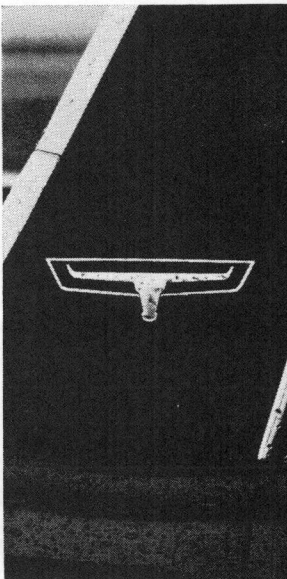

SCOTT MALCOLM PHOTOS

Ford; the cushion is either a shade too low or the steering wheel a shade too high. It is always a bother to adjust to this foible with each new Ford, but in the Ranchero's case, it was quickly accommodated. Staff members agreed, however, that were any of them to buy a Ranchero they would immediately replace the deeply dished steering wheel with one of the sportier, flatter, thicker-rimmed wheels that are available. This, in effect, would lower the wheel slightly as well as place it a trifle farther from the driver's chest—thereby exchanging whatever chest protecting value the deep-dish design may have for the accident-avoiding value of proper control.

Falcon Ranchero V-8

Even so, there were no problems in proper control of the Ranchero. Indeed, this too, was one of the factors which made the vehicle so pleasant. Somewhat surprisingly, the weight distribution of the unloaded Ranchero is a great deal better than the curbside glance would indicate. With the back end doing a fairer share of the work, handling and control do not suffer as might otherwise be expected. But more basic has been the change in front suspension geometry, raising the front roll center for the new chassis structure to improve the precision in handling and roadability. The newly designed steering linkage was quite good, exhibiting none of the full-lock kick that marred earlier power-assisted Falcons, although assistance is still via linkage booster instead of the more modern integral arrangement. Adequate effort and road feel are retained, so that the driver doesn't feel he's twisting the steering shaft in a pile of greased ball bearings.

Brakes are only average in effectiveness, though they exhibited a welcome ability to resist fade. It was possible to lock the rears in a panic stop, but this was more the fault of the power boost than the brakes themselves. Keeping in mind that the vehicle would undoubtedly be used hauling things in the back, the brakes are none too good. It's a pity that the Mustang discs aren't available on Fairlanes or Falcons, too.

One tangible benefit of last season's legislative harassment of Detroit has been the placarding of new cars with decals advising proper tire inflations and load limits. This, together with the fitting of larger tires on many cars, is a welcome move. In the Ranchero, the decal inside the glove box lid warns drivers to carry 24 psi front and 30 psi rear (cold) and to add 4 psi all around for fast driving. It also states that 850 lb. is maximum rated load with standard suspension (driver plus 700 lb. cargo) or 1250 with heavy-duty under-pinnings. It may only be our imagination, but the owner's manual inside the glove box also seemed more thorough and informative than has heretofore been the case.

Larger cross-section tires make the Ranchero sit slightly higher than other Falcons, a factor easing entrance and exit from the sporty interior. And that interior, complete with wall-to-wall carpeting, vinyl door panel inserts and padded everything else, was impressive for its care in assembly. This was a utilitarian vehicle, in Ford's cheapest domestic line, but it illustrated the great strides in assembly quality which the corporation has taken in the past 24 months. There were no gaps, no rough edges, no slap-dash attachings, no dangling wires or doodads that didn't work. Everything was designed to fit and, when it was put together, it did just that. The only flaw we could find was a tiny corner of the seat covering poking out from beneath the chrome side molding; it was easily remedied with momentary application of a razor blade.

ONE THING worked too well: The light in the transmission lever's console quadrant was bright enough to cause distraction when driving at night.

1966 FORD
FALCON CUSTOM RANCHERO

DIMENSIONS

Wheelbase, in.	113.0
Track, f/r, in.	58/58
Overall length, in.	197.5
width	74.7
height	56.2
Front seat hip room, in.	2 x 25
shoulder room	58.0
headroom	38.2
pedal-seatback, max.	46.5
Rear seat hip room, in.	
shoulder room	
leg room	
head room	
Door opening width, in.	45.5
Floor to ground height, in.	12.5
Ground clearance, in.	5.9

PRICES

List, fob factory	$2299
Equipped as tested	3118

Options included: 289/225 engine, auto. trans., power steering, power brakes, bucket seats and console, wheel covers, remote side mirror, exhaust control system, pushbutton am radio, deluxe seat belts, wsw tires.

CAPACITIES

No. of passengers	2
Luggage space, cu. ft.	39.1
Fuel tank, gal.	20.0
Crankcase, qt.	5.0
Transmission/diff., pt.	8.25/4
Radiator coolant, qt.	15.0

CHASSIS/SUSPENSION

Frame type	unitized

Front suspension type: Independent s.l.a. with lower drag strut, ball joints, coil springs over upper arm, concentric tubular shock absorber.

ride rate at wheel, lb./in.	192
anti-roll bar dia., in.	0.65

Rear suspension type: Hotchkiss drive, with variable rate semi-elliptic leaf springs and angle-mounted tubular shock absorbers.

ride rate at wheel, lb./in.	100-160

Steering system: Recirculating ball and nut gearbox; parallelogram linkage, power assisted.

gear ratio	16:1
overall ratio	21.4:1
turns, lock to lock	3.73
turning circle, ft. curb-curb	41.0
Curb weight, lb.	2945
Test weight	3560
Weight distribution, % f/r	53.5/46.5

BRAKES

Type: Single-line hydraulic, self-adjusting duo-servo shoes in cast-iron drums.

Front drum, dia. x width, in.	10 x 2.5
Rear drum, dia. x width	10 x 2.0
total swept area, sq. in.	282.6
Power assist. . .integral, vac. booster line psi @ 100 lb. pedal	760

WHEELS/TIRES

Wheel size	14x5J
optional size available	none
bolt no./circle dia., in.	5/4.5

Tire make, brand: Goodyear Power Cushion

size	7.35-14
recommended inflation, psi.	24/30
capacity rating, total lb.	4080

ENGINE

Type, no. cyl.	ohv, V-8
Bore x stroke, in.	4.00 x 2.87
Displacement, cu. in.	289
Compression ratio	10:1
Rated bhp @ rpm	225 @ 4800
equivalent mph	120
Rated torque @ rpm	305 @ 3200
equivalent mph	79
Carburetion	1x4
barrel dia., pri./sec.	1.437

Valve operation: Hydraulic lifters pushrods and rockers

valve dia., int./exh.	1.78/1.45
lift, int./exh.	0.36/0.38
timing, deg.	16-70, 52-24
duration, int./exh.	266/266
opening overlap	40

Exhaust system: Y type, single muffler

pipe dia., exh./tail	2.0/1.75
Lubrication pump type	rotor
normal press. @ rpm.50-60@2000	
Electrical supply	alternator
ampere rating	38
Battery, plates/amp. rating	54/45

DRIVE-TRAIN

Transmission type: Torque converter automatic, 3-speed with planetary gearset.

Gear ratio 4th ( ) overall	
3rd (1.00)	3.00
2nd (1.46)	4.38
1st (2.46)	7.38
1st x t.c. stall (2.02)	14.9
synchronous meshing	planetary
Shift lever location	console

Differential type: Hypoid; straddle-mounted pinion

axle ratio	3.00:1

IT'S A pleasure to be picked up in this pickup fitted with bucket seats, console and carpeting.

EVEN TAILGATE actuation can be fun with an assist from the Ranchero's counter-sprung lifting mechanism.

Rough edges and runny paint were visible in one place—down behind the seats where a pair of compartments were cut under the cargo deck. One was filled with the spare tire, but the other made an excellent out-of-sight stowage area for valuables being carried in the car. There obviously is little need to finish off such inconspicuous places.

The Ranchero had enough charm about it to make one forget he was, after all, only riding in a pickup truck. It was quite sufficient, in appearance and in grace, for driving to the country club or to a doorman-attended hotel. We suspect that womenfolk wouldn't need much persuasion to be chauffered to a fancy-dress ball in this car. But

more than that, it was fun to drive. There was an exhilaration about the Ranchero, not from a wind-in-the-face sportiness, but in a delightfully capable, nimble and responsive vehicle which performed its assigned tasks with aplomb. The most disappointing thing about it was that we had to return it. ∎

CAR LIFE ROAD TEST

ACCELERATION & COASTING

(Graph: ELAPSED TIME IN SECONDS vs MPH, showing 1st, 2nd, 3rd gears and SS ¼)

CALCULATED DATA

Lb./bhp (test weight)	15.8
Cu.ft./ton mile	114
Mph/1000 rpm (top gear)	24.8
Engine revs/mile (60 mph)	2420
Piston travel, ft./mile	1160
Car Life wear index	28.0
Frontal area, sq. ft.	23.4
Box volume, cu. ft.	431

SPEEDOMETER ERROR

30 mph, actual	31.7
40 mph	42.8
50 mph	54.2
60 mph	65.0
70 mph	75.6
80 mph	86.0
90 mph	

MAINTENANCE INTERVALS

Oil change, engine, miles	6000
transmission/differential	as req.
Oil filter change	6000
Air cleaner service, mo.	12
Chassis lubrication	36,000
Wheelbearing re-packing	30,000
Universal joint service	30,000
Coolant change, mo.	24

TUNE-UP DATA

Spark plugs	BF-42
gap, in.	0.032-0.036
Spark setting, deg./idle rpm	0/950
cent. max. advance, deg./rpm	26/4800
vac. max. adv., deg./in. Hg	15/11.5
Breaker gap, in.	0.014-0.016
cam dwell angle	26-28.5
arm tension, oz.	17-20
Tappet clearance, int./exh.	0/0
Fuel pump pressure, psi	4.5
Radiator cap relief press., psi	12-15

PERFORMANCE

Top speed (3800), mph	95
Shifts (rpm) @ mph	
3rd to 4th ( )	
2nd to 3rd (4400)	75
1st to 2nd (4200)	42

ACCELERATION

0-30 mph, sec.	3.9
0-40 mph	5.6
0-50 mph	7.7
0-60 mph	10.3
0-70 mph	13.9
0-80 mph	18.8
0-90 mph	25.8
0-100 mph	
Standing ¼-mile, sec.	17.7
speed at end, mph	78
Passing, 30-70 mph, sec.	10.0

BRAKING

(Maximum deceleration rate achieved from 80 mph)

1st stop, ft./sec./sec.	22
fade evident?	some, rears lock
2nd stop, ft./sec./sec.	21.5
fade evident?	slight

FUEL CONSUMPTION

Test conditions, mpg	16.8
Normal conditions, mpg	14-17
Cruising range, miles	280-340

GRADABILITY

4th, % grade @ mph	
3rd	10 @ 56
2nd	16 @ 43
1st	30 @ 21

DRAG FACTOR

Total drag @ 60 mph, lb.	214

A PICKUP THAT SWINGS

Want a utility vehicle you can use on weekends? A machine that can be used for towing or a date? It's all right there in the all new full sized 289 powered Ford Ranchero.

TEST TEAM/*Trackers Car Club, Burbank, California*

BY DICK SCRITCHFIELD ■ Being a regular reader of CAR CRAFT, you are aware that we normally test only the high performance models that you would consider buying for a street/strip car. Although the Ford 289 Ranchero might not be classified a "high performance" vehicle, it is becoming extremely popular around the drag strips as a utility car. Anyone that ever owned a competition car soon learns that the tow/push car is as vitally important as the drag car. Without a good tow car, you just don't arrive, at least in time for the meet! Often a lot of consideration must be given before a decision is reached regarding which type of vehicle best suits your particular needs. The first tow car is usually based on what's available, and ends up by being a passenger car, not really suited for the task. As you progress further into drag racing, and a tow car or two has blown up under you, you start thinking about a machine designed and built for towing. □ Deciding to find out how well the Ranchero would act in this capacity, we started searching for a club primarily interested in drag racing. Our search ended at the Trackers Car Club, located in Burbank, Calif. They own a very clean and rapid '34 Ford in C/Altered which they run frequently at the strip with great success. The Trackers were formed in 1957 by school mate drag racing enthusiasts who decided they could have more fun and build a better car by pooling their resources.

Obtaining an eight car garage and a '34 Ford Coupé, got the organization underway. Since '57, members have come and gone, but the coupe remains, receiving changes from year to year as the groups' drag knowledge increases. □ Getting together at the Tracker's garage, they were eager to be given a chance to test the all new Ford Ranchero. They immediately noticed the "Falcon" name plate had been dropped and was not shown anywhere on the car although the car is still in the Falcon line and uses the basic station wagon chassis. Recalling the diminished size of the Falcon Ranchero from the original '57 Ranchero, they were glad to see that the '66 had come back to the normal size of things with its overall length of 197.5 inches. In fact, it's almost as large as the original, having a 113 inch wheelbase, to the '57's 116 inch. In comparison, the wheelbase on the '65 Falcon Ranchero measured only 109.5 inches. The pickup box has grown 7½ inches in length, 4 inches in width and almost 2 inches in depth, giving you a big 39 cubic-foot capacity. Overall, it's three inches wider, and two inches lower, and 16″ longer than the '65. Really quite a change. □ For the test, we had received the "Custom" model which was pretty plush for a utility vehicle. The Standard Ranchero comes to you at about $2300 from the factory and includes a 6 cylinder, 200 cubic-inch engine and three speed manual transmission. With the "Custom" model you get those

44

neat thin twin strips the full length of the body, bright metal window frames, rocker panel mouldings, and wheel-well lip mouldings. On the inside, you step onto deep loop pile carpeting and look into a swept-away instrument panel with perfectly positioned big round gauges. For about $136 more, you can have bucket seats and a console below the "T" handle shifter. The buckets fit you just right giving you support the full width of your back. Power steering and power brakes were a couple of added accessories which proved useful for our tests, and an option well worth the extra cost now that the Ranchero has grown up. □ The pickup was turned over to the Trackers for several days while they used it to chase parts and eventually tow their '34 to the Lion's Drag Strip in Long Beach. Club President Chuck Coulter thought, **"The buckets are really comfortable and place you right where you want to be. I wonder, however, if a bench seat wouldn't be more valuable in a tow car. It seems that at the drags you're always cramming 3 or 4 people in the front seat, and you'd be pretty much out of luck with the buckets.** □ **"The power steering is a big help when backing the trailer or in just driving. It is not as effortless as earlier models so that you feel you're the one who's actually in control. It feels good to me.** □ **"Engine**

power is ideal for towing a light car and trailer, such as a dragster, but I personally feel it could stand a little more power for towing a car as heavy as our 2900 pound coupe and a 7 to 800 pound tandem trailer.** □ **"It's good to see the larger sized Ranchero back on the market again. The compact Ranchero looked nice, but it was too short of space to really make it a good utility car. This one has just the right amount for drag strip weekends."** □ Option engines for the new Ranchero are two and four barrel carbureted 8 cylinder, 289 cubic-inchers with 4 inch bores and 2.87 inch strokes. Compres-

Trackers Car Club racing team loads up the Ranchero preparing for a day at the drags with their Chrysler powered '34 Ford coupe. Club's eight car garage is excellent place to work on projects. Coupe took B/comp at '62 Winternationals.

113-inch wheelbase makes the all new Ford Ranchero just right as a drag tow-push car. Long Beach Drag Strip played host to Car Test Club, giving Trackers a chance to really put the car through its paces as a utility vehicle. No runs were made.

sion ratio is rated at 10:1 with the 4 barrel equipped engine and produces 225 horsepower at 4800 rpm. If you want more horsepower, the options are almost unlimited for this popular engine, either through the dealer or speed shops. □ Fully synchronized transmissions are the stick offerings with both the three and four speed manuals available, or if you've given up the shifting bit, the three-speed dual-range automatic is waiting for your order. The Cruise-O-Matic, as it's called, has ratios of 2.46, 1.46 and 1.00 and topped off with a neat selector box. The instant the ignition switch is turned on, the indicator window on the shift console lights up the red or green letter. Two "D's" (drives) are indicated, one lighting up green while the other lights up red. Seeing all these colors immediately sent us looking for the owners manual. Thumbing through, we discovered that normal Drive position was indicated by the green light and Drive, for slippery roads, was in red along with the rest of the selector positions. Putting the selector in "red" Drive (one notch below Neutral), the transmission started off in second, just right for rain or snow covered pavement. □ "Roller," oops, Rowland Hall, as his parents know him, was quite enthusiastic about the Ranchero. □ **"It is definitely the answer for those trips to the drags, whether it's towing or taking the wife, or both. With that luxurious interior you'd feel as much at home headed for a dance as**

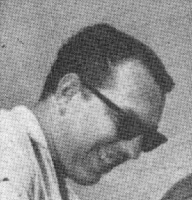

the drags! The ride is as soft as any passenger car and there's certainly no question about the comfort. I like the center console with the storage area. Only trouble is that the seat buckle usually falls against it when it's released, cutting nicks. There should be some type of bracket where it could be attached when not being used. On the other side, the retractor makes the belt act like a piece of spaghetti, causing the metal clasp to nick both the seat and the door sill mouldings as it whips into the keeper. The "Fasten Seat Belt" light under the dash is a good reminder. Haven't quite figured that out yet, but I guess it's on a timer as it doesn't go out when the belts are fastened.** □ **"I was surprised at how solid and air tight the Ranchero felt. It's really hard to shut the doors with the windows rolled all he way up. The spaciousness of the interior is quite remarkable from last year's model, even with the closeness of the rear window, fitting the way it does, into the cab. Speaking of windows, I like the curved glass design of the side windows as it really adds a lot to the modern curves of the car."** □ The suspension is a cross between the Falcon line and the Fairlane which would be useful should some of the heavy duty options be desired by the owner. With such items as stiffer springs and enlarged anti-sway bar being available, this could set the suspension to anyone's needs. Front suspension is the usual Ford design. Independent with lower drag strut and coil springs mounting over the upper "A" arm. An anti-roll bar of .65 inches is standard. Stability could be improved with the heavier Fairlane unit. In the rear, two five-leaf semi-elliptic springs are mounted to handle a maximum load of 700 pounds. By installing the heavy duty option, capacity is increased to 1250 pounds. It seems well worth the extra money. □ What impressed Larry Murphy the most was the positioning of the front seat. □ **"Boy, am I glad to see a seat that will adjust for my 6'7"! This is one of the few vehicles that I've driven that is roomy enough to keep me**

from getting my legs tied in knots and that is really comfortable. The hanging gas pedal takes a little getting used to, with the pedal itself pivoting, but once you're used to it, it's much more comfortable than the normal type. The seat belt warning light is a nice little accessory, lighting as soon as the switch is turned. Although the ride is quite soft and smooth, I feel as though I'm balancing atop a rubber

(continued on following page)

SWINGIN' PICKUP

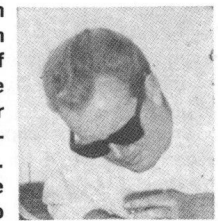

ball. I like a much stiffer suspension than what is standard. Possibly, the heavy duty set-up controls it better. I would prefer the four-speed transmission, but the automatic seems very smooth. With the H-D suspension, it would make a terrific tow car. The instruments have an excellent location being directly in front of the driver while their well-designed round faces are easy to read at a glance. Considering the rate that we were passing cars, it appears that quite a bit of error is present in the speedometer gearing. Even though the car is equipped with "Casler's," a variation that great shouldn't occur." ☐ This is the first year that Falcon has offered power brakes, which should prove helpful on the Ranchero, especially in towing. The vacuum booster reduces pedal effort by 55 per cent and cuts pedal travel to speed up braking response. Also new, is the foot operated parking brake. Front drum braking surface is 10 inches in diameter by 2½ inches, while the rear's are 10 inches by 2 inches, giving good positive control. Tires are Goodyear Power Cushion, 7.35 x 14. ☐ In the body department, the new integral-constructed body shell features isolated torque boxes and a "catwalk" on both sides of the engine for added rigidity. Quality control is superior from past years which is noticeable in the correct panel alignment and overall finishing. Really a marked improvement.

☐ Club Treasurer, Terry Trimble, agreed with "Merf" that the suspension could be stiffer, especially if much towing was involved. ☐ **"I prefer a car with a little more stability. Although the Ranchero rides beautifully over the bumps in the road, it is too soft on the corners and seems to roll excessively. You definitely would need a stiffer suspension for extensive towing. The American "Mags" and Casler tires really set it off and give it the "hot" appearance while the 289 V-8 seems to have all the power you'd need. The inside storage compartments are very handy and quite roomy. At least it gives you a place to store things out of sight. To me, the pickup bed is at just the right height so that you can easily lift things over the side without having to go past the tailgate every time. The tailgate is the easiest I've ever seen to operate. It only takes one hand to lift the latch and the 'gate lays right down. Being counterbalanced is the only answer! With the cable stops and opening mechanism inside the panel, it has a clean, well designed appearance. One thing that bothered me was the super bright shift lever quadrant light. At night it about blinds you! The heater works great in the small tight cab, but the major part of the air seems to be directed at the driver's right leg. Mine nearly burn't up that one cold night. With all the tightness in the door fits, the fiberboard covers behind the seats rattle no end. A little glue in the right places would put a halt to that."** ☐ Tailgate opening and closing is no longer a three man job, as Terry mentioned. A Torsion bar in the hinge provides assistance making it as easy as operating any door on the car. A woman could even use it one-handed. ☐ In all, the Trackers agreed, the sporty pickup performed the tasks it was designed to do. It rode smoother, quieter, and softer than most passenger cars, provided a luxurious interior for driver comfort, yet furnished more than ample carrying capacity. Dual purpose is exactly what it is and certainly gets our vote for the car most likely to succeed in getting that drag car to the strip . . . in style! ©

Test Car was "Custom" model with optional bucket seats and console. Features all loop pile carpet interior, swept-away instrument panel and big round faced gauges. Instruments are all positioned in front of the driver and easily read.

Left — *Pickup box now gives a big 39 cubic-foot capacity having increased 7½ inches in length, 4 inches in width, and almost 2 inches in depth over the '65 Ranchero. Here, Merf finishes tying down coupe as Coulter and Roller help with loading.*

Extra storage compartment has been built into panel behind driver's seat which allows parcels to be hidden from view. Spare fits neatly into right compartment.

Above center — Thin door and curved side glass gives dual purpose pickup the "Modern" look. Fit of the doors and panels was greatly improved from the earlier models.

Above right—American Racing's aluminum wheels mounting Casler slicks help set off the fire-truck red Ranchero as a member of the Trackers makes a part pick up at one of the original speed shops.

Right — Ranchero's clean lines make it a beautiful utility vehicle with it's 289 cubic-inch engine. Optional heavy-duty suspension is recommended for towing.

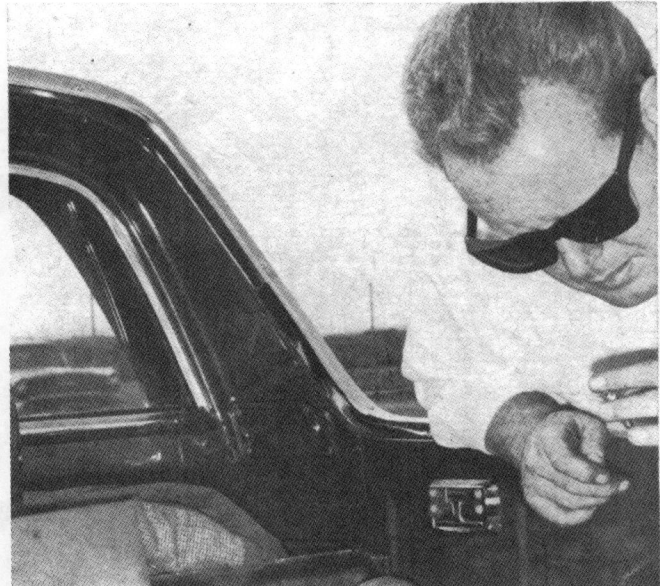
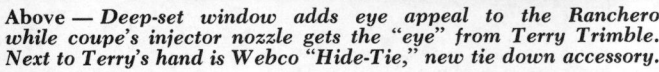

Above — Deep-set window adds eye appeal to the Ranchero while coupe's injector nozzle gets the "eye" from Terry Trimble. Next to Terry's hand is Webco "Hide-Tie," new tie down accessory.

Above Right — You need a lot of spares when you go to the drags! Trackers busily load Ranchero with everything they could possibly need. Came up short anyway, when Chrysler engine blew on run.

Right — It would be hard to improve on these lines. Falcon front end flows into unitized body which mounts on station wagon chassis. Bright metal and stripes are standard on "Custom."

After taking years of bemoaning and bad mouthing about their general ineptitude in the styling salons, the motor-city bunch sneaked up on the customizers and ran 'em down with a flock of classy carriages that ended an era. Like restyling ain't what it used to be baby. Considering this, it would be a real compliment if an enthusiast took one of those same svelte buggies, waved the wand of creativity over it and served up a finished product that gave viewers the impression that that's the way the thing should have looked to begin with. Right? Right.

So when you get ready to throw some bouquets, throw one down Charlotte, North Carolina, way to Ed Skelton, an electrical contractor, who wanted a '66 Falcon Ranchero but didn't entirely buy the overall styling of a rounded front end that somehow failed to square with a more angular back. Ed thought that the Fairlane front saddle and grille represented a likelier choice so he ordered a new Ranchero body shell and went to work tailoring for himself what has become the watchword of the industry these days; a "personalized" vehicle. Knowing that the Falcon and Fairlane lines share a common unit body, Ed felt it would be little more than routine to get the front end pieces from one attached to the other, but, being caught up more than slightly in the total-performance concept (he also owns one of the better running Mustang funny cars), he sought more go and stamina as well.

But first things first. An entire GTA fender assembly — hood, bumper and back bars (Part Nos. C60Z 16612-B, C60Z 16005-6-A) — was added for the biggest sheet metal change. Realizing that the Fairlane options the 390 cube engine and that a 427 possesses identical external dimensions, a brand new medium-riser, Grand National honker-type mill was bolted in. However, this unit has a pretty gung-ho, rump, rump idle as it comes from Holman & Moody; not one you would recommend for towing race cars around. So, a 427 cam blank

ABOVE — From the up angle this S. Carolina chariot looks like a normal Fairlane. But wait! Farther back we can see the Ranchero's utility.

FUTURE FORD

Ford

Text and photos by Eric Dahlquist

AT RIGHT — This is the way a lot of people thought the later model Ranchero should have been done up the first time around. Notice the centered rear wheel.

was reground to hydraulic lifter 406 Ford high performance specs, the tappet bosses were drilled to pump oil in from the main gallery and a set of TZ juice truck lifters (DZ's are regular) were installed. Although it might seem slightly redundant, what with hydraulic lifters and all, the 427 adjustable rocker arms were retained and worked out well. To attain the desired lash once the lifter is filled with oil, the rocker arm adjustment is run down until the clatter disappears, backed off until an audible "click" is heard and then snugged a quarter-turn more.

Either the 390 or 427 engine would fit with equal facility except that on the latter, the exhaust manifold's bolt pattern interferes with the spring towers. There are several ways to circumvent this condition and Ed chose the custom header route, supplied in drag-car profile by Balanger Brothers. Another item that would have fit was the stock 3-speed Cruise-O-Matic transmission but it is a matter of conjecture that it could keep hanging in there under hard usage. If it ever was a possible problem, it won't be now, for a 428-Police Interceptor automatic (Part No. C60P 7000-H) fell in behind the engine. Now Ed had strength but he wanted snap, so the 428 valve body was removed and swapped for the GTA number. While they were at it, the shift linkage was turned in for a floor operated type.

Things were looking pretty good in the drive train now and the only question mark was the stoutness of the rear axle assembly. Just to make sure, a rather large looking, but nonetheless neatly fit-

(Continued on page 122)

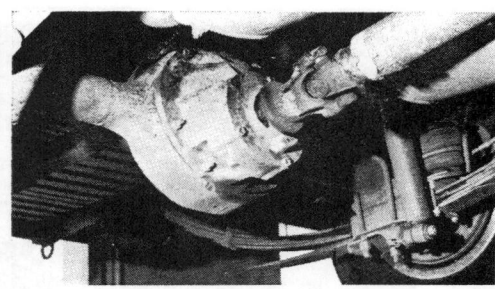

If that rear axle looks on the beefy side, remember that it's one of those elephantine T-Bird jobs. Axles for this honey are super-big 31-spline.

Ed Skelton made some sneaky changes to his Ranchero — both inside and out. The crystal ball shows he may have beaten Ford to the punch with a new model

FAR LEFT — Not satisfied with standard 289 fare, Ed Skelton opted for a faster as well as fancier 427; a unit, incidentally, that happens to bolt right into place.

LEFT — Rear quarter of Ranchero is set off by taut white tarp. Sag is controlled by two tubular aluminum bows.

FAR RIGHT — Inside, conversion consists of GTA instrumentation, Sport Shift and stereo tape facility that is integral with padded panel.

RIGHT — Optional heavy-duty Ranchero rear spring pac is augmented with inflatable Air-Lift arrangement. Combination allows safe ride, loaded.

THE 3 FACES OF FAIRLANE

Although the tamest of our trio, there was nothing Plain-Jane-ish about the Fairlane 500, either in appearance, decor or performance. Hardtop with 289 had best weight distribution, handling of the three Fairlanes tested.

Fairlane's range runs the gamut from the super-sporty convertible to the highly utilitarian Ranchero pickup. By building a wide variety of body styles on its intermediate-size chassis, Ford strengthens position in a popular price range. Two different horsepower versions of 390-cu.-in. engine were used in both the GTA convertible and the Ranchero.

A decade ago movie audiences were stunned by Joanne Woodward's Oscar-winning performance as a woman with three separate personalities. Though the story was true, the condition was a psychiatric rarity.

Multiple personality may be rare among humans, but in automobiles it is now as routine as a case of good scotch in Jackie Gleason's dressing room. Seemingly endless permutations of engine, transmission, body styles, and trim option combinations give any particular model more potential personalities than Kellys in a St. Patrick's Day parade. This is no less true of Ford's intermediate size Fairlane line than any other marque.

To attempt to exercise all the possible combinations would put both the MOTOR TREND staff and a great many people at FoMoCo on the couch, so we settled for a trio of Fairlanes to illustrate the diversity that may be found under one nameplate. These were a Fairlane 500 hardtop, a GTA convertible, and a Ranchero pickup.

The Fairlane 500 was selected to represent the Plain Jane branch of the family, but we got a surprise; poor old Jane may not be as exotic as some of her relatives, but there's nothing plain, dowdy or old-maidish about her. With the 289-cu.-in., 200-hp engine burning regular gas we felt no power shortage until a sojourn in the 390s spoiled us. The little 289 is a pretty reasonable animal to feed, with about a 2-mpg edge over the 390 and with regular 3c a gallon

cheaper than Ethyl. To keep it running well on regular, however, requires that it be in good tune, with special attention to timing, so for the performance tests we switched to the higher-priced pump. This didn't improve performance, just assured that it did all it was capable of doing.

Just how much it is capable of we discovered in a hurry. Frankly skeptical of what the 289 could do, we arrived at the Carlsbad Drag Strip on the first clear morning after several days of rain. One side of the strip seemed reasonably dry, with no puddles and only a few damp spots, which seemed unlikely to bother us, especially with such a tame car. One run proved how wrong we were and how right the Fairlane was. Any spot moist enough to reflect light provoked wheelspin. Even on the dry pavement near the starting line we could break the tires loose getting off the line. We got the message; we unhooked our 5th wheel, packed our gear, and retreated from the field like the Philistine army until things dried out.

Over the years we've always been very impressed with the consistently good handling of Fords. The ride, as in the days of the transverse leaf springs, has sometimes been harsh, but we could always count on the car going where we pointed it. This one was no exception. There's a strong case to be made for the school of thought that says the so-called "intermediates" are the right size for a car, and in terms of agility with reasonable elbow room this may be so. The convenient size, plus the weight-distribution advantage of the smaller engine, makes this car the steadiest of the three. It was a natural for Ford to switch to this chassis for stock car racing when NASCAR rules were changed to permit it, although we wonder what the huge 427-cu.-in. engine does for weight distribution.

In 1966 certain sporty Ford and Mercury models offered Sport Shift automatics as an option. Now all Fords and Mercs have this feature which allows the gearbox to be used as a regular automatic by putting it in "D," or shifting it manually through the three speeds. All three of our Fairlanes were so equipped and all revealed a noteworthy item during performance tests. For all the jazz disseminated by the pseudo-sporty car types, the Sport Shift won't do a cotton-pickin' thing for performance. Not unless you consider the opportunity to overrev the engine "doing something for performance." The fact is that on none of these cars were we able to turn a time going through the gears that we couldn't equal or better in "Drive." A firm foot brings the revs up to the red line anyway before shifting automatically and the stopwatches don't lie, more than can be said for some of the stoplight Winternationals drivers.

When we said that this Jane wasn't plain we weren't just talking about equipment and performance. Interior decor and comfort features are as dressy as any. Our test car had the optional vinyl interior, but the cloth types we looked at certainly didn't seem like poverty pocket castoffs. Our 500 had a bench seat rather than the sportier buckets found in the GT series, but a bench has certain advantages, particularly when courting.

Convertibles, once *the* car for the would-be playboy to own, have fallen on hard times in recent years. Sports cars and personal cars have had a lot to do with the downgrading of the full-fledged, 5-passenger ragtop as a status symbol. Among the convertible's disadvantages was the drill that went with raising or lowering the top, something akin to preparing a 280mm atomic cannon for firing. The rear window was either a tiny glass panel that provided very little visibility, or a large plastic panel that soon became opaque and provided none. Tops were ill-fitting and, if raised and lowered very much, wore out with biennial regularity.

Our GTA indicates that Ford is looking toward a resurgence of convertibles, however, and they have obviously been hard at work to make them more appetizing to a larger number of people. The rear window, for example, is now large and made of glass. A hinge of silicon rubber divides the glass horizontally so that it folds neatly for stowage. This arrangement, developed by Corning Glass (for which they received a MOTOR TREND Special Achievement Award), makes it possible to lower the top without the ritual of unzipping the back window. This is a boon, as there is one frustrating condition in which a human being can maintain no leverage, and that is kneeling on a back seat trying to budge a jammed window zipper. Top latches are also simple and operate smoothly. The GTA had the great thumping 335-hp 390-cu.-in. engine. Although we had been very happy with the 289 in the hardtop, this reminded us of what power is all about. That old adage about power corrupting is automotive as well as political.

As good as it felt, that big engine has other subtle disadvantages besides economy. Power steering masks the fact that the 390 adds a hefty chunk of iron over the front end, but it is clear that handling is not the same as in the 289. Not terrible, or brutish, or dangerous, just not as good. This manifests itself in the kind of front-end pushing that makes it tricky turning into a narrow street at speed.

Power tends to overcome the awareness of weight, but the effect of the extra avoirdupois of the big engine, along with the heaviness that goes with all convertibles, was driven home to us most forcibly in the brake tests. Although the 390 convertible had disc brakes, it took longer to stop than the drum-braked 289 at 60 mph. Curiously, the 289's stopping advantage was even better at 30 mph where it amounted to almost a car length.

That 390 gives mechanics fits when it is stuffed into the hole meant for a 289. Even the smaller engine has some accessibility problems for mechanics changing spark plugs; the rear plug on the left-hand bank is difficult (in the Fairlane) or impossible (in the Mustang) to get at without removing the power brake unit. Mechanics are of varied opinions about how to change plugs on a 390, but ideas like cutting a hole in the wheel well crop up. Opinions among mechanics do not vary about the ancestry of the engineers who designed this nightmare. Check the labor charges on this operation before you have it done; some shops charge straight time and it takes plenty of that.

One Ford move that received virtually universal applause this year was switching their high-style pickup, the Ranchero, from the Falcon series to Fairlane. Introduced a decade ago on the full-size chassis, the Ranchero has been in and out, up and down, and now can claim to have been in every Ford chassis line. The marketing philosophy behind this move was clear: Chevrolet had reintroduced its El Camino in the intermediate Chevelle chassis, hence Ford had to follow suit to compete. This has made the Ranchero heftier as a pickup and opened up bigger engine options. Having driven the Falcon Ranchero a few years ago, our reaction to the Fairlane version was that anyone against the change must also be against the American Way of Life, Mom's apple pie and Sunday double headers.

The whole Ranchero is an almost bewildering combination of compromises that come off beautifully. The engine is a prime example of this. It was a 390, which assured performance, but it had only a 2 bbl. carb as a sop to practicality. With 270 hp, the balance of virtues came right in as hoped for. Performance on the strip was decidedly inferior to the GTA, but just as obviously superior to the Fairlane 500. In the lower speed ranges (0-30, 0-45) the Ranchero was either dead even with or just behind the GTA, thanks to tighter gearing. At 0-60 and the quarter-mile, the pickup fell off about a second. All of which attests that the Ranchero is a hauling hauler, while the slight compromise pays off at the gas pump like a playboy in a paternity suit. Typical of this is a comparison of miscellaneous city and expressway driving done with the cars, where the Ranchero was almost 3 mpg better than the GTA, and was actually better than the 289 as well. All of which is sort of like having one's cake and eating a large chunk of it too.

We had no opportunity to drive the Ranchero loaded, but the suspension was definitely intended to suit the vehicle in its working state. The ride was quite good, especially compared to the full-fledged pickups we've owned and driven, but the combination of a soft-sprung front end and hard-sprung rear end makes it quite different from the other two Fairlanes. In turns the Ranchero has a distinct body lean when pushed hard, but all on the front end.

Because of our earlier experience comparing the heavy GTA with its discs to the lighter 500 with drums, we were interested in how the drum-braked Ranchero would stack up. Again, weight and weight distribution are as much of the story as the hardware. Although the light, unladen Ranchero stopped better than either of the others, the light rear end tended to come out of line slighly in the 60-mph stop. The hardtop and convertible, on the other hand, had been as straight as the hero in a Roy Rogers Western. At 30 mph this condition never showed up in the Ranchero, however.

To get some estimate of what a load would do to stopping distance, we checked back on a station wagon test we did last year (MT Sept., 1966) in which tests were made both loaded and unloaded. The Mercury Comet Villager, built on the same chassis, required an extra 17 feet at 60 mph after we added a 720-pound payload. This data is less than expert testimony, but gives some clue to the curious.

We've always hesitated to refer to the Ranchero as a

pickup because of the image such vehicles have as being stark, unlovely and uncomfortable. The Ranchero is none of these. The interior is identical to that found in a Fairlane 500 XL, complete with bucket seats, vinyl trim and console-mounted shift quadrant. There is none of the echo sometimes found in a small cab, and if the driver could be equipped with blinkers to prevent him from seeing behind him, he need never know he was in a pickup.

The bane of the pickup driver's existence has always been where to hide valuables. Ford has thoughtfully opened an area behind the seats that goes under the bed for about a foot or so. The right side is for the spare tire, but behind the driver there is an equal amount of room. Is it possible that someone connected with designing the Ranchero has actually owned a pickup himself?

The bed itself is bigger than the old Falcon versions, but still slightly smaller than a real pickup. It is not a bad compromise between utility and style, the basic premise of the Ranchero. The sides of the bed are fairly high, but there are no provisions for sideboards. The station wagon chassis background of this car is borne out by a look under the

bed where the well for the feet of third-seat passengers is still present. It is covered over by the bed floor and now contains the gas tank which is located in the fender of the wagon. One place where Ford missed the boat here is not using their highly desirable 2-way tailgate.

We compared notes with other staff members who had time in the Ranchero and all of us had the same reaction: none of us would want to have one or could use one as our only car. Even as a second car, there are other body styles more useful to us. Despite these considerations, all of us liked the Ranchero, and to a man, wished there was some way we could have one. This is a pretty emotional response to a vehicle with such a practical purpose, but the looks we got from other motorists were pure admiration and had nothing to do with how much top soil it could carry.

Like Topsy, the intermediate size car "jest growed," the result of compacts being too small to exploit the full market of people who didn't want a big car. It is a natural for all these variations because, economically, it can draw from several directions. No telling where that personality is likely to split next.

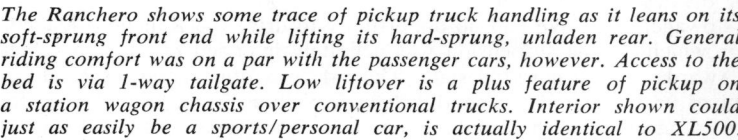

The Ranchero shows some trace of pickup truck handling as it leans on its soft-sprung front end while lifting its hard-sprung, unladen rear. General riding comfort was on a par with the passenger cars, however. Access to the bed is via 1-way tailgate. Low liftover is a plus feature of pickup on a station wagon chassis over conventional trucks. Interior shown could just as easily be a sports/personal car, is actually identical to XL500.

On the road the 500 was pleasant, the GTA exciting. GTA's convertible top lowers easily, stows neatly without great effort or fuss. Some indication of the wet surface that delayed acceleration and brake tests is still seen as 500 starts quarter-mile run. Acceleration tests were about as expected, surprises came comparing stopping distances.

A 289-cu.-in. V-8 in the 500 (top) had satisfactory power and is the easiest of the three to work on, but did not show any economy edge over the Ranchero (center) with its 390. Two-bbl. carb plus light weight of small pickup contributed to its good mileage, while extra inches, 270-hp contributed lively performance. The GTA convertible with 390 and 4-bbl. (bottom) was the best performer, despite weight handicap inherent in ragtops. Note the engine accessibility problem of the 390s due to suspension mounts, accessories, and plumbing of modern American cars.

performance . . .

ACCELERATION (2 aboard):	500	GTA	Ranchero
0-30 mph (secs.)	3.8	3.5	3.5
0-45 mph (secs.)	6.6	5.6	5.9
0-60 mph (secs.)	10.6	8.1	9.4
0-75 mph (secs.)	16.1	12.1	14.5
¼-mile from rest (secs.) & (mph)	18.0 & 79.0	16.2 & 89.0	17.0 & 80.0
TIME & DISTANCE TO ATTAIN PASSING SPEEDS:			
40-60: (secs.) & (feet)	5.6 & 410	4.2 & 301	4.5 & 329
50-70: (secs.) & (feet)	6.6 & 580	5.1 & 459	6.2 & 546
SPEEDS IN GEARS:			
1st (mph) @ (rpm)	51 @ 4500	51 @ 5000	40 @ 4500
2nd (mph) @ (rpm)	84 @ 4500	84 @ 5000	70 @ 4500
MPH PER 1000 RPM:	25.6	24.6	21.3
STOPPING DISTANCES:			
From 30 mph (feet)	34.0	48.0	33.0
From 60 mph (feet)	169.5	176.0	168.0

SPEEDOMETER ERROR:

Calibrated speedometer	30	45	50	60	70	80
Fairlane 500	30	46	51	61	72	83
GTA	32	45	50	60	70	80
Ranchero	33	49	54	63	73	83

specifications . . .

	500	GTA	Ranchero
ENGINE:			
Bore & Stroke (ins.):	4.00 x 2.87	4.05 x 3.78	4.05 x 3.78
Displacement (cu. ins.):	289	390	390
Horsepower @ rpm:	200 @ 4400	320 @ 4800	270 @ 4400
Torque (lbs.-ft.) @ rpm:	282 @ 2400	427 @ 3200	403 @ 2600
Compression ratio:	9.3:1	10.5:1	9.5:1
Carburetion:	2V	4V	2V
TRANSMISSION:			
Type: 3 speed automatic with torque converter			
Ratios: 2.46, 1.46, 1.00; 2.20 reverse			
FINAL DRIVE RATIO:	2.79	2.75	3.00
STEERING:			
Type: Recirculating ball & nut, power-assisted			
Turning dia., curb-to-curb:	41.45	41.45	41.45
Turns lock-to-lock:	5.25	5.25	5.25
WHEELS:			
Type: Stamped steel disc			
Size:	14 x 5J	14 x 5.5J	14 x 5J
TIRES:			
Type:	Rayon 2-ply 4-ply rated WSW	Nylon 2-ply 4-ply rated WSW	Rayon 2-ply 4-ply rated WSW
Size:	7.35 x 14	650/8.95x 14	7.75 x 14
BRAKES:			
Type:	Duo-Servo hydraulic self adjusting power assisted	Disc front, drum rear, power assisted	Duo-Servo hydraulic self adjusting power assisted
Front dia. (ins.):	10	11.375	10
Rear dia. (ins.):	10	10	10
Effective lining area (sq. ins.):	126	235.5	165
FUEL CAPACITY (gals.): 20			
MILEAGE RANGE (mpg):	11.5-14.2	10.8-12.5	11.1-14.5
USABLE TRUNK CAPACITY (cu.-ft.):	15.2	12.2	——
WHEELBASE (in.):	116	116	113
FRONT TRACK (ins.): 58.4			
REAR TRACK (ins.): 58.1			
LENGTH (ins.): 197.0			
WIDTH (ins.): 74.0			
HEIGHT (ins.):	54.2	54.4	54.2

SUSPENSION: Independent Front with Coil Springs. One piece rear axle with longitudinal leaf springs.
BODY & FRAME: Unit Construction

prices and accessories . . .

MANUFACTURER'S SUGGESTED RETAIL: (Includes federal excise tax, but excludes state and local taxes, license, options, accessories, and transportation)
Fairlane 500: $2439.14 GTA: $3063.67 Ranchero 500 Deluxe: $2474.40

OPTIONS & ACCESSORIES	500	GTA	Ranchero
Base 289 2V V-8	$105.63	std.	n/a
390 2V Thunderbird V-8	74.30*	74.30*	104.00
390 4V Thunderbird V-8	150.10*	150.10(1)	n/a
Select Shift Cruise-O-Matic	220.17	220.17	220.17
Power steering	84.47	84.47	84.47
Power brakes	42.29	std.	42.29
Disc brakes	85.00	std.	85.00
7.75 x 14-4PR WSW tires	48.35	(2)	48.35
Radio AM	57.51	57.51	57.51
Stereosonic tape system	128.49	128.49	128.49
Selectaire Conditioner	356.09	356.09	356.09
Limited-slip differential	37.20	37.20	37.20
Closed crankcase emission system	5.19	5.19	5.19
Exhaust emission control	45.45	45.45	45.45

*Above price of 289 V-8
(1) 335-hp on GT series, 320-hp on others. (2) F-70-14 Wide Oval tires standard

AMERICA'S NEW FUN CARS

El Camino and Ranchero have established a new trend in the fun car market, and people all over the country are getting on the band wagon.

By Lee Kelley

Seldom has one type of vehicle captured the imagination of so many varied age groups as has the so-called "semi-pickup" produced by both Ford (Ranchero) and Chevrolet (El Camino). These vehicles are becoming more and more popular

throughout the country as people seek a multipurpose car to be both functional and nice-looking.

Ford hit the scene early in 1957 with its Ranchero, but public acceptance was not the greatest and it was discontinued from the big car line in 1959. Chevrolet introduced their El Camino in 1959, but it, too, was discontinued a year later (1960). Sales on both these early efforts were not up to expectations, although in some parts of the country, notably Southern California, the Ranchero and El Camino did as well or better than most other models. In the 1961 model year, Ford reintroduced the Ranchero, this time in the Falcon line, and the results, saleswise, were much more rewarding. The Ranchero continued in the Falcon line until 1967, when it was upgraded to the Fairlane series, its present state. Chevrolet brought the El Camino back to life in 1964 in the Chevelle series and found the public reaction much more favorable. Both the Ranchero and El Camino have enjoyed a fair amount of success the second time around, and it's been due mainly to the changing ideas of the automotive public.

The Rancheros and El Caminos of today offer a little something to everyone without catering to

Motorcade editors gave El Camino thorough testing on GM's test track. New '68 version has redesigned pickup bed section.

EL CAMINO and RANCHERO:

a specific buyer. To the housewife, it's a glorified grocery-getter; to the street rodder, it's the hot setup on a Saturday night; and to campers, racers, boat enthusiasts and anyone else who tows a trailer or needs additional space, it's the perfect compromise between a passenger car and an all-out truck.

Engine and transmission options are so varied in these two vehicles that they can be tailored to fit the needs of almost anyone. This is especially true in the '68 models because both Ford and Chevrolet are offering everything from six-cylinder economy models to storming high performance V-8s. Why do these particular cars appeal to so many varied groups? There's no simple answer to that question because what attracts one group may be totally ignored by others. Perhaps a look at some of the various segments may shed some light on the subject.

Consider the housewife. With all her errands and shopping to do, she needs something that will provide plenty of space and yet offer some degree of comfort. Rancheros and El Caminos certainly fit this bill with their adequate pickup beds and luxurious interiors. It might be pointed out that station wagons also fit this description, but the

"semi-pickups" are usually second cars where a family is concerned and are much easier to handle than the heavier, bulkier station wagons. These cars are becoming more and more popular as runaround fun vehicles, and in suburban life the Rancheros and El Caminos are popping up in the driveway very frequently.

One of the strongholds (and getting stronger everyday) of these fun cars is the street rodding set. It's very "in" to have one of these cars to tool through the drive-ins on Saturday nights, and when they're set up, they're very competitive on

Ranchero has good handling characteristics, considering its light weight over rear wheels.

Severe wheel hop and smoky runs occur when clutch is dropped on high-performance engine. Traction problems can be cured with traction bars and heavier shocks.

Ranchero for '68 also has all-new interior featuring instruments mounted in four pods directly in front of driver.

New grille design and dual headlights highlight front end treatment on '68 El Camino. Semi-hemi 396 engine is optional.

Interior of '68 El Camino has also received major revisions. Luxury is keynote of new fun cars.

the local race track. These models aren't in the cheap category, either. They are usually ordered with the most expensive interiors (bucket seats, padded dashes, full set of gauges, etc.) and a full complement of high performance equipment including the most powerful engines, four-speed transmissions, disc brakes and heavy-duty suspension systems. These cars are good looking, sound great and give the owner something a little different in the way of a high-performance machine.

To that large group of people who frequently tow trailers, boats or cars, these fun cars are the answer to a big problem: what about additional space? To the racer, the Rancheros and El Caminos offer a place to put extra tires, gas, fuel, tools and extra race car parts. This same advantage is afforded to the camper who has quite a bit of extra equipment that can't be stored in the camp trailer or to the boat enthusiast who needs additional room to store equipment for that long week-end trip to the lake. The needs of all these people are similar, and the Ford and Chevrolet people are catering to these groups.

So, to answer the original question, the Rancheros and El Caminos appeal to so many varied groups for three major reasons: they provide additional space while being easy to handle in traffic; they satisfy the ego of the street rodder who wants something different in a high- performance machine; and, most importantly, they're just plain fun to own and drive. Call them handy, call them a necessity; they're the new trend in America's fun cars! ■

The fellas at Ford aren't making life any easier for us. Last month we sampled a Chevy El Camino, and came away wanting one, or at least a comparable passenger car type pickup. Trouble is, now the only way we'd be happy is to have two: a Ranchero and El Camino. We may wind up owning neither, but that's our fault.

This latest in the series of Ford Rancheros is on the Fairlane chassis. It's been through most of the Ford lines since its inception in '57 on the regular line, then over to the Falcon in the early 60's, and switched to the Fairlane in '67. But never has it looked as good or worked as well.

Our test truck was fitted out with almost every conceivable option. Air-conditioning, bucket seats, console, automatic transmission, GT interior and trim, 390 V8, disc brakes and on and on. This puts the suggested list at a rather steep angle, but it can be purchased quite reasonably in basic form.

Straight-line and cornering stability is extremely well balanced. There's very little tendency for the rear end to leave the intended direction of travel. This was a problem on earlier haulers, but seems to have been cured on the present generation. High-speed freeway running finds the car "settling" into a relaxed position and staying with the course set from within. While there've never been any serious shortcomings here in the Ranchero, the front suspension has undergone a redesign in recent years, insuring even more high-speed stability. And gone is the "plastic" steering response we noted on earlier '68's.

Brakes on our test car were of the disc front/drum rear variety first introduced on Fords in '66. These latest units are "floating" caliper type, meaning that the caliper centers itself on the disc during application rather than being shimmed and rigidly held in place. They work on a par with an aircraft carrier landing cable. After repeated hard stops from 60 mph and above on Irwindale's shut-off area, we lost any fear of brake fade or an imbalanced system that would cause the tail to go first in quick traffic stops. And we've had our share of this in pickups. Last year's El Camino really had a problem in tail-end stability and even this year's issue will move slightly. But the Ranchero stopped over and over in sub-130-foot dis-

tances from 60 mph without even locking up the wheels. That's some kind of a pleasant surprise and it sure is nice when the back end stays behind the front.

Addition of a load to the bed will bring the tail clearance down somewhat, but it isn't at all serious so long as the load rating is maintained. This means don't load a ton into a half-ton hauler and then gripe about how badly the tires wear. The Ranchero uses semi-elliptic rear leaf springs, instead of coils as in the Camino. Use of the leaves allows them to be built to withstand heavy loads as well as provide a good ride when the car is unladen. Proper configuration and the right amount of spring leaves do this. The tail rides a bit high when there's no load, but on the other hand, doesn't drag bottom with a cargo. Just as the regular Ford truck line incorporates progressive rate springs, this is the theory behind the Ranchero's semi-elliptics. There's an H-D suspension option, which is never a bad idea to include on any car, but "air" shock absorbers (like in the Camino) aren't factory available. But should they be needed because of repeated heavy loading, or are desired for the owner's particular use, identical Delco Pleasur-Lifts (parts No. P3044) are parts-house available.

Generally speaking, the all-round good ride and driving behavior of the GT Ranchero impressed us most. Unfortunately, its performance was below what we'd expected.

This machine came with a 390 cubic inch V8, rated at 335 hp. This is more commonly referred to as the 390-4V GT engine. Mated to it was one of Ford's well-proven Cruise-O-Matic 3-speed automatics. Our initial quarter-mile pass at Irwindale Raceway felt good, but turned out to be a 16.32 seconds e.t., and carried a speed of 85.38 mph. This was done by shifting the gearbox manually at 5000 rpm, and due to the slight lag between movement and shift, brought about a 5200-5300 rpm shift. Trying the car in "Drive" really slowed things down to 16.48 seconds because the fully-automatic blast shifted at 4500-4700 rpm, just below the peak horsepower mark.

Seriously wondering if we could be running on seven cylinders, we closely went over every detail. Checking wiring, dis-

(Continued on page 60)

SUPER HAULER
390 RANCHERO

Pioneering the passenge

by Steve Kelly

r-pickup field, Ford's Ranchero still has a few "ideas" left for others to follow

The question of the hour: "How ya gonna keep 'em down on the farm after they've run this machine down the Great White Way?" Ranching may not hurt the Ranchero, but it sure looks a lot better on Sunset Blvd. GT stripes, styled wheels and trim styling make this hauler valuable as a nighttime cruiser as well as daytime workhorse. TOP LEFT—Engine compartment is virtually "stuffed" with equipment, due to addition of optional power goodies like air conditioning, power steering and brakes, etc. Plug access—simply stated—isn't the greatest. BELOW LEFT—Bed-to-tailgate gap isn't much, especially in comparison to El Camino. TOP RIGHT—Safe and handy inside door lock release is in use on bigger Ford products. Armrest is generously padded and long enough for full arm support. CENTER—Fiberglass Stockland canopy top can be had with fold-out windows, tinted or plain glass, or none at all. Tab for well-built cover is around $300.

photography: PPC Photographic and Steve Kelly

59

SUPER HAULER

tributor, plugs, carburetor, etc., we found everything set to spec. Next item was to disconnect air-conditioner and power steering drive belts. This brought about a best of 15.98 e.t., with a speed of 89.90. Removing the top half of the air cleaner, actually just the lid, helped induce more air and this was what the Holley 4-bbl was waiting for. Then the V8 started working, netting a best of 15.60 and speed of 91.80. Still slow on the mph, but improving the elapsed time. Jacking the advance up a few notches, for a total centrifugal of 33 degrees at 4000 rpm versus the stock 29, and lowering the tailgate helped even more, giving us a best for the day of 15.52 seconds elapsed time, and speed of 98.34 mph. While this may not be all that bad, compared to the 350 hp 396 cubic inch V8 in the Camino, the best run here is about a half-second from that car's poorest, and over a second slower than its best. Also, the Ranchero is about 500 pounds lighter. Engine to engine, we'd have to say — and a good deal of Ford engineers will agree with us — the 396-427 Chevy engine is better for pure acceleration. On the other side of the coin though is economy, and here's where the 390 Ford does a better job. Our lowest mileage figure was 12.0 mpg and our best was over 16 (but not by much). All in all, the average fuel consumption figures were far better for the Ranchero.

In a non-comparison vain, the Ford engine needs better exhausts, a bit wilder hydraulic-lifter cam, and possibly some carburetion refinement before it'll cut the 14's on every run — or any run.

We made no attempt to mount slicks on this car. Having a 3.00:1 rear axle wasn't a good starting point and any slick addition would've only cut that gear to the detriment of performance. Besides, we didn't have any wheel-hop problem and our 7.75 x 14 tires were giving us a relatively good bite. They worked best at 31 pounds pressure on both sides, slipping very little on take-off from our 1000 rpm maximum starting point. With a higher stall speed or a manual shift car, slicks would be mandatory for decent acceleration times.

It took us no time to get tuned-in on the Ranchero styling. This goes back to last summer when we first saw the car at a pre-introduction preview. Right away we knew it had the right lines. It's a bit ironic to note how Ranchero and Camino styling have sort of "traded off" this year. In '67, the Ford had thick rear top pillars and the Camino's were

VEHICLE
Ranchero GT 390

PRICE

Base	$2964.26
As tested	$4012.76

ENGINE

Type	OHV V8
Cylinders	8
Bore & stroke	4.05 x 3.78 in.
Displacement	390 cu.in.
Compression ratio	10.5:1
Horsepower	335 @ 4800 rpm
Torque	427 lbs.-ft. @ 3200 rpm
Valves: Intake	2.03-in. dia.
Exhaust	1.560-in. dia.
Camshaft:	
Lift	.4809-in. intake; .490-in. exhaust
Duration	270° intake, 290° exhaust
Overlap	46°
Tappets	Hydraulic
Carburetion	Holley 4-bbl
Exhaust	Single: 2.00-in.dia. branch, 2.50-in. -dia. main pipe

TRANSMISSION

Type	Cruise-O-Matic 3-speed automatic, torque converter with planetary gears
Ratios: 1st	2.46:1
2nd	1.46:1
3rd	1.00:1

DIFFERENTIAL

Type	Semi-floating design, straddle mounted pinion, Equalock limited slip
Ring gear diameter	9 in.
Final drive ratio	3.00:1

BRAKES

Type	Front disc/rear drum with power assist
Dimensions:	
Front disc	11.3-in. dia.
Rear drum	11.0-in. dia.
Total swept area	228 sq. in.

SUSPENSION

Front	Independent single lateral arm with ball joints & coil springs
Rear	Single-unit Hotchkiss design axle with semi-elliptic leaf springs
Shocks	Direct-acting tubular type
Stabilizer	Front only, link type, .85-in. dia.
Tires	7.75 x 14 conventional pattern
Wheel rim width	5.5 in.
Steering:	
Type	Recirculating ball & nut with linkage booster power assist
Gear ratio	16:1
Overall ratio	21.6:1
Turning circle	41.45 ft., curb to curb
Wheel diameter	16 in.
Wheel turns lock to lock	3.5

PERFORMANCE

Standing start quarter-mile (best)	15.60 sec., 91.80 mph

FUEL CONSUMPTION

Best reading	16.20 mpg
Poorest	12.00 mpg
Average	13.4 mpg
Recommended fuel	Premium

DIMENSIONS

Wheelbase	113.0 in.
Front track	58.8 in.
Rear track	58.1 in.
Overall height	55.2 in.
Overall width	74.0 in.
Overall length	203.9 in.
Test weight	3375 lb.
Body/frame construction	Unit
Crankcase capacity w/filter	5 qt.
Cooling system	20.5 qt.
Fuel tank	20 gal.

NOTE: Data listed is for car tested, and reflects optional equipment in some cases.

slim. Now it's the other way around. After driving both for some time, we're still not sure which design makes more sense, but one thing's for sure — you can see more out of the Ranchero cab than from the Chevy design.

Interior finishing on the GT Ranchero is A-1. There're no unnecessary frills and/or adornments, though it is in the "sports" motif. Each bucket seat is genuinely comfortable, and seat height relative to the floor allows many different leg/foot positions, should one become uncomfortable. That's one thing we've liked on recent Fords, the generous amount of leg room. Ranchero is no exception. Dash treatment is so naturally good, yet naturally simple, we wonder why it's taken so long for someone to use it. The four instrument clusters are buried deep below the padded surface while the entire right-hand facing is blank except for padding. Putting the radio where a driver can reach it isn't a bad idea either, but reaching the glove box is virtually impossible while belted in the driver's seat. But Ford certainly has no exclusive on this feature. This Ranchero came with a floor-mounted console and shifter. The two-compartment storage bin in the console will take all you'll ever need while driving. When the '68's first hit the scene, we weren't

too impressed with the "horseshoe" floor shifters on automatics. We're still not altogether won over, but they at least don't have protruding ends — as did this car — on the shifter handle, to lodge in a long sleeve shirt. (We've got a torn sleeve as evidence that it can happen.)

Ford's integral air-conditioning will cool off the Ranchero cab almost as soon as it's turned on. It really pumps out the cold. Placing the ash tray just below the center outlets could be looked upon as a bit of poor planning, and forgetting to put a light in the tray is cause for another bad mark.

Aft of the seats is a sizable floor area, taken up by the horizontally-placed spare on the right, and nothing on the left. Rear panel finishing is better than in the Camino, and includes a flap over the "under bed" compartment behind the left seat. This area is large enough to hold a briefcase or small toolbox, and the flap helps hide them from outside. Though the spare takes up most of the right-hand area, it is at least flat and not upright, so small stuff can rest on top. The Ranchero suffers the same bumper-jack dilemma as the Camino. It lays with one end protruding over the floor tunnel with a very sharp end interferring with the space on the left. It will scratch or cut just about anything with less than a 45 Rockwell hardness. Why tailgate space isn't utilized for jack storage on both Ranchero and Camino is still an unanswered question.

The one major design change that causes more comments than all else is the absence of vent side windows on the '68 Fairlane. We like their absence because of the cleaner appearance it gives the car and there's no additional draft caused by their not being there when the glass is down. But we don't like not having them because getting just a breath of fresh air means the entire edge of the window, all the way around, must be opened. There's a flow-through ventilation which works OK, but being human, we — and many like us — can't seem to keep from wanting smog-filled

height from the ground with an empty truck and the side-panel measurement is consistent all the way back. The El Camino, on the other hand, has a sloping side which ranges from a floor-to-fender-top height of about 17 inches to a low of around 13 inches. The straight-down roof pillars of the Ranchero don't extend back into the forward bed area, meaning straight drop-in nearly anywhere, into the bed. The tailgate doesn't come down level with the bed, but stays slightly higher as well as angled down slightly into the load area. There's no large gap here as in the Camino floor-to-gate, but a "flap" as in MoPar wagons would still be a good idea. Finish of the cargo hauling sheet metal is excellent, though it'll scratch with abuse. A pair of drain holes are fitted at each forward corner to get rid of trapped rain or car wash water, and this is a real "better idea."

It'd be impossible not to compare the Ranchero and El Camino after driving them both. But it's also impossible to really come up with a positive comparison. We know the 396 V8-powered Camino will outrun the 390 V8-engined Ranchero, but that's not always the reason cars are bought. We received a comment from a man who owns both and he likes the Ford pickup better. While

speeds under 40 mph will reveal a "roaring" noise from the drivetrain. Yet everything continues to operate smoothly and there's no hint of a "thump-thump" anywhere along the line. About all our calculating minds can figure is that there's a harmonic vibration set up in this speed range, and it's integral in the design. However we didn't notice it after about a thousand miles of running the car, indicating it either fixed itself — or us.

With the windows closed tight, cockpit interruptions are only a product of the radio. Cruising along at 70 mph and feeling the urge for some of that smog-filled air, the outside noise really is startling when the window is lowered. Though Ford's gone on to other areas of concentration, they're still remembering the "quieter than a Rolls" bit conjured up a few years ago which helped sell quite a few cars.

Pricewise, the Ranchero starts in the $2700 range, and continues up to just short of $3000 for base models. There're three of them listed: Ranchero, Ranchero 500 and Ranchero GT (like our test vehicle). Only three engines are offered — a 200 cubic inch 6-cylinder, a 302 V8 and the 390 4-bbl. A three-speed manual gearbox is standard with the lower two engines, and a 4-speed floor-shift stick

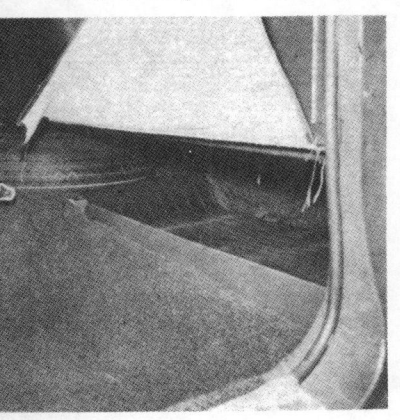

LEFT — Second-gear starts are possible with full-manual controlled automatic. Big help on slippery surfaces. Interior finishing is superb. CENTER — Behind-seat storage area has drop-down flap to hide valuable goods. Note jack end protruding over tunnel. RIGHT — Body lean is severe in tight corner with no load. Secure any cargo before giving this maneuver a try.

air hitting us in the face on occasion. Guess we'll have to get used to this as more and more car models will be switching over in the future.

Back in the work-area, the pickup bed, length checks out at 70.4 inches from back window to top of tailgate. Measured at floor level, the actual floor length is 79.8 inches. The angle of the tailgate really cuts off some room. Width of the bed is 59.8 inches at its widest point, but a slide-in load of 51.6 inches is the most that'll pass over the gate and through the rear opening. And then the bed narrows to 44.9 inches between the rear wheelhouses, and these start only about two feet in from the gate. Side loading shouldn't be much of a problem since the panel height is only 15.6 inches above the bed floor, 40 inches liftover

admitting Chevy engine and power-train seemed much better, he emphasized that as a "truck," the Ranchero was better designed. We go along with him to a point. Neither one can be a "truck" compared right down to the nitty-gritty. They're designed for more than that. Each is supposed to do a comfortable job of hauling people too, and they both do this in equal measures of comfort. Realizing that they're passenger oriented also is one big reason our Ranchero or El Camino would have a three-passenger bench seat and not two buckets.

Both machines aroused more comment from passersby than most other cars we've tested. Owners of Rancheros reflected the same noise transfer subject we noted. For some peculiar reason,

or automatic can be had with V8's.

Like we said at the beginning, the Ford people have really given us an upset. It's not likely we'd take to draggin' our passenger car-pickup, so, short of having both of them, we probably wouldn't be happy owning just one. Can't auto-makers get together? Why not let one company build a real bad car this year, and the other a good one? Then everything would be easy for us and for them. No more worrying about how sales will be in the coming year, or the year after. This way they'd be able to count on good and bad seasons. But no, they won't go for this idea at all. They'd rather have us worry. They'd also like to see us buy both cars. At least that appears to hold true for Chevy and Ford. ■■

Death Valley Daze

Or, How Four Recreational Vehicles Spent Their Easter Vacation Looking for a Home
By Julian G. Schmidt

Something's wrong.

The moment you find yourself and four other virile, red-blooded males of unquestionable romantic heritage sitting innocently in the Corkscrew Saloon 187 feet below sea level at midnight in Death Valley discussing epistemology, theoretical physics and the insidious road to Beatty, Nev., with two swell blondes — one who sings Madame Butterfly like Bob Cousy played basketball, and the other who has a provocative speech "deflect" and supports herself in one manner with college term papers that she free-lances on the sly, and in another manner with a 34 double-D — you know, just know, that this neat little progressive civilization of ours screwed up somewhere along the way.

Off-the-road? Remote? Bull. There we were, cursed with a 4-wheel-drive Jeep Wagoneer, a rugged Ford Ran-

Opposite page: (Top) At lowest spot in the U.S. — 287 feet below sea level, known as Badwater, Calif. — vehicles performed best. (Left center) GMC carried bikes; Ford Ranchero (bottom left) was nimble; Travco/Dodge (right) was homey; Schmidt, Sanders & Sussman were contemplative. (Below) Jeep was great for sand dunes.

chero GT with a 390-cu.-in. engine, GMC's new Golden West Special pick-up prepared for the worst and carrying four trail cycles, and an Orange-County-Modern Dodge A-108 camper van outfitted luxuriously by Travco with everything but palm bearers and milk baths . . . while outside, the Memphis Washboard Co. throbbed out songs about 4-letter words, college kids from all over the state mobbed in to pinch each other and drop acid, and 40-year-old cadaverous couples, going on 80, sat around with ascots and intolerance on the siccaneous veranda of nearby Furnace Creek Inn — another Fred Harvey cyanosis sanatorium — oblivious to it all. No doubt John C. Portman was sweating away in some nearby suite, planning another Appletree Center to handle the tourist trade. *Death* Valley?

But we had to learn the hard way, getting ourselves all worked up before

the trip by staring at the glistening hot chrome pipes of the bikes, the indomitable, monolithic sculpturing of the GMC, the total providence of the Travco Dodge, the sleek and rigid Ranchero, the highpockets stance of the Jeep. But it was good. An honest escape from the noise and pressure of hot cars, from the choking smog of the city, from teeming humanity. "Recreational" vehicles, indeed!

THE MOUNT

Just entering them was a welcome escape — as though they were intentionally designed along plans diametrically opposed to those for the family car. No slithering under the steering wheel until you're pressed procumbent against the floor like the rest of the super-cool slick kids of the pseudo-GT generation . . . no delicate steering to avoid chuck holes that might disintegrate the suspensions of lesser vehicles.

Instead, you mount the ladder-like steps into the Dodge and GMC and climb onto firm vinyl seats that tower above the freeway. Your legs are straight down, your back is straight up, and you swing — not steer — those big horizontal steering wheels from side to side. For braking and acceler-

(Left) And the beat goes on, even in Death Valley — especially in Death Valley and its Furnace Creek Ranch. Jeep is very stout, able to support entire Memphis Washboard Co. plus chorus under vibrant strains of folk rock. (Right) Badwater was one extreme of terrains encountered on trip — sand, salt pools, heat, borax. Other extreme was mountains.

DEATH VALLEY *continued*

ating you virtually stand on the pedals. They, too, are nearly vertical.

All vehicles fortunately had 3-speed automatic transmissions, which resulted in a clumsy pedal arrangement on the Dodge that wouldn't have been noticed with a gearbox: if you use your left foot for braking, it must be moved consciously around the steering column.

The GMC is very cramped for leg and arm room, but this, we eventually noticed after two days' use and no fatigue, was more the effect of an awkward seating position than lack of space.

At the other extreme was the Ranchero — low, comfortable — in fact, the new Torino with a truncated passenger compartment. The interior is very stylish and designed for excellent fatigue reduction with plenty of leg and elbow room. It was the one vehicle that kept us in contact with the sporty set, but it did it pleasantly with such items as full carpeting, center console for the SelectShift Cruise-O-Matic, radio, and power disc brakes.

The Jeep Wagoneer was the compromise of the group. You still climb high onto the seat, and once there, you retain an impression of Olympian superiority very much like the GMC. But the seats are soft, and successful attempts have been made to impart all the convenience and comfort of sedans with a tasteful dash and refined fabrics.

Chaos reigned as initial driving stints were chosen, and brains clicked in deciding whether it would be best to sacrifice some comfort by driving the Jeep on the freeways at the beginning in order to use the Ranchero in the mountains, or to utilize total comfort while one could.

It was almost time, and when someone draped the map over the fender of the GMC, the mere names of towns aroused primitive excitement from deep in the gut of every member of the expedition . . .

. . . Honby, Solemint . . .

. . .past Salt Wells and Dry China Lake to Mojave, we wound out of the city and were thankful for the solid-shifting automatic transmissions on all vehicles. The Ranchero's SelectShift Cruise-O-Matic, operated by a horseshoe handle on a center console, was quick and direct between shifts. It required some concentration in locating reverse, but that's typical with any mechanism of the horseshoe type. The Dodge van upheld the singular reputation of TorqueFlite's positive, immediate action, but it didn't have the performance to utilize it. The Jeep lacked sufficient power to enhance quick shifts, so it simply lugged interminably onward, anxiously anticipating the time when it would undoubtedly receive more affection. The GMC was quite the opposite — too rugged for town, and it couldn't disguise its muscle. Shifts were firm and definite, even loaded with four cycles.

. . . Saltdale, Red Mountain, Borosolvay . . . the powerplants proved one thing: this is the age of specialization. Performance is provided only where you expect to use it most, and even then, it seems to be done strictly by gearing. Each vehicle had a V-8, but the only one with adequate performance for freeway driving was the Ranchero, and perhaps by grasping at straws — the GMC.

Ranchero's 325-hp, 4-bbl. engine had more than enough power both in traffic and on the open road. And even with all accessories operating, it did not overheat, though air condition-

ing is a painful and noticeable drag on power, completely eliminating wheelspin from a standing start.

The GMC had only sufficient power to remain at the speed limit on hills. However, this lack of responsive performance at speed was a result of gearing, for its 310-hp (235 hp net) 396-cu.-in. engine put out a *net* torque of 288 lbs.-ft. to provide power where it was needed later on in more demanding, rugged terrain.

Dodge's 318-cu.-in. engine is a lightweight, flexible, high-torque powerplant that works well in a light sportstype vehicle designed for handling and response, but its 230-hp and 340 lbs.-ft. of torque were not quite enough to give the heavy Travco van an acceleration margin at freeway speeds.

An analysis of the Jeep's performance is unfair at present, since our Wagoneer was equipped with last year's American Motors 327-cu.-in. engine. Newer models use Buick's 350-cu.-in. unit which should be more satisfactory in all aspects.

Traffic was still heavy, even with 150 miles of pathetic villages and lifeless, transitory topsoil between us and metropolitan Los Angeles. Still, the recreational vehicles lumbered on, the GMC now riding much smoother and very quiet with a full load, its 950 x 16.5, 8-ply tires with their thumb-deep tread humming uncomfortably on the pavement. Surprisingly, however, they built and insulated the cab for distance driving, and thus far it boasted the quietest interior and the one most conducive to conversation. With the bed empty, the GMC's wide tires often set up disturbing modes of vibration, but now the only sounds and sensations were the air conditioner that could operate comfortably in the Mojave Desert at one-third its capacity due to the small cab, and the AM-

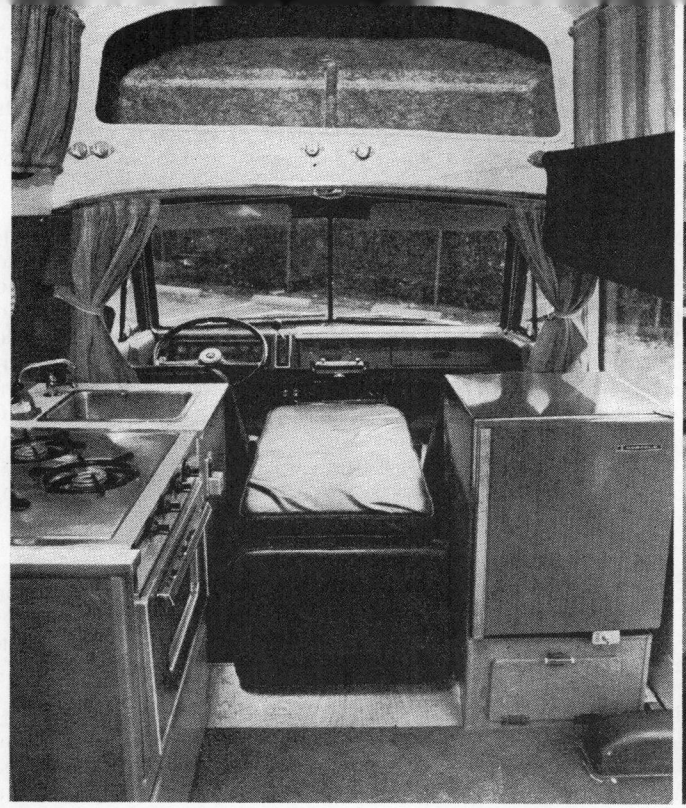
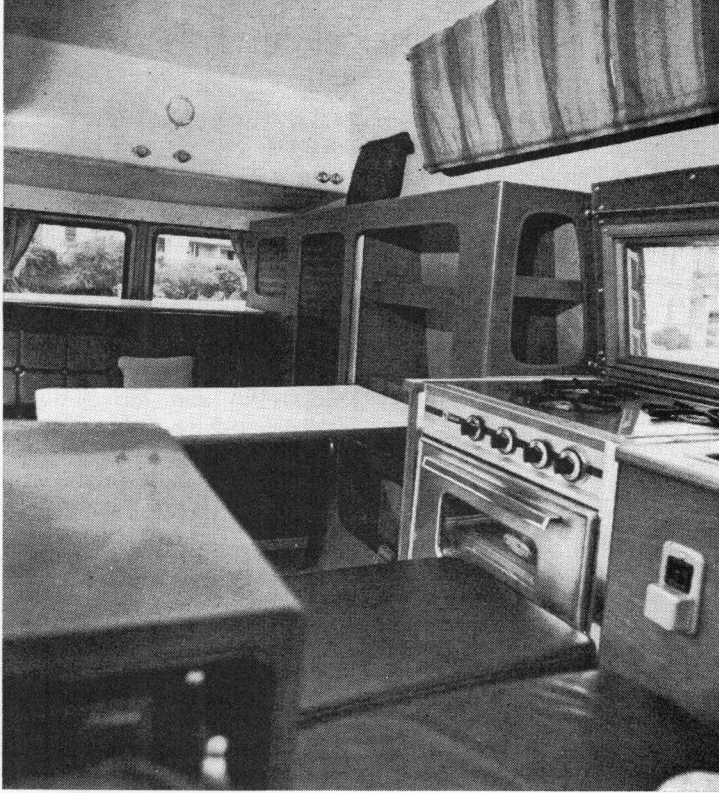

(Clockwise, from top left) Dodge van was equipped by Travco with kitchen appliances, including running water and refrigerator, sleeping room for entire crew, and virtual recreation parlor. A/C electrical outlet is on body, outside. Doors contain bar items.

FM radio with its impressive fidelity confirmed by tight cab construction.

Even on the road the pickup anatomy of the Ranchero is unnoticeable. Ride is still very sedan-like and its low profile adds to stability. As in the GMC, air conditioning for the small cab is more than adequate, regardless of temperatures. However, three sets of vibrations — hood, air conditioner and engine — gave us concern, though no problems developed even though the Ranchero began the trip with nearly 6000 miles on the odometer.

The Jeep had no air conditioning, but as long as we were moving at freeway speeds, it was comfortable. By opening two windows on each side, plus the tailgate window which is electrically operated from the dash, all available air could be captured. But it was obvious this vehicle was designed for duty, not pleasure. The ride was good, but still had that truck-like feel, the AM radio had poor fidelity, and wind noise was high with the windows open, and even worse with the windows closed.

The same with the Dodge. Fully equipped, it is ideally suited for stationary use. The ride is quite hard, even with a weight of well over two tons, but at least the safety and handling virtues of its stiff suspension are well worth the sacrifice of a little comfort, especially with the Travco addition placing it 100 inches above the ground. Air conditioning is modestly effective for front passengers, even with scores of cubic feet of space behind them. As fatiguing as the driving position and instability of the vehicle may be, its stereo tape and AM-FM radio qualify it as a kind of Mobile Met, and running water, stove, refrigerator, beds, cupboards, table, drapes, etc., in the rear allay any fatigue-consciousness by reminding you that you can stop and live it up any time you so desire.

. . . Argus, Trona . . .

. . . and we had now penetrated deep into the Mojave Desert. Gasoline stops were dictated by the GMC, its air conditioner and heavy cargo dragging economy down to as low as 8.0 mpg. On only one leg were we able to break 10 mpg, and then by only two tenths. At all other times, it hovered close to 9.5, while the Ranchero, Jeep and Dodge achieved as much as 14.0, 13.5 and 13.2 respectively.

Civilization was hours behind us, and the city's fever was difficult to recall. Ah, virgin America, with nothing but endless salt beds, thousands of mesquite bushes breaking the magnificence of unoccupied space, amorphous hills of boulders, each one defaced by inane Graffiti and high school initials.

It was mid-afternoon and the burning sky was beginning to lose its intensity from California's ubiquitous mustard haze of smog. But at least there was space — unoccupied space permeated with sulphur dioxide belching from the arrogant anal-stacks jutting triumphantly above sterile, antiseptic laboratories of the Stauffer and Trona chemical works.

According to the map, an unpaved road led to the ghost towns of Ballarat, four miles from Highway 178 at the toe of the Panamint Mountains, and Panamint City, 12 miles further

DEATH VALLEY

up the slopes. Through the dust — the blessed, glorious dust whose purity we savored as it drifted across hoods and gushed through the Jeep's open windows — Ballarat materialized . . . eerily, briefly . . . and it was a genuine California ghost town, complete with unrecognizable, pathetic, decrepit carcasses of red-earth buildings that meant something back in 1807 when they rang with spirit and inspired men by their very presence.

Ballarat 1968: vague, vestigial remains of Chris Wick's Saloon, built by the man in 1817, were prostituted by a brazen, fresh modern sign blaring its name — a recent opportunist's execrable attempt to exploit history. Across the street another crumbling foundation was filled to the brim with fetid trash. In the middle of it all, the new air-conditioned aluminum and concrete resort headquarters shone like a polished scalpel.

Behind town, the Panamint Range beckoned deliciously, and before we could unload the cycles and squeeze off four rounds from a .22, the sheriff/mayor/owner swaggered up, confiscated our Road Test Editor's peace medallion and aimed us for Panamint City, far above.

Another couple of hours, a little strategy, and some food and water, and the Jeep, in 4-wheel-drive-Low, maneuvered easily up the narrow, 35%, rock-covered, rivulet-laced path. The others, with the exception of the GMC loaded with cycles, simply lacked sufficient traction.

It was 18 miles to pavement, and the road race was on, led by the GMC as it hugged the rough, rolling, anguiform road. The Jeep was next, never at a disadvantage, and the Dodge van, towering above clouds of dust from those ahead, was able to follow as closely as it wished while dozens of appliances and utensils crashed with deafening percussion in accompaniment to Andy Williams' "Moon River" on the stereo tape deck. Only the Ranchero, which had started late, lagged deliberately behind — its sleek, low profile was swallowed by the dust and visibility was gone.

. . . Pinto Peak, Skiddo . . .

Death Valley. Aguerreberry Point, Stovepipe Wells . . . the road through the Panamint Range provided a first opportunity to observe high-speed roadholding and handling behavior. From near sea level to almost a mile high, the GMC retained the lead. More than two tons, well-distributed, pressed its enormous tires to the pavement.

But it was terrain for which the Ranchero had been waiting, and with its limited-slip differential, heavy-duty suspension, power disc brakes and potent engine with 427 lbs.-ft. of torque, it could dive deep into turns, braking late, power slide around hairpins and exit from sweepers in a full, controllable drift — the only one of the vehicles able to do so. Because of its lighter weight, it handled better than many supercars. If it hadn't been for the traffic, it could have overtaken the pickup within minutes.

But analyses aside, it was that lumbering, outrageous Travco Dodge that stole the hearts of the staff. It crashed and rattled around rough turns, and the driver was almost standing while spinning the steering wheel mercilessly. But the van hung on, and when we finally pushed it far enough to lift the inside rear wheel, it made the entire trip, the thousands of campers, even smog in Death Valley, worthwhile.

High-speed maneuvering, is not the Jeep's forte. A high degree of camber at the rear wheels combined with the vehicle's high center of gravity, causes some anxious moments on unpredictable turns.

From The Pan Into . . .

The temperature rose, and the cause was soon apparent, though the "Sea Level" sign was not the only reason. Death Valley . . . Ft. Lauderdale West . . . The New Scene . . . Lucifer's anointed land of depravity and desolation, the one spot on earth for which he didn't have to battle the Almighty. Surrounded by borax, salt pools and alluvial fans, and blanketed wall-to-wall with the cold alloys of trailers and campers belonging to every mitty-

Suzuki rode smoothly, but should have had trail sprocket connected.

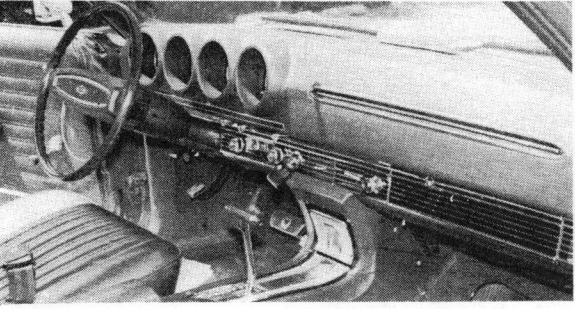

(Clockwise, from above) GMC Golden West Special had most abundantly equipped dash, with tach, all gauges, A/C-D/C converter. Jeep dash had idiot lights, with column shift for automatic box, floor shift for 4-wheel-drive hook-up. Ash tray on back of Ranchero seat is a nice idea, but difficult to reach by either passenger. Its sophisticated dash, however, could pass for luxury GT car.

minded mini-man who can't find liberty anywhere but 307 miles from his boss, Death Valley has become the new Mecca.

It is also irony. The trail cycle set drives 307 miles for elbow room. The camper set drives 307 miles for privacy. The college kid drives 307 miles for a sexual sabbatical. Ergo: Death Valley *Lives*.

The sun was barely up on the second day when, with bated breath, we threw the cycles from the GMC's bed —one Kawasaki 120 Road Runner, one Hodaka Ace 90, one 120cc B-105 Suzuki Bearcat, one 100cc Yamaha— and donned our genuine certified original Grant competition helmets that saved us several times from our inexperience. Soon, the valley reverberated with the "ree-e-e-e-e-e-n-nga ding ding ding ding" quartet of 2-stroke engines as four figures with shiny white domes rolled toward the rose-cotton horizon.

"Keep off" signs, "restricted area" signs, "motorcycles-not-allowed-in-this this - area" signs, "do - not - take - motorcycles - off - authorized - designated - paths" signs, led us over 2-lane paving protected by a "speed limit 35 mph" sign — past a group of 26 chaperoned members of the Southwest Inyo County Audubon Society on the left, 14 members of the Association for the Preservation of Ordovician Disconformities to the right, and a flurry of aging Supporters of the Herbal Beauty of Pahrump Valley a few hundred feet farther

At least two choices remained. We could ride 1½ miles to Zabriskie Point and shoulder our way through throngs of parents who left their kids bored

and bawling in station wagons and campers to walk to the edge and gaze excitingly upon thousands of square miles of borax, salt pools and alluvial fans, or we could follow the endless queue of vehicles a full mile off the highway along the authorized designated official "scenic trail," paved with sand and more borax, that shielded mankind from misdeeds by its strictly enforced, well-regulated one-way traffic.

We chose both and broke the law besides. One by one we slammed the cycles into low gear and sadistically ripped up the unauthorized non-designated desert hillsides. The Kawasaki and Hodaka screamed loudest and rode roughest but went farthest because they were the only ones connected to trail sprockets, while the Yamaha and Suzuki contented us with comfort, quietness and fatigue-free touring.

Accompanying us for the day was the Dodge camper, its refrigerator loaded with ice and beverage, its reservoir topped with water, and its air-conditioned living area affording a comfortable retreat from the 100° smog-filtered sunlight and desperate vacationers outside. Any of the other vehicles could have penetrated deeper into wilderness, but Death Valley's restricted lands rendered this advantage void.

Reasons For Being

Opinions were beginning to form. The GMC was most suitable for carrying trail cycles and passengers in reasonable comfort; the Dodge van promised existence under all condi-

tions, even though none of the bikes would fit inside; the Ranchero was by far the most versatile, able to haul two bikes to the hills during the day and two lovers to a semi-formal party at night, and still receive plenty of admiring comments; and the Jeep was the only one capable of penetrating inviolable aras.

Since nothing was allowed off the authorized, designated roads, the 4-wheel-drive of the Jeep was not needed. But inspiration from the prior day's experience when the Jeep had ground its way up the Panamint Mountains, had infused our blood. With spirits high, we headed for Stovepipe Wells 22 miles away to romp and play in the ephemeral sand dunes.

. . . According to reliable sources, the sinister "do-not-leave-designated-road" signs surrounding the dunes were what provoked the third day's notorious action: early in the morning the roads were already rife with travelers, so again we packed the Dodge's refrigerator with ice and followed the mindless cortege, led on by signs into Golden Canyon, Artist's Drive, Devil's Golf Course, down a borax road into the Black Mountains where fawning pawns of progressivism could walk a quarter of a mile to stand beneath an ersatz natural bridge whose beauty is desecrated daily by thousands of feet that scrape its surface, by hundreds of hands that carve indelible names in its sides.

"Do-not-drive-beyond-designated-parking-area," threatened the sign. But the reason was clear, and this time legitimate. If the Ranchero or Dodge

Photos by Pat Brollier

GMC was the true workhorse of all vehicles, yet, equipped with all the comfort items necessary for a trip like this, it also proved to be the most comfortable for all-around driving.

Extra heavy-duty suspension gave it excellent road handling, with no indication of nausea in mountains. Enormous 9.50x 16.5 tires were valuable option. 4 wd would make it perfect.

DEATH VALLEY *continued*

had left the road, they would have submerged axle deep into soft gravel and sand, or pierced their pans on jagged boulders that filled the valley winding beneath the bridge. The GMC, with its wide tires, had sufficient buoyancy but not enough traction.

But for three days the Jeep had ached for this opportunity. We kicked the 4-wheel-drive lever and dove into the canyon, spraying rocks on all sides while hiking sightseers plastered themselves against the cliffs and shrieked forbidding threats. "Hey, that's against the law!" "You're not supposed to leave the authorized, designated areas!" "Ya oughta be reported to the Rangers!"

Our eyes were glazed, our palms perspired from the grip, and the saliva of ecstasy oozed from the corners of our banzai sneers. For a full half-mile, we plowed through the canyon, the Jeep growling and churning, sometimes almost faltering, but we rode it out to the very end. It conquered nature. We conquered Man. Fulfillment.

As if unrequited, the wind followed us home . . . Baker . . . Barstow . . . blowing with such fury that the top-heavy Dodge was tossed playfully from lane to lane on the freeways, and twice the Ranchero's hood was loosened from its latch. But we could not be delayed by petty problems. We had done it . . . met the challenge . . . rather made our own . . . and won.

. . . Outside, the deluge of campers and trailers poured profusely into stark, uncontaminated hinterlands— mankind's last outpost of solitude and freedom. . . .   /MT

Recreational Vehicles — How They Compare

	TRAVCO DODGE	FORD RANCHERO	GMC PICKUP	JEEP WAGONEER
Manufacturer's Suggested Retail Price:	$2500	$2964	$2447	$4041
Price as Tested — equipped with:	5900	4012	4161	4782
	318-cu.-in. V-8; Torque-Flite automatic transmission; air-conditioning; stereo tape; AM-FM radio; power steering; power brakes; heavy-duty suspension.	390-cu.-in. V-8; air-conditioning; Select-Shift automatic; power steering; power brakes; radio; limited-slip differential; center console.	396-cu.-in. V-8; automatic transmission; air-conditioning; power brakes; power steering; Golden West package; limited-slip differential; tinted glass; tachometer; radio; heavy-duty suspension.	327-cu.-in. V-8; automatic transmission; radio; heavy-duty tires; limited-slip differential; power steering; power brakes; power tailgate window.
Engine Displacement:	318	390	396	327
Bore & Stroke:	3.91 x 3.31	4.05 x 3.78	4.094 x 3.76	4.00 x 3.25
Hp @ rpm:	230 @ 4400	325 @ 4800	325 @ 4800	250 @ 4700
Torque: Lbs.-Ft. @ rpm:	340 @ 2400	427 @ 3200	410 @ 3200	340 @ 2600
Compression Ratio:	9.2:1	10.5:1	10.25:1	8.7:1
Transmission:	3-speed automatic	3-speed automatic	3-speed automatic	3-speed automatic
Steering Wheel Turns — Lock-to-Lock:	3.8	4.6	4	4
Turning Diameter — Curb-to-Curb	37 ft.	42 ft.	43.8 ft.	38 ft.
Brake Type:	Power drums	Power front disc rear drums	Power drums	Power drums
Tire and Wheel Sizes:	8.15 x 15	7.35 x 14	9.50 x 16.5	7.75 x 15
Rear Axle Ratio:	3.55:1	4.09:1	4.10:1	3.31:1
Wheelbase — Ins.:	108	113	127	110
Height — Ins.	100	54.4	74.5	65.0
Width — Ins.	78.6	59.8	77.8	75.60
Length — Ins.	189	203.9	200.5	183.7
Road Clearance — Ft.:	7.31	6.5	11.6	11.04
Weight — Lbs.:	3950	3680	4035	3816
Bed Dimensions — Width:		51.6 in.	65.0 in.	52.5 in.
Bed Dimensions — Length:		79.8	98.0	66.3
Inside Height:	74 ins.			39.54 in.
Sleeping Capacity — Standard:	4 persons	2 persons	2 persons	2 persons
Sleeping Capacity — Optional:	6 persons			
Fuel Capacity	23 gal.	20 gal.	22 gal.	20 gal.
Mileage Range:	10.5-13.2 mpg	10.2-14 mpg	8-10.2 mpg	10.6-13.5 mpg

well-spaced ratios, teamed with a 3.5 to 1 rear axle ratio which is an important aspect of the car's passenger-car feel: it is not undergeared, as most pick-ups are.

On the other hand, the high-compression engine (9.3 to 1) has tremendous spread of torque, so that the Ranchero can idle along at 20 m.p.h. in top with the greatest of ease—loaded or not.

The Test car was standard in all

Ford
* A practical, economical and versatile dual-purpose car...

A CAR ROAD TEST

RANCHERO 3·6

THERE is increasing emphasis in South Africa on the dual-purpose type of vehicle—particularly in the rural areas.

Transport which can be both prestige conveyance and husky load-carrier is in demand, and one of the best suited to this dual role is the Ford Ranchero, based on the redoubtable Australian Fairlane.

Derived from a sedan, the Ranchero combines clean appearance, passenger-car comfort and tough load-carrying abilities.

It looks good about town or parked in front of the homestead, with its modern lines and detail finish; it cruises and handles like a strong big car—seating three in comfort and four at a pinch—and it is strong on ¾-ton working ability.

RACING TOW-CAR

For this quick Test we are indebted to Team Meissner, which made available the Ranchero used for towing Peter Gough's trailer-mounted racing Ford Escort on the annual motor sport circuit in Southern Africa.

This Ranchero—in team colours—has already completed 27,000 towing miles at high speed (carrying also a load of spares, fuel and team equipment) yet it came up for testing fresh as a daisy and bursting with eager power.

The Team Meissner people have

been delighted with it, rating it as by far the best towing vehicle of their long experience in this field.

CAB AND LOAD

The Ranchero has a roomy cab with bench seat, closely resembling the front passenger compartment of a comfortable big car. With its stylish looks it appears a bit of a dandy, but this is belied by its firm heavy-duty suspension, and the tremendous response of the high-torque, 3.6-litre, six-cylinder engine.

The load platform is 80.6 in. long and 45 in. wide between wheel arches, giving a total load area of about 31 sq. ft.

The tailgate can be opened with one hand, station-wagon fashion,

DATA AT 70

Min. Noise level	84.0 dBA
0–70 through gears	19.8 sec.
M.p.g. at 70	18.0 approx.
Reserve power at 70	0.103 g.
Max. gradient at 70 (top)	1 in 9.7
Speedo error at 70	7.2— over
Speedo at true 70	75
R.p.m. at 70 (top)	3,210

and drops flush with the load platform. Sides are 16.4 in. deep, and a useful option (fitted on the Test car) is a neat and durable vinyl cover which laces down with nylon rope to enclose the load space.

PERFORMANCE

The three-speed, all-synchromesh transmission with column shift has

respects, except that the 6-in. wheel rims had been widened and massive 185, 70-ratio Dunlop SP Sport tyres fitted for all-weather towing.

It tore away from rest with free use of the throttle and lots of wheel-spin, to reach 60 in 13.8 sec., and has a maximum speed potential of well into the nineties.

FUEL ECONOMY

Its strength in 2nd and top gears proved astonishing, and is the reason why it has proved an outstanding and economical tow-car.

We were unable to test fuel consumption in the short run, but Team Meissner reports an average of about 18 m.p.g. in fast towing over long distances—which should be pretty representative!

We were also unable to test brakes, as the linings were due for replacement after 27,000 miles of extra-hard use, but the team drivers report that the big drums have proved quite satisfactory.

SUMMARY

Our outstanding impressions of the Ranchero are its attractive appearance and easy control, its huge reserve of mechanical strength, moderate noise levels by pick-up standards, and load-capable suspension which retains comfort in riding light.

Practical, economical, versatile and competitively-priced, it must rate highly in the dual-purpose car class.

ENGINE :

Cylinders	6 in line
Carburettor	Single choke
Bore	3·68 in. (93·5 mm.)
Stroke	3·46 in. (88·0 mm.)
Cubic capacity	221 cu. in. (3,624 cc.)
Compression ratio	9·3 to 1
Valve gear	o.h.v., pushrods
Main bearings	Seven
Aircleaner	Paper element
Fuel rating	Premium
Cooling	Water, 12·5 pints
Electrics	12 -volt AC

ENGINE OUTPUT :

Max. b.h.p. SAE	135
Max. b.h.p. net	114·8
Peak r.p.m.	4,400
Max. torque/r.p.m.	208/2,400

TRANSMISSION :

Forward speeds	Three
Synchromesh	All
Gearshift	Steering Column
Low gear	2·95 to 1
2nd gear	1·68 to 1
Top gear	Direct
Reverse gear	3·67 to 1
Final drive	3·50 to 1
Drive wheels	Rear
Tyre size	7·75 x 14, 6-ply

BRAKES :

Front	10·0 x 2·25-in. drums
Rear	10·0 x 1·75-in. drums
Total lining area	153·6 sq. in.
Boosting	Nil
Handbrake position	Under dash

STEERING :

Type	Recirculating ball and nut
Lock to lock	5·0 turns
Turning circle	36·5 ft.

MEASUREMENTS :

Length overall	187·4 in.
Width overall	73·5 in.
Height overall	55·6 in.
Wheelbase	110·9 in.
Front track	58·0 in.
Rear track	58·0 in.
Ground clearance	8·0 in.
Licensing weight	2,937 lb.

SUSPENSION :

Front	Independent
Type	Coil springs, extra heavy duty
Rear	Live axl
Type	2-stage, 7-leaf, semi elliptic springs.

CAPACITIES :

Seating	Three
Fuel tank	12·8 gal.
Load space	31·0 sq. ft.

SERVICE DATA :

Sump capacity	6·0 pints
Change interval	2,500 miles
Oil filter capacity	1·7 pints
Change interval	5,000 miles
Gearbox capacity	2·9 pints
Change interval	Nil
Diff capacity	2·3 pints
Change interval	Nil
Air filter change	Up to 10,000 miles
Greasing points	Nil

(These basic service recommendations re given for guidance only, and may vary ccording to operating conditions. Inquiries hould be addressed to authorised dealer- hips.)

TYRE PRESSURES :

Crossply:	front		26 to 30 lb.
	rear		26 to 36 lb.
Radial ply:	front		26 to 32 lb.
	rear		26 to 36 lb.

ngine is that of the Australian Falcon dels: a very flexible "six" in a vast gine compartment.

INTERIOR NOISE LEVEL

ACCELERATION

ENGINE SPEED

MAKE AND MODEL :

Make	Ford
Model	Ranchero

PERFORMANCE FACTORS :

Power/weight (lb./b.h.p.)	25·5
Frontal area (sq. ft.)	26·7
Drag at 60 m.p.h. (lb.)	120·5
M.p.h./1,000 r.p.m. (top)	

(Calculated on licensing weight, gross frontal area, gearing and net b.h.p.)

INTERIOR NOISE LEVELS :

	Min.
Idling	51·0
30 m.p.h.	67·0
45 m.p.h.	71·0
60 m.p.h.	78·5
Full throttle	See graph

(Measured in decibels, "A" weighting, averaging runs both ways on a level road; "Minimum" with car closed.)

ACCELERATION FROM REST :

0–30	4·2
0–40	6·6
0–50	9·6
0–60	13·8
0–70	19·8
¼ mile	18·9

OVERTAKING ACCELERATION :

	2nd	Top
20–40	4·8	7·0
30–50	5·4	7·6
40·60	—	8·3
50–70	—	9·7

(Measured in seconds, to true speeds, averaging runs both ways on a level road, car carrying test crew of two and standard test equipment.)

MAXIMUM SPEED :

True speed	94·0*
Speedo reading	100

Calibration :

Indicated	20	30	40	50	60	70
True speed :	18	27	36	45·5	55·5	65

(*Calculated to the nearest 0·5 m.p.h.)

FUEL CONSUMPTION :

In high-speed towing . 18 m.p.g. approx.

GRADIENTS IN GEARS :

Low gear	1 in 2·1
2nd gear	1 in 3·0
Top gear	1 in 4·8

(Tabulated from Tapley g readings, car carrying test crew of two and standard test equipment.)

GEARED SPEEDS :

Low gear	00·0
2nd gear	00·0
Top gear	00·0

(Calculated to true speeds, at engine peak r.p.m.—4,400.)

TEST CONDITIONS :

Altitude	At sea level
Weather	Fine and mild
Barometric reading	30·04
Fuel used	93-octane
Test car's mileage	27,000

WARRANTY :

Six months or 6,000 miles.

BASIC PRICE :

National	R1,915

PROVIDED TEST CAR :

Team Meissner, 1969, Paarden Eiland, Cape.

HOT '71 FORD RANCHERO GT

Fast hauling for two in passenger car comfort.

For the car buyer with a long list of transportation needs, some seemingly in conflict with others, but all wanted in the same vehicle, there's one Ford Motor Company offering which deserves very close consideration. That's Ford Division's 1971 Ranchero which, in one package, neatly combines the most desirable attributes of an intermediate-size passenger car with the very broad application flexibility of a small, open-bed truck.

With Ranchero, the performance, handling and roadability of a first class muscle car can be had. So also can solid measures of passenger car comfort and luxury. At the same time, there's all the utility of a truck with ½-ton-plus (1,035 or 1,245 lb.) payload capacity.

This is possible because from the back of the cab forward the Ranchero is almost pure Torino and from the cab rearward, it's all truck and fashioned from basic wagon quarter panels. Its 114-inch wheelbase gives excellent maneuverability.

Beginning with the base version, which is simply called Ranchero, this little car/truck is available in four models, each with added standard and/or luxury equipment to justify the higher price tag. In ascending order these are the Ranchero 500, the GT and the top-line Squire. The latter is clearly the plushest and provides the most no-extra-cost features.

As with Torino cars the Ranchero buyer can choose from a list of options extensive enough to dent just about anybody's pocketbook. In short, there's a version for just about everybody, both taste and budget-wise. This ranges from those which will be at home (and win) on the drag strip to others which will draw envious glances at posh country clubs.

Our test Ranchero was built to our order and in turn, we ordered exactly what Ford sales experts said would be the "typical" package. This Ranchero was the GT series, one step up the price ladder from the most popular (with buyers) Ranchero 500 which in turn, is No. 2, cost-wise, to the base Ranchero. Engine was the optional Cleveland 351 V-8 with four-barrel carburetion and the tuned full dual exhaust system which comes with it. Most buyers specify either the 351 or the 302, Ford reports. Between 70% and 80% of all Rancheros are ordered with the three-speed automatic transmission and our car had the Select Shift version with its floor mounted stick.

A stormer by title and appearance, our GT was a car for all seasons and equipped to put to shame nearly any

Extra-cost laser stripes on sides of Ranchero GT adds flashy touch as well as a measure of safety for it is moderately reflective at night.

truck and many cars. To the Ranchero GT (base price $3,247.07) had been added automatic temperature control air conditioning, a Traction-Lock rear axle, power brakes with discs up front, bumper guards, tinted glass, concealed headlamps, "Laser" side striping, racing mirrors, AM/FM radio (with stereo), Shaker Hood with ram-air induction, black vinyl roof, high-back bucket seats, and console between, power steering, tachometer, intermittent windshield wipers, G70×14 Firestone raised-letter glass-belted tires and a visibility group. All together, it was $5,142.67 worth of machinery which is some pickup truck!

There could have been more. A canvas tonneau, to shelter the big 79.8 by 51.6-inch load box, is a dealer option at $49. So is 2-way Citizens Band radio, a product of subsidiary Philco-Ford. The big new (in 1970) 429-cubic-inch 370 hp V-8 power plant with 4-speed manual transmission and standard Hurst shifter may also be ordered, as can every six-cylinder and other V-8 plant in the Torino stable.

Clearly, the Ranchero can have

ing to a Ford analysis of 1970 buyers, the majority consider it a car. They don't buty it for commercial use, but in the great majority of cases the vehicle regularly carries a load. Most often this consists of recreational equipment like surf boards, cycles and lightweight campers. About one out of every four Rancheros is used to tow a boat or recreational vehicle, Ford finds. Clearly sales have been helped by the strong upsurge of other recreational hardware.

Over half of all Rancheros sold, incidentally, are registered in the so-called "warm weather belt" from the Southern Pacific coast into the Southwest and the Southern coastal states. Ford hopes to expand popularity into other areas of the country where the vehicle can serve equally well for warm and cold weather work and play.

In basic configuration, the GT version of the Ranchero is given a performance edge over the others in this car/truck line. Standard GT engine is the 302-cubic-inch 2v V-8, producing 210 horsepower (4,600 rpm) and 296 lbs.-ft. of torque (2,600 rpm). Ranchero, Ranchero 500 and the luxury-line Ranchero Squire all get (as standard) the 250-cubic-inch 1v six, providing 145 horsepower at 4,000 rpm and 232 lbs.-ft of torque at 1,600 rpm.

The 302 is available with either a three-speed manual transmission, optional four-speed stick shift or three-speed automatic, with a 3.00-to-one rear end standard. The six-cylinder powerplant comes with a three-speed manual box and 3.25 to one axle or

From head-on view, Ranchero looks like a Torino despite fact it is legally a truck. As with Torino, concealed headlights are an option.

GT series of Ranchero is identified by chrome emblem on lower right of rear deck door. Ruler was used to measure spring deflection loaded and unloaded.

many price tags and be many things to many people. On the performance end, for example, it earned the accolade as "fastest truck in the world" in 1969. With the much less powerful and now discontinued 428-cubic-inch 335 hp engine, Mario Andretti was clocked in an unmodified version on the Bonneville Salt Flats at 191.7 mph for a two-way average. With one of the small six-cylinder plants, the Ranchero can be both a low cost, docile workhorse and comfortable economical personal transportation.

Legally (for registration purposes) the Ranchero is a truck. But, accord-

In hard braking from 60 mph Ranchero's nose dips a little and there's fairly moderate rear end rise when vehicle is not loaded. Stability in maximum deceleration was found to be very good to excellent.

extra cost automatic with 3.00 to one ratio.

Optional engines for Ranchero run the gamut, power-wise from warm to hot. To pull all the stops there's the 429-cubic-inch plant with 4V carburetion providing 370 horsepower at 5,400 rpm and 450 lbs.-ft. of torque at 3,400. This well-proved stormer can be ordered with either a four-speed manual box with a Hurst shifter or optional automatic and standard 3.25 axle or 3.50 option. The 429 also comes in the Cobra Jet or Cobra Jet-Ram Air versions. The latter includes the Shaker hood/ram-air induction package. All Ranchero power teams can be ordered with the Traction Lock differential.

Ford is predicting the Ranchero with 4v1-351 power will be the most popular GT. This engine has a 10.7-to-one compression ratio and offers near maximum performance at an appealing initial outlay cost in terms of insurance premiums and miles per gallon. That, Ford feels makes the 351-4V a winner. With Shaker hood and direct dual exhaust, we tend to agree; the package makes for heady driving.

Our test car had the three-speed automatic transmission and floor mounted SelectShift, a $232.80 option. This box is a very acceptable compromise of performance with convenience. The T-bar shift lever utilizes a thumb button to isolate Park and Reverse at the top, and 1st and 2nd at the bottom, from drive and neutral. The "T" shifter is one of the most comfortable to the hand to be found anywhere.

With the SelectShift automatic, of course, you don't exactly burn your way from the starting line. In fact, we were unable to induce any wheel spin at all even with high transmission loading, in part because the test vehicle had the bigger tires and a locking rear. But from about 5 mph up, performance was quite lively, though obviously no match for the same car with a three- or four-speed manual box.

Still, the driver of a big-engined Ranchero who forgets he has a payload on board could, in jumping away from a light, leave much of the rear deck contents behind in the street. The vehicle's dual personality requires respect. You can drive it like a performance car when empty, but when carrying a load it is preferable to think of the Ranchero in terms of a truck.

Our test GT was checked on Ford's Dearborn (Mich.) electronically-timed quarter-mile strip in two different ways, empty and carrying 450 pounds of antifreeze (in cases) to simulate a moderate load. At test time the vehicle, which had 36 miles on the odometer when we picked it up, showed slightly over 700 miles, nearly all in typical city and freeway travel. The 351 seemed to be running smoothly, so we declined the Ford Division's offer of a minor retune.

Two techniques were tried for all runs. Best time (15.8 sec.) was made running empty with a driver and passenger weight of 365 pounds and a transmission pre-load (as registered on the optional tachometer) to 2,200 rpm. The transmission was permitted to do the thinking for shifting which occurred at about 5,000 rpm from 1st to 2nd and 5,100 from 2nd to 3rd. With similar pre-loading and shifting manually at 5,200 rpm (redline is 5,600) the best time was about half a second slower. Empty, without transmission loading cost about half a second more for the quarter.

Runs with the 450 lbs. of antifreeze were all under 20 seconds which is more than adequate to keep right in there with most cars in average traffic. With the added weight, it might be noted, the Ranchero tipped the scales at just under 4,000 pounds and had almost the

Ranchero GT features extremely comfortable bucket seats identical to those optionally available also on Torino. Only significant flaw uncovered in Ranchero test involved the closeness of brake and accelerator pedals.

Ranchero spare tire is stowed behind passenger seat where it is both out of weather and not as likely to be stolen if cab is locked.

Cargo bed of Ranchero is lower than that of some pickup trucks, permitting access. Test included performance checks with and without 450 pounds of cargo aboard.

Regular rear suspension has 1035-pound load capacity. Heavy duty springs, an option, can carry 1,245 pounds. Loading standard suspension with 450 pounds of cargo produced slightly under two inches of deflection.

optimum 50-50 front-rear weight distribution.

Unless the Ranchero buyer wants to extract every last bit of capability from whatever engine is selected, we recommend the automatic transmis-

In hard cornering Ranchero exhibited fair amount of lean (to camera) but felt good to driver, with very little tendency to understeer or oversteer.

sion. It's a sturdy unit, even for a load carrying vehicle. SelectShift provides near what the powerplant can deliver and also takes a lot of effort out of workaday driving, especially in urban traffic. With that box and the 351-4v pushing, the Ranchero—even loaded—can run with any car, leaving the common breed of trucks behind.

There's an overall tight, sporty feeling to the Ranchero GT whether empty or moderately loaded. The heavy duty suspension is one of the better to be found in a U.S.-built car. It offers the firmness of imported and domestic performance vehicles without approaching the board-hard ride of some conventional pickups. The shorter 114-inch Torino station wagon wheelbase no doubt also contributes to the tight-knit feel.

In fast cornering, the GT gives the impression of staying fairly flat, with or without a payload, as far as the driver is concerned, though the camera picks up evidence to the contrary. One reason for the deception is the Ranchero's high level of control even when pushed hard. As with the Torino, which got a much changed suspension for the '70 models, un-

dersteer-oversteer tendencies are minimal. This was a major objective in that rework of front end geometry.

Ranchero suspension remains unchanged from last year. A .72-inch diameter sway bar is teamed with front independent coils rated at 225 lbs./in. The Hotchkiss and four-leaf semi-elliptic set-up at the rear is rated at 126 lbs./in. Higher rate front coils are part of the package when everyone of the 429 engines is ordered, to compensate for the extra weight of these lusty powerplants.

The heavy duty suspension package (*Road Test's* vehicle didn't have it) is available with all versions of the Ranchero. It provides a 1,245-pound load capacity at the rear, compared with 1,035 pounds for the standard hardware. With this extra-cost springing, the larger "F" or "G" tires are a required option.

Because of advanced suspension geometry, and no doubt because there's comparatively less side sheet metal and glass than on a station wagon, the Ranchero is relatively immune to cross winds. However, for ideal high speed roadability the optional tonneau cover for the pickup box is recommended. This minimizes aerodynamic drag.

If the Ranchero is going to be used very much to carry loads of say 500 pounds up to the rated 1,035 or 1,245 pound capacity, front discs with mandatory power assist are recommended. They characteristically provide no-swerve stops which are especially desirable when the vehicle is carrying cargo. Our test car had the discs.

For lighter duty, the standard Ranchero brakes should be quite adequate. They consist of 10-in. × 2.50-in. drums in front and 10-in. × 2.0-in. in the rear, except for models with the 351 or 429 engines. They get the 2.50-inch drums in the rear too.

Braking performance from 60 mph was checked empty and with that 450-pound load of antifreeze. As expected, empty performance was best, with the minimum distance 174 feet but with moderate rear end rise. There

was also a tendency for one rear wheel to lock until the right amount of line pressure for maximum deceleration was found. With the load, the Ranchero's rear stayed pretty well down and, with improved traction on the back tires, the tendency of a wheel to lock up early was gone. Best stop in this (loaded) test was 197 feet, a distance attained after several practice tries.

Visibility from the Ranchero cockpit is great. Support posts are relatively unobstructive, and that big rear window just over your shoulder offers a panoramic view of nearly everything behind. Our test car had the optional dual racing mirrors which completely eliminate what few small blind spots there are in a Ranchero.

We were very pleased with the intermittent windshield wipers, which at $26.70 extra are a tremendous aid in poor weather conditions. Michigan in the fall is particularly drizzly, and these time-delay units encourage the driver to use the wipers at times when he would normally leave them off, putting up with the occasional drops of rain.

There's an overall quality throughout the Ranchero GT interior that indicates it gets the same interest and attention on the assembly line as do passenger car versions of the Torino. If you think of the Ranchero as a truck, it's one of the plushest production models you can buy. If, on the other hand, you think of it as a passenger car (most buyers do, according to Ford), it is still one of the fanciest around.

The optional high-back bucket seats are extremely comfortable, providing excellent non-fatiguing support. They were of a houndstooth woven vinyl, trimmed in solid black, well fitted and carefully stitched. The deep-pile black carpeting, also nicely trimmed out, incorporated permanent black rubber floor mats to form a good looking, highly practical one-piece floor covering.

Because of the narrower rear support ("B") pillars, flow-through ventilation is not applicable to the Ranchero or Torino wagon. Evidently, it is too costly to build relief valves into

these members. This presents no major problem with an air-conditioned Ranchero, but to achieve maximum air flow in other models, the driver must slightly open one of the side panes. The resulting wind noise at highway speeds may be objectionable to some motorists.

The Ranchero equipped with Select-Air (climate control) air conditioning has no independent below-dash fresh air vents. These are incorporated in the optional system. Fresh outside air is directed, by means of a "Fresh" setting on the Select-Air lever, through the climate control system, and can be made either cool or warm by adjusting the temperature selector. With this arrangement, the driver also has the option of warming the interior by way of the conventional heater outlets centered at the drive-shaft tunnel, or via the waist-high cooler vanes.

The car is unexpectedly quiet with windows up. That's a little surprising in light of the low-impedence dual exhausts on the 351 version tested, since they produced a deep-throated rumble at idle and low speed. That sound becomes little more than a hum with the windows up, resulting in excellent acoustics for the AM/FM Stero radio. Within the Ranchero two-passenger compartment, stereo speakers produce super sounds.

Storage room inside the Ranchero is as clever as it is plentiful. There's a conventional locking glove box plus a large area for tools behind the

driver's seat, concealed by a vinyl flap. Behind the passenger seat, a similar tunnel holds the spare tire with a fitted vinyl cover over the part of the wheel that juts into the passenger area. The jack is well secured to the floor in back of the buckets, leaving room on both sides for an attache or brief case, or objects of similar size. In addition, the GT offers a generous console compartment. It's an ideal spot for small miscellaneous items like sun glasses. The GT, in fact, actually provides more out-of-the-way inside storage space than many full-size passenger cars.

Ranchero interior lighting is also a bit more than you might expect. There are two entrance lights beneath the dash, and a map light positioned in front of the passenger seat. An optional console, which is the same unit used for standard Torinos, has illumination too. Inherited from the passenger car, though, is an out-of-reach second ash tray at the back. It would serve rear-seat passengers in the normal Torino installation; in the Ranchero it makes a nifty spot to hide an extra set of keys.

The Ranchero GT is a scene stealer everywhere you drive it. Parking lot attendants at the swankiest places give you special attention even over the luxury cars. Enthusiasts continually gather around for a closer look. The GT is near the ultimate "personal" car for anyone who has a need (or excuse) for the pickup box. Apparently more and more people do.

1. *Shaker ram-air system*

2. *Servo brake assist*

3. *MacPherson-type coil springs*

4. *Air-conditioning compressor*

5. *Heavy-duty shrouded fan*

6. *Retractible headlights*

7. *351-4v ''Cleveland'' engine*

'71 FORD RANCHERO GT 2-DOOR PICKUP

PERFORMANCE AND MAINTENANCE

Acceleration: Gears:
  0-30 mph .3.1 secs.— I
  0-45 . . . . .5.9 secs.— I
  0-60 mph . . . . .9.3 secs.—I, II
  0-75 mph . . . . .13.1 secs.—I, II
  0-¼ mile . . . . .15.9 secs. @ 88 mph
Ideal cruise . . . . 74 mph
Top speed (est) . . . . .121 mph
Stop from 60 mph . . . . .184 ft.
Average economy (city) . . . . .13.2 mpg
Average economy (country) . . . . . . .19.2 mpg
Fuel required . . . . .Regular
Oil change (mos./miles) 6/6000
Lubrication (mos./miles) 12/12,000
Warranty (mos./miles) 12/12,000
Type tools required . . . . .SAE
U.S. dealers . . . . .5775 total

SPECIFICATIONS AS TESTED

Engine . . . . .351 cu. in., ohv 4V V8
Bore & stroke . . . . .4.002 x 3.50 ins.
Compression ratio . . . . .10.7 to one
Horsepower . . . . .285 (SAE gross) @ 5400 rpm
Torque . . . . .370 lbs.-ft. @ 3400 rpm
Transmission . . . . .3-speed, automatic
Steering* . . . . .3.5 turns, lock to lock
                     42.33 ft., curb to curb
Brakes* . . . . .disc front, drum rear
Suspension . . . . .coil front, leaf rear
Tires . . . . .G70 x 14, belted-bias
Dimensions (ins.):

Wheelbase 114.0	Front track 60.5
Length 209.0	Rear track 60.0
Width 75.8	Ground clearance 6.0
Height 53.4	Weight . . . .3929 lbs.

Capacities: Fuel . . . .18 gals.   Oil . . . .5.0 qts.
    Coolant . . . . . .15.4 qts.   Trunk . . . . .N/A

**Power-assisted as tested.

RATING

	Excellent (90-100)	Good (80-90)	Fair (70-80)	Poor (60-70)
Brakes		85		
Comfort	91			
Cornering	93			
Details		88		
Finish	95			
Instruments . .		82		
Luggage (Inside)			70	
Performance . . .	91			
Quietness		84		
Ride		86		
Room		90		
Steering	94			
Visibility	98			
Overall	93			

n/a — not available

BASE PRICE OF CAR

(Excludes states and local taxes, license, dealer preparation and domestic transportation):
$3,247 at Detroit.
$ 95   351 4-V
$ 232   SelectShift Trans.
$ 112   Power Steering
$ 71   Power Front Disc Brakes
$ 14   Heavy Duty Suspension
$ 67   G70-14 Tires
$3840   TOTAL
$.91 per lb. (base price).

ANTICIPATED DEPRECIATION***

(Based on current Kelley Blue Book, previous equivalent model): $240 1st yr. + $560 2nd yr.

N/A — not applicable

In 1957, Ford came up with the brilliant idea of a dual purpose vehicle for folks who could afford only one car. The Ranchero. But, there were certain drawbacks. Since it is virtually impossible to throw Stilson wrenches, tool boxes, pieces of sewer pipe and horse manure in and out of a vehicle all day without scratching the paint and dinging sheet metal, the bed appearance tended to suffer. Also, because the thing was to be a car when it wasn't a truck, it had to accommodate both unloaded and loaded situations and not forfeit ride and handling. Somehow, they struck a good balance.

It worked out so well that Chevrolet was quick to follow suit with the El Camino and promptly outsold Ford like all Chevys must do. In fact, current sales figures for 1970 put El Camino out front with 38,286, followed by Ranchero at 20,537. Sales for both makes are increasing yearly, constituting an irrefutable barometer of public acceptance of the dual-purpose concept of these cars.

With the advent of Kennedy, Johnson, the space program and a big boost to military support industries imparted by the Vietnam exercise, Ranchero-type vehicles assumed a different role. Good pay and more leisure time inspired such toys as dune buggies, go-karts, surf boards and most recently, All Terrain Vehicles and snomobiles. All of these neat little mechanized tranquilizers, however, require a means of transportation to get from up-tight to far-out, and they are too big to stuff into even a Chrysler trunk. The Jekyll-Hyde pickup became a weekend magic carpet.

In spite of the popularity upswing of the Detroit coat-and-tie trucks, it remained a home show until two major events kicked open the door to the oriental imports. The item having the single greatest impact on the recreational market was the invention of the birth control pill. Young singles of amorous bent were seldom surprised with the sudden and immediate necessity to face the cost of setting up a home; and young marrieds did not have to share their combined incomes and leisure time with a gnarled little noisemaker requiring more support gear on a trip than a platoon of Green Beanies.

The second factor welcoming the aliens was the free-thinking attitudes held by the independent young marrieds. They would not knuckle under to Detroit when there was such a neat little alternative available at just over half the price.

Along came Datsun with its big bed, low price and cute little cab, all of which fit very nicely into cramped apartment parking slots. Swinging singles bought them as the principle means of transportation, and the cool marrieds who worked at opposite ends of town bought them as second cars. Datsun had been around since 1957, but they really didn't catch on until 1969, when sales took a marked upswing. Current sales are running 50,954 annually with future prospects even better. With the success of the L'il Hustler, Toyota took a long look at the market, a short sip of sake, turned up the sleeves of their kimonos and out rolled the Hilux. Japanese have a reputation for shortcutting research and development by taking a good foreign product and copying it in an improved version. They also do it to their domestic competition. Hilux initially entered the U.S. market in 1970 with first year sales of 11,566. At present, the only thing restricting further sales growth is the availability: they sell everything they import.

In spite of a commonality of function, the Detroit product can be compared with the imports in concept only. The most salient difference is in the price. A stripped Datsun goes for $1,966, POE while Toyota eats a slightly larger hole at $1,998. The base price of a stripped Ranchero is $3,172, the El Camino, $3,074. No one buys stripped vehicles for private use, but it does give an idea of the gap.

Size, of course, is the most obvious difference between the domestics and the imports. An item of note is the surprising similarity in useful cargo space among all four vehicles. The 17-ft. domestics have only 4 sq. ft. more bed area than the 14-ft. imports. The ride and handling bring to the fore the distinctly different design concepts employed by Detroit and Nippon. Both El Camino and Ranchero are basically passenger cars with passenger car suspensions and interior decor, designed to function comfortably and adequately in the unloaded configuration: in essence, a commuter car capable of hauling a load on weekends for recreation, or as a part of a business requirement. Heavy-duty suspensions are a mandatory option. They not only permit safe hauling, but they also improve the unladen handling characteristics.

When El Camino has a rated load on board, the rear end droops. This has been very nicely provided for by the inclusion of air inflatable shocks on the rear. The shocks are inflated by means of a valve protected by the rear bumper, until the vehicle regains a level attitude. The ride is a bit mushy and bump rebound is longer in duration, but still quite safe and comfortable. Handling is not measurably affected.

Ranchero does not incorporate this feature, but the air shocks are available through Autolite parts which can be ordered from most Ford dealers.They are not a factory option. Dearborn solves the droop problem by means of their heavy-duty suspension. The Ranchero has leaf springs in the rear, which tend to resist distortion to a greater degree

Roller Derby Special

Hollywood Haulers vs. Tokyo Rough Riders

Two sedans with cargo bodies match tailgates with a pair of Nipponese pickups masquerading as commuter cars. Ranchero — El Camino — Datsun — Toyota

By Jim Brokaw

Utilitarian configuration of Toyota Hilux extracts 28.48 sq. ft. of bed area from overall dimensions of 13.8 ft. by 5.26 ft. Tailgate has open hook chains to permit lowering below horizontal.

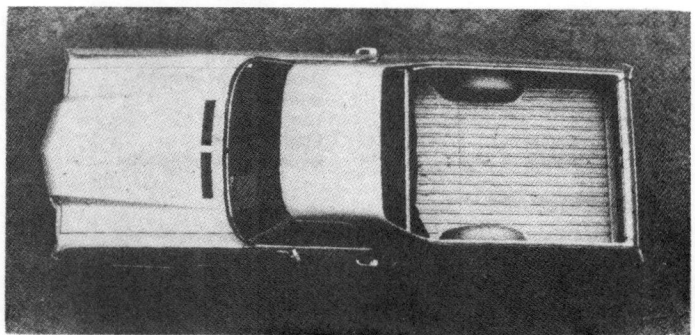

In spite of El Camino's 3-ft. edge in length, the bed is only .5 ft. longer than imports'. Bed area on domestics is less than 4 sq. ft. larger than minis'. Tarpaulin (rolled) is dealer installed; will protect both bed metal and cargo.

Datsun Li'l Hustler has same bed dimensions as Toyota but is a bit longer overall at 14.19 ft. Peripheral tie-down dogs on both abbreviated models permit securing of an infinite variety of loads.

Hood scoop induction system on Ranchero is superfluous, but dual mirrors are necessary for rear visibility with loaded bed. Both domestics have inside mounted latches, which are hard to reach with load flush against tailgate.

ROLLER DERBY

than the coil spring in the rear of the El Camino. Under a full load, the Ranchero settles down on its haunches, but not excessively. The ride is virtually unaffected, but the front end does get a hair light on the steering. Cornering capability is, surprisingly, improved. In the unloaded configuration, the Ranchero corners quite well. In the loaded setup, the vehicle develops an almost neutral understeer/oversteer condition and just rockets around corners. The Traction-lok differential is a decided asset in this situation, although there is a real question whether the 1957 Ranchero wasn't a better compromise.

The imports react in a totally different manner. One short trip around town is enough to convince your tortured body that they are very definitely designed to be operated with a load in the back. Both have short, sharp spring rates which jar the spine on every bump. This is a built-in safety feature though. You must wear seat belts over 25 mph or you will crack your skull on the headliner if you hit a bump of any decent magnitude. If you are unfastened and encounter a large bump or series of bumps while cornering, you will return to the seat in a different location than your launch point. Datsun has the roughest ride, but also has the best seat. There is more spring action to absorb jolts, but it falls far short of the mark. The seat in the Toyota is nothing more than an upholstered slab. Instead of jarring the spine, the Toyota beats all the contour out of your posterior. An ex-

Toyota

GOOD POINTS
General economy
Superior load capacity to size ratio
Resale value
Handling
Power (relative)
Ease of loading
Braking
Serviceability
BAD POINTS
Ride comfort (empty)
Shifter
Leg room
Engine noise
Back window reflection

Specifications

Engine	SOHC in-line 4
Bore & stroke	3.38 x 3.15 in.
Displacement	113.4 cu. in. (1900cc)
HP @ RPM	108 @ 5500 rpm
Torque	117 lbs.-ft. @ 3600 rpm
Compression ratio/Fuel	9.0:1/regular
Carburetion	2V
Transmission	4-speed manual
Final drive ratio	4.11:1
Steering type	Recirculating ball
Steering ratio	19.48:1
Turning diameter	31 ft. (curb-to-curb)
Wheel turns	3.9 (lock to lock)
Tire size	6.00-14/6-ply radials rated
Brakes	Drum/drum
Front suspension	Coil/stabilizer bar
Rear suspension	Leaf springs
Body/frame construction	Box section girder
Wheelbase	99.8 ins.
Overall length	165.9 ins.
Width	63.2 ins.
Height	61.8 ins.
Front track	50.8 ins.
Rear track	50.8 ins.
Curb weight	2,435-3,380 lbs.
Fuel capacity	12.1 gals.
Oil capacity	4.3 (1) qts.

Cargo Area

Length	6.06 ft.
Width	4.7 ft.
Square area	28.48 sq. ft.

Performance

Acceleration

0-30 mph	4.4 secs.
0-45 mph	8.5 secs.
0-60 mph	15.2 secs.
0-75 mph	30.8 secs.

Standing start 1/4-mile 69.28 mph
Elapsed time 19.39 secs.
Passing speeds:

40-60 mph	7.0 secs.
50-70 mph	9.8 secs.

Speeds in gears*

1st	24 mph @ 5500 rpm
2nd	38 mph @ 5500 rpm
3rd	62 mph @ 5500 rpm
4th	79 mph @ 4500 rpm

Mph per 1000 rpm (in top gear) 17.5 mph
Stopping distances:

from 30 mph	38.8 ft.
from 60 mph	140.2 ft.

Gas mileage range 23.55 mpg
Speedometer error:
Electric speed-
ometer 30 45 50 60 70 80
Car speed-
ometer 31 46 51 62 72 —

Datsun

GOOD POINTS
General economy
Superior load capacity to size ratio
Handling
Gearbox
Ease of loading
Serviceability
Resale value
BAD POINTS
Braking (empty)
Ride comfort (empty)
Engine noise
Lack of power
Back window reflection
Leg room

Specifications

Engine	SOHC in-line 4
Bore & stroke	3.27 x 2.90 in.
Displacement	97.3 cu. in. (1600cc)
HP @ RPM	96 @ 5600 rpm
Torque	99.8 lbs.-ft. @ 3600 rpm
Compression ratio/Fuel	8.5:1/regular
Carburetion	2V
Transmission	4-speed manual
Final drive ratio	4.375:1
Steering type	Recirculating ball
Steering ratio	19.8:1
Turning diameter	34 ft. (curb-to-curb)
Wheel turns	
Tire size	6.00-14/6-ply rated
Brakes	Drum/drum
Front suspension	Torsion bar
Rear suspension	Leaf springs
Body/frame construction	Box section girder
Wheelbase	99.6 ins.
Overall length	170.3 ins.
Width	62.0 ins.
Height	60.8 ins.
Front track	50.7 ins.
Rear track	50.7 ins.
Curb weight	2,436-3,538 lbs.
Fuel capacity	10.8 gals.
Oil capacity	4.3 (0.75) qts.

Cargo Area

Length	6.06 ft.
Width	4.7 ft.
Square area	28.48 s

Performance

Acceleration

0-30 mph	6.1
0-45 mph	11.1
0-60 mph	19.6
0-75 mph	32.5

Standing start 1/4-mile
Elapsed time
Passing speeds:

40-60 mph	8.5
50-70 mph	14.9

Speeds in gears*

1st	23 mph @ 5500
2nd	37 mph @ 5500
3rd	61 mph @ 5500
4th	82 mph @ 5000

Mph per 1000 rpm (in top gear) 16.4
Stopping distances:

from 30 mph	40
from 60 mph	200

Gas mileage range 23.7
Speedometer error:
Electric speed-
ometer 30 45 50 60 7
Car speed-
ometer 34 49 54 63 7
*Speeds in gears are at points (limited by the leng track) and do not represent mum speeds.

tended trip in either vehicle while empty is a very fatiguing experience. The simple solution is to carry a dummy load when there is no cargo to haul. The addition of four sandbags placed directly over the rear axle, some 240 lbs., converted both machines into docile little beasts. Datsun and Toyota are each capable of carrying 1,100 lbs. of cargo, and, as far as the ride goes, it becomes almost tranquil.

Tire pressure is fairly critical with both trucks. When inflated to the upper limits, handling at high speeds was ex-

cellent with neither model having an edge. In an effort to soften the ride before use of the dead load, tire pressure was reduced to the minimum limits. An immediate reduction in directional stability at high speeds was experienced. So, the hot tip is to keep the tires well inflated – your owner's manual will have the correct pressures for the type tires mounted – and purchase about 200 lbs. of cheap sand at your local hardware – bagged, not bulk.

The interior of the El Camino is strictly Chevelle, with which any Chevy

fan is familiar. The primary addition in both Detroiters is a little hole in the back wall behind the driver's seat. This is very handy for storing bulky little items, such as briefcases, thermos jugs, six-packs, books, and cameras. There is a slight amount of storage space between the seats and the back wall, but it is limited. The primary disadvantage to the Ranchero concept is the lack of storage area for items subject to weather damage. The toting of a brief-
text continued on page 83
how to buy overleaf

text continued on page 83

CAMINO

RANCHERO

GOOD POINTS	BAD POINTS
...ating comfort	Price
...pty performance	Load capacity compared with
...aded performance	imports
...trument panel layout	
...king	
...ling	
...el economy (relative)	
...sale value	

...pecifications

		Cargo Area	
...gine	OHV 90° V8	Length	6.6 ft.
...e & stroke	4.00 x 3.48 in.	Width	4.87 ft.
...placement	350 cu. in.	Square area	32.14 sq. ft.
@ RPM	245 @ 4800 rpm		
...que	350 lbs.-ft. @ 2800 rpm		
...npression			
...atio/Fuel	8.5:1/regular		
...buretion	2V		
...nsmission	3-speed automatic		
...al drive ratio	2.73:1		
...ering type	Power,		
	recirculating ball		
...ering ratio	Variable 18.5-12.4:1		
...ning diameter	42.0 ft.		
	(curb-to-curb)		
...eel turns	2.9 (lock to lock)		
...size	(F78x14B) G60x15		
	Goodyear Polyglas		
...kes	Power disc/drum		
...nt suspension	Coil/		
	stabilizer bar		
...ar suspension	Adjustable air		
	shocks Coil/control arm		
...y/frame			
...onstruction	Welded perimeter		
...eelbase	116 ins.		
...erall length	206.8 ins.		
...th	75.4 ins.		
...ght	54.4 ins.		
...nt track	60.2 ins.		
...ar track	59.2 ins.		
...rb weight	3,472-4,272 lbs.		
...el capacity	19 gals.		
...capacity	4 (1) qts.		

Performance

Acceleration
0-30 mph	3.7 secs.
0-45 mph	6.7 secs.
0-60 mph	10.3 secs.
0-75 mph	16.3 secs.
Standing start ¼-mile	77.98 mph
Elapsed time	17.57 secs.

Passing speeds:
40-60 mph	5.3 secs.
50-70 mph	6.6 secs.

Speeds in gears*
1st	53 mph @ 4800 rpm
2nd	88 mph @ 4800 rpm
3rd	92 mph @ 3500 rpm
Mph per 1000 rpm (in top gear)	26.3 mph

Stopping distances:
from 30 mph	32.7 ft.
from 60 mph	109 ft.
Gas mileage range	16.23 mpg

Speedometer error:
Electric speedometer	30 45 50 60 70 80
Car speedometer	34 49 54 65 75 85

GOOD POINTS	BAD POINTS
Power steering	Seats too low
Handling	Price
Empty performance	Fuel economy
Loaded performance	Lack of interior space
Control accessibility	Load capacity compared with imports

Specifications

		Cargo Area	
Engine	OHV 90° V8	Length	6.65 ft.
Bore & stroke	4.02 x 3.50 in.	Width	4.95 ft.
Displacement	351 cu. in.	Square area	32.92 sq. ft.
HP @ RPM	285 @ 5400 rpm		
Torque	370 lbs.-ft. @ 3400 rpm		
Compression			
ratio/Fuel	10.7:1/premium		
Carburetion	4V		
Transmission	3-speed automatic		
Final drive ratio	3.25:1		
Steering type	Power,		
	recirculating ball		
Steering ratio	20.64:1		
Turning diameter	42.33 ft.		
	(curb-to-curb)		
Wheel turns	3.5 (lock to lock)		
Tire size	F70x14 Firestone		
	Polyglas		
Brakes	Power disc/drum		
Front suspension	Coil/		
	stabilizer bar		
Rear suspension	Leaf springs		
Body/frame			
construction	Unitized		
Wheelbase	117 ins.		
Overall length	206.2 ins.		
Width	75.8 ins.		
Height	53.4 ins.		
Front track	60.5 ins.		
Rear track	60.0 ins.		
Curb weight	3,464-4,314 lbs.		
Fuel capacity	18 gals.		
Oil capacity	4 (1) qts.		

Performance

Acceleration
0-30 mph	3.7 secs.
0-45 mph	5.8 secs.
0-60 mph	8.5 secs.
0-75 mph	12.0 secs.
Standing start ¼-mile	88.14 mph
Elapsed time	16.14 secs.

Passing speeds:
40-60 mph	3.7 secs.
50-70 mph	4.9 secs.

Speeds in gears*
1st	58 mph @ 5400 rpm
2nd	97 mph @ 5400 rpm
3rd	103 mph @ 4000 rpm
Mph per 1000 rpm (in top gear)	25.7 mph

Stopping distances:
from 30 mph	33.4 ft.
from 60 mph	116.2 ft.
Gas mileage range	12.83 mpg

Speedometer error:
Electric speedometer	30 45 50 60 70 80
Car speedometer	32 47 52 61 71 80

DATSUN

We could make it sound like there is more than one version but there isn't. You have to buy the economy version and add your own bolt-ons — like mags and wide tires — from after-market suppliers. But, just to give you the full run of Datsun's mini-option list, here's a sample recommendation on equipment:

Economy Version

Start with the 97-cu.-in. in-line four mated to a four-speed and add the heavy-duty battery. To make it more comfortable inside, we'd add the AM radio, the dome light door switch, and arm rests. For increased visibility, add the outside mirrors. And even after opting for all this, you're **still** in the economy market, price-wise.

1971 DATSUN PICKUP POWER TEAM

Engine	Transmission Available	Torque	Carburetion	Compression Ratio	Fuel Required	Rear Axle Ratio
96-hp 97 4-cyl.	4-speed	100 @ 3600	Two-barrel	8.5	Regular	4.11

TOYOTA

Economy Version

What else is there? Let's go whole hog and order the big 113-cu.-in. four linked to Toyota's rugged 4-speed. For wheels and tires, we suggest asking the dealer what kind of deal he's got on mags and wider treads. Fortunately, on its miniscule option list, Toyota does have outside mirrors. Order them, because if you have a tall load in back, you need the extra visibility to see around it. For sounds, we'd skip the ordinary AM radio and order the AM radio with the built-in 8-track stereo tape deck and then order the FM cartridge in addition. The latter plugs into the tape deck so you can have FM in your AM. Simple, isn't it?

1971 TOYOTA HI-LUX POWER TEAM

Engine	Transmission Available	Torque	Carburetion	Compression Ratio	Fuel Required	Rear Axle Ratio
108-hp 113 4-cyl.	4-spd. only	117 @ 3600	Two-barrel	9.0	Regular	4.11

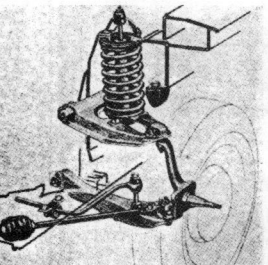

Far left: Ford puts front coil spring and shock on top of upper A-arm. Left: Chevrolet prefers to mount front coil and shock on lower control arm. Right: Datsun follows Chrysler route with front torsion bar and shock. Far right: Toyota front suspension is the same as Chevrolet.

RANCHERO

Economy Version

Try the 302-c.i. V8 with its easy-on-gas 2-V and mate it to a four-speed manual trans. Add power front disc brakes if you can afford it.

Moderate Version

"Moderate" means performance with economy, so we'd choose the 351 two- or four-barrel V8, mated to Ford's Cruise-O-Matic. Again, power discs and power steering.

Luxury Version

To power the accessories you're going to hang on this dude, we'd advise the big 429 four-barrel Cobra-Jet (non-Ram Air variety). Cruise-O-Matic, power steering, power disc brakes, air, the high capacity radiator and a HD battery are recommended, too.

Performance Version

Could be this is a trick way to get past your insurance man who says "no" to your having a hot two-door hardtop. So order the 429 Cobra-Jet with Ram-Air, add the four-speed and power disc brakes and beef it up with the Traction-lok rear axle. You'll want the wide G70x14 treads and we wouldn't be without the tachometer.

1971 RANCHERO POWER TEAMS

Engine	Transmission Available	Torque	Carburetion	Comp. Ratio Fuel	Rear Axle Ratio
145-hp 250 6 Hydraulic lifters	Manual 3-spd; Cruise-o-matic	232 @ 1600	one-barrel	9.0/R	2.79 3.00
210-hp 302 V8 Hydraulic lifters	Manual 3-spd; Cruise-o-matic	296 @ 2600	two-barrel	9.0/R	3.00 3.00 3.25
240-hp 351 V8 Hydraulic lifters	Cruise-o-matic only	350 @ 2600	two-barrel	9.0/R	2.75 3.00 3.25
285-hp 351 V8 Hydraulic lifters	Manual 4-spd; Cruise-o-matic	370 @ 3400	four-barrel	10.7/P	2.75 3.00 3.25
370-hp 429 V8 Hydraulic lifters	Manual 4-spd; Cruise-o-matic	450 @ 3400	four-barrel	11.3/P	3.25 3.50

EL CAMINO

Economy Version

That's what the 250-c.i. one-barrel six is there for, so check that first on your order blank, coupled to a three-speed. But, if you plan on hauling 500 lbs. or so around, we urge a V8, preferably the 350-cu.-in. two-barrel model.

Moderate Version

If you're ordering power steering, power brakes and air, opt for the 400-c.i. four-brarrel V8. With fewer options, the 350-c.i. 2-V or 4-V would suffice.

Luxury Version

For luxury, we'd add the tamer 454 — the 365 horsepower model — and mate it to a TurboHydra-matic with the floor-mounted shift. We'd also add power disc brakes, power steering and Positraction. For comfort, include tinted glass and AM/FM stereo radio with tape player.

Performance Version

Mate the 425-hp four-barrel to an HD 4-speed, add power disc binders and spec the HD suspension and Positraction.

1971 EL CAMINO POWER TEAMS

Engine	Transmission Available	Torque	Carburetion	Comp. Ratio Fuel	Rear Axle Ratio
200-hp 307 V8 Hydraulic lifters	Manual 3-spd.; 2-speed Powerglide; TurboHydra-matic	300 @ 2400	two-barrel	8.5/R	2.73 3.08 3.31
245-hp 350 V8 Hydraulic lifters	Manual 3-spd.; Manual 4-spd.; TurboHydra-matic	350 @ 2800	two-barrel	8.5/R	2.56 3.08 3.31 3.36
270-hp 350 V8 Hydraulic lifters	HD Manual 3-spd.; Manual 4-spd.; TurboHydra-matic	360 @ 3200	four-barrel	8.5/R	2.73 3.08 3.31
300-hp 400 V8 Hydraulic lifters	HD Manual 3-spd.; Manual 4-spd.; TurboHydra-matic	400 @ 3200	four-barrel	8.5/R	2.73 3.08 3.31
365-hp 454 V8 Hydraulic lifters	HD Manual 4-spd.; TurboHydra-matic	465 @ 3200	four-barrel	8.5/R	3.31
425-hp 454 V8 Hydraulic lifters	HD Manual 4-spd.; TurboHydra-matic	475 @ 4000	four-barrel	9.0/P	3.31 4.10

case, overnight case, suitbag, and camera case pretty well converts the vehicle into a one-man deal, since none of the aforementioned items can be placed in the bed. The overnight bag was too large to stick in the little storage hole.

Ranchero was attired in Torino GT clothing, which is great for the soul but doesn't do much for the limited space. The console as well as the bucket seats are luxuries I could do without. Unless you are running solo most of the time and use the passenger seat only rarely in the evening, a bench is definitely the only way to go. It seems that when serious (heavy) cargo is hauled in the bed, there are two other people who wish to accompany it, one to help you lift it, and the other to tell you where she wants it. Can't be done with buckets. The Ford buckets are set too low for good visibility anyway.

Our El Camino had a small diameter sports steering wheel which was a decided asset. Tight or awkward maneuvering can be frequently anticipated for cargo pickups and such tasks are more easily accomplished with the small steering wheel. The utilitarian bench seat in the El Camino underscored the vanity and wasted space of buckets.

Both Datsun and Toyota have spartan cabs. Datsun's upholstery is of a higher quality than Toyota, but their floor mat is decidedly low-buck and poorly anchored. The seats have been previously discussed, but not the seat backs. Neither model provides any lumbar support. This old spine had some heavy discomfort down in the lower end after a week of 90 miles a day on the freeways. Controls are easily accessible in both and are inscribed with international symbols. Datsun had a radio, which was of good quality, but Toyota did not. It would have been wise of Toyota to have included a radio as it would have helped to mask the bothersome engine noise.

The Datsun shifter was well placed and easy to manipulate. The only hang-up was the wide gate. On a rapid shift between second and third, it was possible to hang the shifter in the detent, thereby having to do it again. When climbing an incline under a load, rapid shifting is mandatory. Toyota's shift linkage leaves a lot to be desired. Mainly a new linkage. The shifter is placed too far back toward the seat and requires too much effort to get into second gear. The location of fourth is uncertain and easy to miss.

Datsun was without benefit of arm rests. Granted, one should always drive with both hands on the wheel, but while trundling through city traffic, it would be pleasant to have an arm rest. (Economy can be very bare bones.) They are

available as an extra cost option. The inscrutable orientals have picked up another little sales tip from us.

Power is strictly buyer's option. Ranchero had a 351-4V with an air scoop of the shaker variety. It didn't really need it. A normal, everyday 351-4V would have been fine. Power in the unloaded condition was instantaneous and smooth. Response was excellent. With a heavy load, reduction in performance was quite marked. The old air grabber would get a little sluggish in mid-range applications. There was always enough power to keep your place in line, and cruising or high speed operation was undiminished, but you have no doubt when there is a load in the back.

El Camino had a 350-2V, which was surprisingly agile without a load. El Camino's torque curve peaks out 600 rpm lower than Ranchero's. This was most evident in the quickness of the Chev at low speed acceleration. Ford's 351-2V has a torque peak at an even lower rpm than the Chev and would really be a better engine for the Ranchero if hauling and economy are of prime consideration. Chev suffered under a load, but it was a general reduction with no specific areas of noticeable loss. Very adequate for the task though.

Datsun and Toyota have limited power. Their work is accomplished through the four-speed gearboxes and the 4.11 rear ends. The Toyota's 1900cc engine is more suited to the task than the 1600cc Datsun. Both are too noisy, and both tend to struggle on a grade when loaded. Level ground power is fine, but hills are sticky. Both engines show the results of desmogging, or detoxing if you will. They are cold-blooded little hummers, requiring liberal applications of the manual choke. The Datsun is set so lean that a touch of choke is needed to really get it on at freeway speeds. The manual choke is a functional part of engine operation at all speeds. When lugging up a grade at a speed too high for a down shift and too low for the next gear, a little choke helps to ease the strain. Toyota has a long step between first and second, while Datsun's long stretch is between third and fourth.

Heater controls are the essence of simplicity in the Toyota. There are two control knobs on the dash. One controls the air direction — heat or defrost — with a pull function for blower control; the other selects the air mix, ranging from fresh, through recirculation. Datsun has three levers and a preset heat switch on the heater itself for environmental control. Instructions are contained in the owner's manual.

Fuel economy can only be compared laterally, not vertically. Datsun and

Toyota were in a virtual dead heat, with the edge going to Datsun's 23.7 mpg to 23.5 mpg for Hilux. The big boys weren't even in the same class. The best that Ranchero's 4V could manage was 14.23 mpg, while the more economical 2V in the El Camino leaned out at 17.23 mpg. Neither was even in the ball park with the mini-engined imports. Sharp-eyed readers will cry "foul" comparing a 2V with a 4V, but as previously stated in other articles, we test what we can get. In this case, the relative merits of each configuration are worth investigating. Power performance unladen went to the 4V, but surprisingly, with a load, the 2V Camino more than held its own.

Square area load capacity is similar in all four vehicles. The basic difference is in the wheel well area. All four load through a full width tailgate which lays down flat. Datsun saves a buck by using a single layered gate with the support ribs showing. Toyota uses a double sheet gate as do the Detroiters. The double sheet is mighty handy when struggling with a hernia-sized piece of cargo. The imports have tie-down dogs all around the periphery of the bed sides, invaluable when securing a load of multiple boxes and assorted paraphernalia. There are auxiliary tie-down hooks available for the domestics, but they are not as effective as the built-in ones.

El Camino has an integrated roll back tarpaulin, but you'll have to find your own for the Ranchero. A tarp is really a necessity if it ever rains in your home town. Not only does it keep the load dry, but it will add to the longevity of the sheet metal in the bed.

Your choice of vehicles depends primarily on your income and intended utilization. If you plan to use the machine primarily as a commuter vehicle and you spend more than 45 minutes one way, the Detroit models are the way to go in spite of the price. If most of your driving is going to be short range, the little ones will get the job done at a much lower cost. The imports are fun to drive, and their rough ride can be softened, either by removing a couple of leaves from the rear springs if your loads are going to be light, or deadloading them. Their biggest attraction is price.

Of the Detroit models, there is little choice. The Ranchero handles better, but with similar power plants there is little else to choose from except styling. With the imports, we'll have to give the edge to Toyota. Except for the gearbox, it has just a bit more power and a little more sophistication. They may have copied Datsun, but they have improved the product.   /MT

RANCHERO-HACIENDA V8 AUTOMATIC

We put the combination through a cornering test at 45 km/h, with very satisfactory stability.

Ford

TEST HIGHLIGHTS

- Clever combination of car and camper
- Easy mobility, full caravan amenities
- Adequate handling and braking safety
- Poor attachment, heavy fuel consumption
- Verdict: Rough edges, but a winner!

FORD — well provided with a range of towing vehicles — is going into the leisure business in a big way in South Africa this summer. Capri, 20M and Ranchero are all being promoted as towing vehicles and — as something really special — the "Hacienda" Ford camper conversion is being offered for the Ranchero utility car.

The Ranchero, with powerful 6 and V8 engines, heavy-duty disc front brakes, and rugged suspension providing load-capability and stabi-lity, makes a great tow-horse. In fact, last year it was voted "South African Towing Car of the Year" by our contemporary, *Caravan* magazine.

These same virtues lend it to pick-up camper conversion, and Ford has shown considerable enterprise in offering the four-berth Ranchero Hacienda as a package for family holidays in the Republic.

Ranchero and its camper make a highly-practical and roadworthy travelling/living unit. There are some disabilities and points for criticism, but a thorough test has shown that the combination meets normal safety requirements under road conditions: it handles cleanly, is stable and has sound stopping ability. With the 5-litre V8 engine and Cruise-O-Matic transmission it is also easy-driving and well-powered.

We found that under good open road conditions the unit can be cruised safely at between 100 and 120 km/h, but as stopping distances are increased by about 30 per cent and the high-up weight limits swerv-ing ability, it would be best to regard 80 to 100 km/h as a fair cruising speed when traffic is around, and/or when there might be con-cealed hazards — that is, under average holiday-traffic conditions.

THE RANCHERO

The Ford Ranchero is a sleek three-seater utility car, available with six-cylinder or V8 engines, and either four-speed manual or three-speed automatic transmission. It is well-geared and a powerful per-former, with a high standard of safety and stability.

Test unit was the V8 Automatic, so that performance figures are comparable with the Road Test of this model published in June, 1970. (A Road Test of the 6-cylinder model was in CAR of September, 1969).

The cab offers a reasonable stan-dard of comfort, with bench seat which takes three adults, and a column selector for the transmission. There is a good capacity for acces-sories and special equipment to in-crease comfort and convenience.

The Ranchero is rated for a load of 790 kg (1 735 lb) and takes the 426-kg Hacienda comfortably, with only mild rear suspension drop, and plenty of resilience left in the heavy overload springs.

THE HACIENDA

The Hacienda — built under con-tract by Caravans International — is tailored to the Ranchero, with tail-gate dropped, and overall length of the vehicle is raised by about 60 cm. It is 2 metres wide (increasing overall width by about 45 cm) and when it is mounted, the overall height of the vehicle rises to a lofty 2,6 metres (about 8 ft.). The combined unit will not fit into a normal garage, because of height.

The raked forepart of the Hacienda protrudes over the cab to form a raised double bunk, so that in

KEY FIGURES

Accel. 0–100 km/h .		15,1 seconds
Maximum speed .	.	127,9 km/h
Cruising fuel range	.	263 km
National prices:		
Ranchero V8 A/T		R2 421
Hacienda . .	.	R1 585
Together . .	.	R4 006

addition to the big increase in gross frontal area (from 2,48 to 4,40 m²) an air-trap is formed above the cab, causing severe curtailment of performance and fuel economy.

The Hacienda looks and feels heavy on the road, but the Ranchero copes with it well.

We did not like the side extension mirrors on the test car: these did not clamp firmly enough, and were deflected by wind at speed.

ATTACHMENT

The means of attaching the Hacienda to the pick-up body is our main point of criticism. It is done in rather home-workshop fashion, with four bottle-screws linking to anchor points on the car coachwork. It is firm enough, but on the test car the coachwork was being distorted by the tension.

We understand that this is being modified in production to single bottle-screws on either side, with anchors in the coachwork above each rear wheel spat, but this (although tested and approved by Ford, we are told) is not likely to be much improvement. We would have expected more sophisticated and positive means of attachment, using the robust load space surround and the reinforced floor.

There was also a tremendous volume of body squeaks — rising to well beyond 90 decibels, C (high-frequency) weighting, in the test unit. We were told that two wooden friction strakes will be fitted in production to eliminate this, but we imagine that with two heavy bodies

IMPERIAL DATA

Major performance features of this Road Test are summarised below in Imperial measures for comparative purposes:

ACCELERATION FROM REST

	(seconds):
0–60	14,5
¼ mile	18,6

MAXIMUM SPEED (mph):

True speed	79,5

FUEL ECONOMY (mpg):

60 mph	13,1
75 mph	9,7

temporarily joined, some form of friction noise is bound to occur when travelling.

DETACHMENT

The Hacienda can be parked on a camping or caravan site using three steel jack legs which come with the unit. These are carried rather untidily when travelling on the side of the combination vehicle, and have to be unbolted and re-bolted in position for detachment. The camper can then be raised an inch or two, and the Ranchero driven out to be available for normal use.

Compared with setting up a caravan, this is a cumbersome arrangement, but this is one of the drawbacks to be expected with a compromise camping/touring vehicle.

The Hacienda has been recognised by the Caravan Club of South Africa as a caravan, and can therefore be used in caravan parks.

ADVANTAGES

Besides its mobility, the advantages of the Hacienda and similar pick-up campers over the conventional caravan are manifold: it is part of the vehicle load, therefore needs no separate licence or third-party insurance; regulations allow passengers to be carried inside the camper, where four seats are available; and a boat or standard trailer can be added to the Ranchero Hacienda for holiday touring.

In addition, it is easy to manoeuvre and reverse the unit, and the driver has a degree of see-through vision via the interior rearview mirror.

LIVING UNIT

Standing on its three legs — and with two extra stays at the front for stability — the Hacienda is pure caravan: as would be expected of a cousin of the well-known Sprite, Gypsey and Bluebird caravans. It has limitations on floor space, and a rather high entrance step, and the layout is dictated by its required shape.

Inside the rear entrance, the sides above the wheel arches are devoted to kitchen unit (including two-burner gas stove and gas refrigerator) and storage space, with lockers and a deep wardrobe. All is neatly finished in wood panelling and formica topping.

At centre is a four-seater dinette with folding table, which converts into a double bunk, and the raised frontal portion contains another double bunk with ether-foam mattress. With five windows and a big

CRUISING AT 120

Mech. noise level . .	.	82,5 dBA
0–120 through gears	.	31,8 seconds
km/l at 120	. . . .	3,5
litres/100 km at 120	. . .	28,0
Braking from 120	. .	5,3 seconds
Max. gradient (top)	. . .	1 in 26,3
Speedo error	. . . .	4,2% over
Speedo at true 120	. . . .	125
Rpm (top)	. . . . .	2 810

roof ventilator, the living unit is airy and comfortable, and comparable with a conventional four-berth caravan.

There is 1,8 metres (more than 7 ft.) of headroom inside, and width is close to that of a standard caravan, so the interior does not feel cramped.

A rear awning is available as an option to provide a covered outside living space.

PERFORMANCE

The Mustang-powered Ranchero V8 Automatic retains quite respectable performance with the Hacienda on board, being affected more by frontal area than by mass. This means that performance is impaired progressively as speed rises and drag builds up. A comparison with the standard car:

	Ranchero V8 Solo	Ranchero Hacienda
0–100 km/h	11,5	**15,1**
0–120 ..	17,2	**31,8**
400 m ..	16,3	**18,6**
Speed ..	164,0	**127,9**

For comparison in Imperial measures, the 0–60 mph time drops from 10,4 to 14,5 seconds, while speed potential comes down from 102,0 to 79,5 mph. This is not serious, as no-one would want to drive the Ranchero Hacienda at 100 mph, anyway, even if it was permitted — but the fuel economy penalty is severe.

FUEL ECONOMY

With the camper riding pick-a-back, the Ranchero becomes heavy on fuel (the more expensive 98-octane kind, too!) as comparative figures (in miles per gallon) show:

		Ranchero V8 Solo	Ranchero Hacienda
30 mph	..	31,8	**21,8**
45 mph	..	29,3	**18,9**
60 mph	..	24,7	**13,1**
75 mph	..	18,0	**9,7**

The importance of moderating cruising speed is well illustrated here: at 120 km/h fuel consumption increases by 45 per cent, while at 100 km/h the rise is only about 36 per cent. Either way, cruising range is rather short, requiring frequent refills of the 75-litre tank.

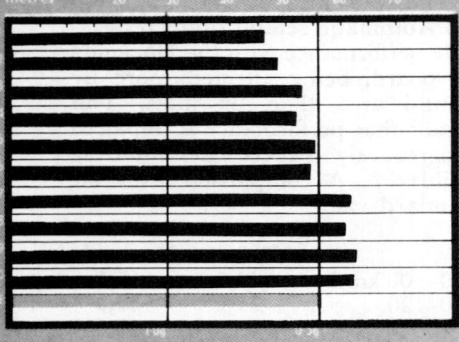

BRAKING DISTANCES

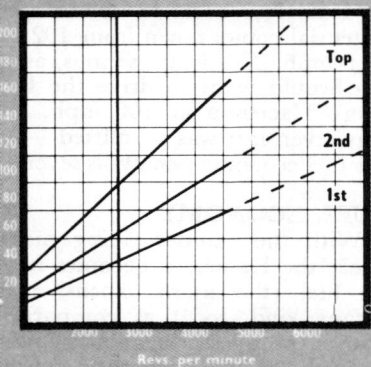

(10 stops from 100 km h)

ENGINE SPEED

Revs. per minute

GRADIENT ABILITY

MAX. TORQUE 2600 RPM

1st
2nd
Top

(Degrees inclination)

MAKE AND MODEL:
Make . . . . Ford
Model Ranchero V8 Automatic Hacienda

PERFORMANCE FACTORS (combination):
Power/mass (W/kg) 75,2
Frontal area (m³) 4,40
km/h/1 000 rpm (top) 42,7
(Calculated on licensing mass, gross
frontal area, gearing and net power output.)

INTERIOR NOISE LEVELS:

	Mech.	Wind	Road
Idling . .	49,5	—	—
60 km/h .	67,0	—	—
80 km/h .	72,5	—	—
100 km/h .	78,0	—	—
120 km/h .	82,5	88,0	88,0
Full throttle			See graph
Average dBA at 120			86,2

(Measured in decibels, "A" weighting,
averaging runs both ways on a level road;
"Mechanical" with car closed; "Wind" with
one window fully open; "Road" on a coarse
gravel surface.)

ACCELERATION FROM REST:
0–60 5,7
0–80 9,0
0–100 15,1
0–120 31,8
400 m sprint 18,6

OVERTAKING ACCELERATION
(A/T):
40–60 2,8
60–80 3,3
80–100 6,1
100–120 16,8
(Measured in seconds, to true speeds,
averaging runs both ways on a level road,
car carrying test crew of two and standard
test equipment.)

MAXIMUM SPEED:
True speed . . . . . 127,9 km/h
Speedo reading 133
Calibration:
Indicated . . 60 . 80 . 100 . 120
True speed . . 52 . 74 . 95 . 115

FUEL ECONOMY (km/l):
60 km/h 7,4
80 km/h 6,1
100 km/h 4,5
120 km/h 3,5
Full throttle . . . . . . See graph

FUEL CONSUMPTION (litres/100 km):
60 km/h 13,5
80 km/h 16,4
100 km/h 22,3
120 km/h 28,0
(Measured in kilometres per litre, averaging runs both ways on a level road.)

BRAKING TEST:
From 100 km/h:
First stop 3,7
Tenth stop 5,1
Average 4,48
(Measured in sec., with stops from true
speeds at 30-sec. intervals on a good bitumenised surface.)

GRADIENTS IN GEARS:
Low gear . . . . 1 in 3,0
2nd gear . . . . 1 in 4,2
Top gear . . . . 1 in 8,1
(Tabulated from Tapley g readings, car
carrying test crew of two and standard test
equipment.)

GEARED SPEEDS:
Low gear 80,0
2nd gear 135,0
Top gear 196,6
(Calculated to true speeds, at engine peak
rpm — 4 600.)

MECHANICAL NOISE

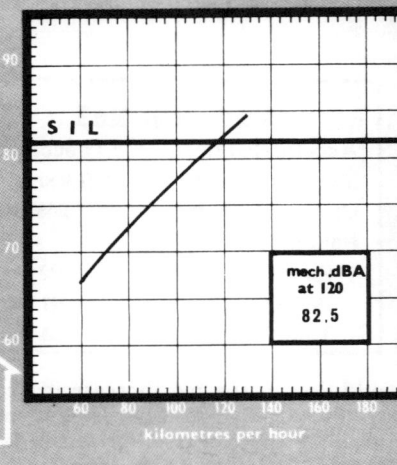

SIL

mech .dBA
at 120
82,5

kilometres per hour

NOISE VALUES

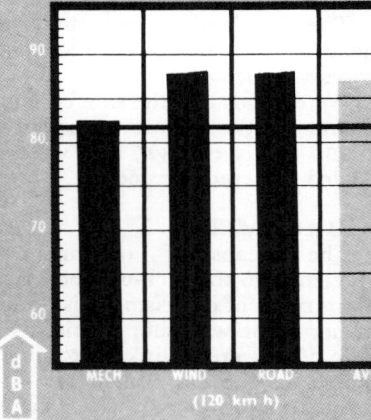

MECH   WIND   ROAD   AVE
(120 km h)

FUEL ECONOMY

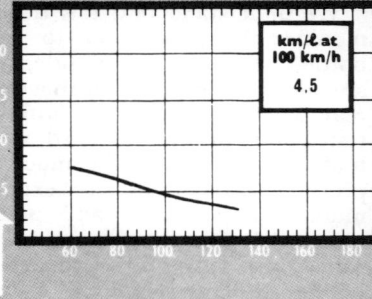

km/ℓ at
100 km/h
4,5

FUEL CONSUMPTION
(litres 100 km)

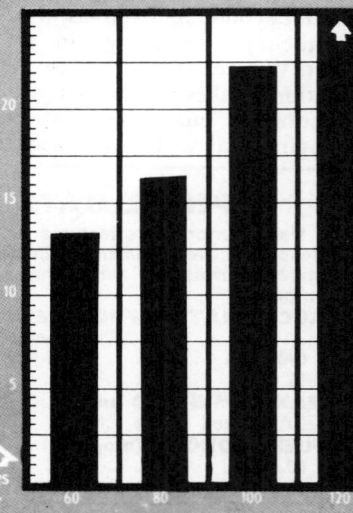

litres
per
100 km   kilometres per hour

ENGINE:

Cylinders	V8
Carburettor	Twin-choke Autolite (Ford)
Bore	101,6 mm
Stroke	76,2 mm
Cubic capacity	4 950 cm³
Compression ratio	9,3 to 1
Valve gears	Ohv, pushrods
Main bearings	Five
Aircleaner	Paper element
Fuel rating	98-octane Coast, 93-octane Reef
Cooling	Water
Electrics	12-volt AC

ENGINE OUTPUT:

Max. output SAE (kW)	156,8 (210 bhp)
Max. bhp net	133,4
Peak rpm	4 600
Max. torque (N.m) at rpm	406/2 600

TRANSMISSION:

Forward speeds	Three, Cruise-O-Matic
Selector	Column
Low gear	2,46 to 1
2nd gear	1,46 to 1
Top gear	Direct
Reverse gear	2,20 to 1
Final drive	2,93 to 1
Drive wheels	Rear
Tyre size	7,75L x 14

BRAKES:

Front	285 mm discs
Rear	254 mm drums
Boosting	Vacuum servo
Handbrake position	Under dash

STEERING:

Type	Recirculating ball
Lock to lock	5,25 turns
Turning circle	11,1 metres

MEASUREMENTS:

Length overall	m (Hacienda; 3,53 m)
Width overall	2,0m (Hacienda: 2,0 m)
Height overall	2,60m (Hacienda: 2,0 m)
Licensing mass (Ranchero)	1 350 kg
Road mass (Combination)	1 776 kg

SUSPENSION:

Front	Independent
Type	Coil springs, extra-heavy-duty
Rear	Live axle
Type	2 stage, 7-bladed, leaf springs

CAPACITIES:

Seating	Three/seven
Fuel tank	75 litres
Sleeping berths	Two double

EQUIPMENT:

Two-burner stove and grille, 3,6 ft.³ refrigerator, washup, wardrobe, roof lockers, wall cabinet, dinette table, 4 floor lockers, large roof vent, five windows, gas bottle, two fluorescent 12-volt lights, access step, three jack legs.

TYRE PRESSURES (with Hacienda):

Crossply:	Front	2,5 bars (36 lb.)
	Rear	2,8 bars (40 lb.)

PROVIDED TEST CAR:

Ford Motor Company of South Africa, Port Elizabeth.

TEST CONDITIONS:

Altitude	At sea level
Weather	Fine and cool
Fuel used	98-octane
Test car's odometer	2 240 km

STOPPING ABILITY

In America, there has been severe criticism recently of pick-up campers combined with conventional ¾-ton pick-ups, on grounds that both stability and braking capacity was inadequate.

The Australian-derived Ranchero, on the other hand, passes all reasonable tests with the comparatively light Hacienda on board. We did the full series of 10 crash stops from 100 km/h, and while the brakes developed some fade they held up reasonably well. One penalty is that the composite vehicle pitches heavily in hard stops, enabling rear wheels to snatch occasionally. This is a feature to watch, as a broadside in a Hacienda could be quite something!

We would suggest that an owner practise some emergency stops on a clear roadway before embarking on holiday.

HANDLING AND RIDE

After some preliminary tests, we became so confident of the stability of the Ranchero Hacienda that we did quite severe cornering tests, with satisfactory results. The Ranchero suspension resists sway and roll firmly, but nevertheless, owners should avoid sharp swerving with this high-up load, as the vehicle could come unstuck with little warning.

Directional stability was surprisingly good: with 2,8 bars (40 lb.) in the rear tyres there is not much sway tendency, and even in a light crosswind the combination ran arrow-straight at speed. Strong side-winds might affect it, but we would not expect it to be serious, particularly at speeds up to 100 km/h.

The ride is rather heavy and gentle, but the unit went through rough stuff very comfortably.

SUMMARY

The Hacienda — a Spanish-American word in the "Ranchero" tradition, and meaning "homestead' — is quite neatly-styled and serviceable. Attachments and other details could be improved, but in general, Ford has come up with a winner.

It provides a new form of not-too-expensive access to outdoor life for the modern family: a sort of super-safari-wagon, with full mobility and versatility. For anyone who can use a Ranchero for daily purposes as well, it is a most attractive proposition, and for the nomadic, it could be an answer to their prayers! ∎

Side-mounted jack legs are untidy, and anchorage points distort the car's coachwork.

At either side inside the door are cupboards, wardrobe, stove and refrigerator.

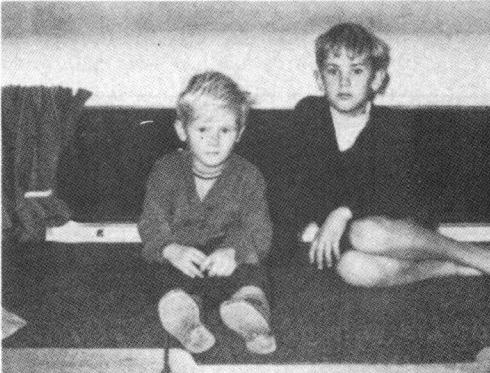

Interior view shows the high double bunk at front, above the car's cab.

The Hacienda can be jacked on its three legs, freeing the Ranchero for car use.

By Ed O'Brien

In 1957 Ford started a completely new concept in light-duty trucks — the Ranchero. The Ranchero is still very much a part of the American automotive scene along with a GM counterpart, but very few of the originals remain in use. One of these belongs to Anaheim, Calif. resident Jim Light.

It only takes a quick glance to determine that Jim's a real Ford fan and a proud Ranchero owner. The truck looks like it belongs either in a new car show or on a dealer's showroom floor. If you're a curious person, a little more research into this car will show that it's probably more like what the engineers envisioned than what the public could actually buy in '57.

Pride kept Jim from reconstructing the styling on his vehicle and from making it into a flashy race-only thing. The body was brought up to mint condition, and removable panels like the small section above the grille and some parts of the bed were removed and chromed. In fact, all the stock chrome components were refinished. In keeping with the custom stock appearance rather than modified, Jim had Clyde Morgan paint the car in a beautiful silver grey. Then Ted's Upholstery finished the interior in black naugahyde and carpeting.

Under the hood is enough power to help Jim run 120 mph quarter-mile speeds in .11.70 seconds, considerably under the national record for D/HR. This car fits closest to the E/HR class by weight and engine size but is not recognized because that particular engine/chassis combination didn't come from Detroit. The car weighs 3850 lbs. and Jim estimates 550 hp output from his engine. Because of the class discrepancy (not to mention his wife's pleading), Jim says that most of this truck's futur will be spent on the street rather than on the strip.

The engine is a '67 model of the 427-cubic-inch variety with just a few modifications and a lot of time both on assembly and tuning. Non-stock components include a Sig Erson 234-degree duration, .525-inch lift cam with Erson single springs. A 780 cfm Holley carburetor is used atop one of Ford's medium riser manifolds. The heads were set up by Ed Flechall. Otherwise the engine remains stock. It runs with 12.5-to-1 compression ratio, and the ignition is set up with a healthy 38 degrees lead.

Even a true Ford fan has to give in once in a while to a better part, and Jim Light was no exception. He may have been able to use a stock Ford flywheel (the clutch is a Weber), driveshaft and Ford Detroit Locker rear end, but not the transmission. There was nothing from Ford that fit his needs, so a Chevrolet Muncie four-speed with a 2.56 low ratio was installed. A Trans-Dapt adaptor mated the trans with the Ford engine. The rear end houses 4.56 gears, and for added strength, Henry's axles make the link to the rear wheels. All four wheels on the car are Cragar S/S, with 8.00 x 15 Goodyear front tires and nine-inch-wide 8.00 x 15 Firestone slicks in the rear.

It takes plenty of patience and ability to reconstruct a car to better-than-new condition as this one is. It also takes outside help, and for that Jim depended on the likes of Hollins Machine Shop and veteran racer/builder Louie Unser. When you talk about a time investment of four years, you have to put the car into the full-time hobby category because at an hourly rate the cost would be staggering. As it is Jim estimates his investment at $5500, a pretty good price to pay for a 1957 model truck. Though that may be a high price to pay for revamping a car, look at it from another angle: what's it worth to have something you can show and about which you can say, "It's my creation and I'm proud of it."?

Dragmaster traction bars, Cure/Ride shocks, nine-inch Firestone tires and about 550 hp put the truck through some wild motions off the starting line.

LIGHT'S

Removable body parts like the inner wall of the tail gate and all brackets and panels were chromed.

Photo by Richard Pucillo

The interior, as clean and attractive as the exterior, is finished in black naugahyde and carpeting. Additions include a Grant steering wheel, Hurst shifter and a Sun tach.

HAULER

OLD FORDS NEVER DIE —
THEY JUST "GIT IT ON"!

Powerplant is a near-stock '67 model with 427 cubic inches. For under-the-hood tuning, a fuel pressure gauge was installed.

Jim over-restored his '57 Ranchero, retaining its stock appearance. It's finished in a beautiful silver grey.

TORINO RANCHERO 1973

Following with the Torino, having been changed in '72, the Ranchero styling changes were only in the front end. New seats were fitted to the vehicle and mechanical changes made. Once again, three models are offered; Ranchero 500, Ranchero GT and Ranchero Squire.

RANCHERO 1972

The Ranchero has a completely new contemporary exterior design, yet it retains the long sporty look that has made Ranchero popular. It is four inches longer in wheelbase with a widened front and rear tread. Top of the line model will be the Squire with semi-transparent wood-tone paneling allowing a tint of the body color to show through. Two other models, the Ranchero 500 and GT complete the lineup. Many options are scheduled.

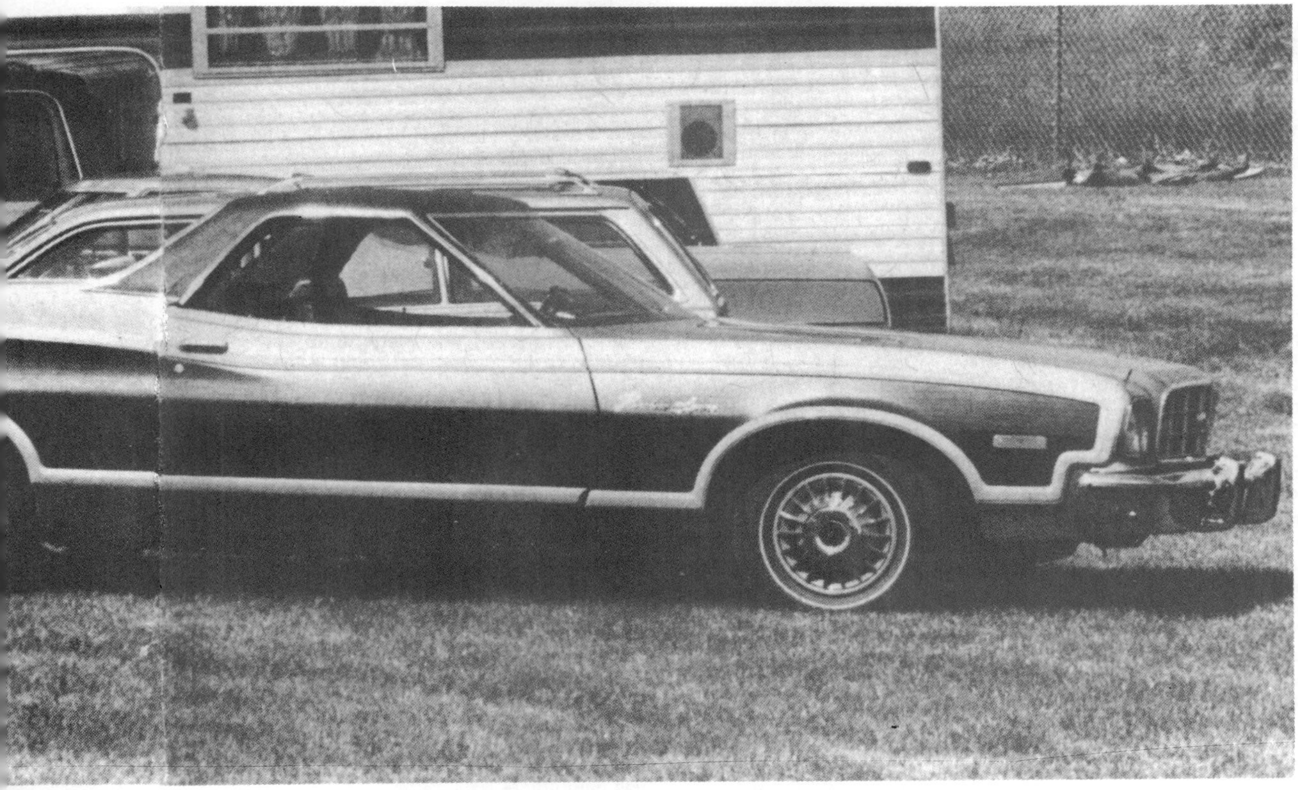

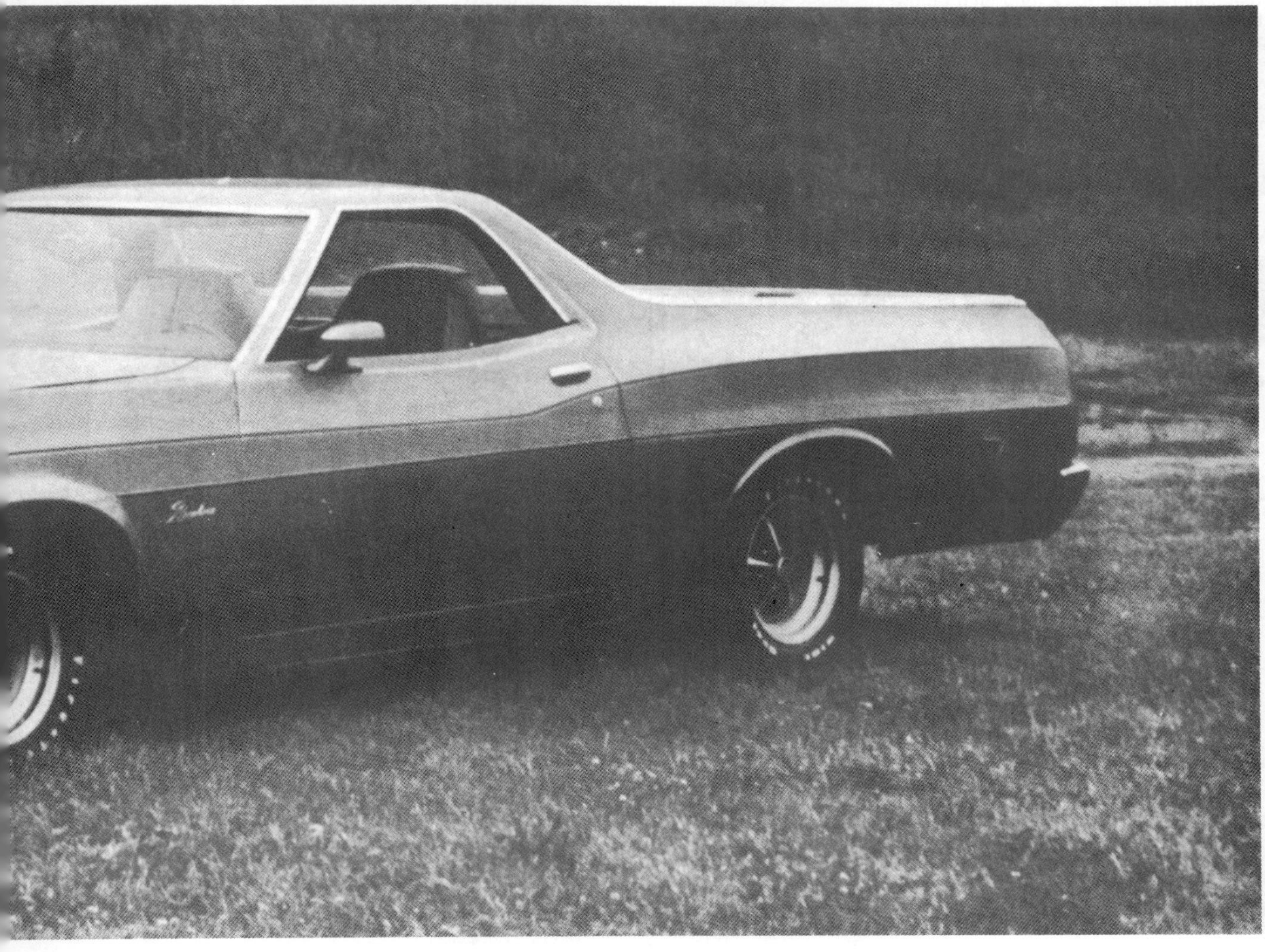

The El Camino/Ranchero Hassle

Chevy played the waiting game—and lost!

by Spence Murray

Chevrolet, traditionally the industry's innovator, was forced by Ford to bide its time until GM's divisional market researchers, engineers, and stylists could find out what their arch rival over at Dearborn was up to when they popped with their revolutionary Ranchero for 1957. Could a pickup truck disguised as a passenger car (or was it vice versa?) find favor throughout America's outback—or wherever? Usually swift Chevrolet, known for its one-upmanship, spent 2 years trying to find the answers and arranging for production, and not until the 1959 model year did anything resembling Ford's by-then popular workhorse/car come to light via Chevy's assembly lines. But though it was heralded as the styling ultimate for a commercial, workaday hauler, the expected hordes of buyers weren't out there, and the original El Camino was quietly phased out of production after only a short 2 years.

Why? That was a question that Chevrolet suffered over for a long time before their second generation El Camino was gingerly announced, no doubt with mild embarassment, for the 1964 model year where the marque surfaced on the medium-size Chevelle chassis where it remains today.

A need had been instantly created for a utilitarian, around-town light-duty truck with a sporty automotive flair when the Ranchero first appeared. Establishments that delighted in putting up a strong visual front grabbed Rancheros for one-upping their commercial rivals. Service stations wanted a fleet, handsome errand-runner, and repair shops and other trades felt a yen for a practical service vehicle that wouldn't be an eyesore among a background of high-priced passenger cars. Ford had found an untapped market that was admittedly limited, but nonetheless certain. Trips around town and to the high rent district could be made without the embarassment associated with the more truck-like trucks, and gentlemen farmers could haul fodder for their thoroughbreds by day yet visit their nightly watering spots without looks of disdain from their neighbors and cohorts.

Unfortunately for Chevrolet, whatever pipeline they had into Dearborn's inner sanctums didn't drain any news back their way, and while the giant was funneling untold dollars into readying their own version of the car-like truck to be called El Camino, Ford was simultaneously preparing to phase the Ranchero out—or, at least, downgrade it to small car (Falcon) status where by then Ford's statistics showed that the real selling market waited.

Ford, with considerable foresight, had given birth to the Ranchero almost effortlessly, since their design for a car/truck was based on their then-current full size 2-door station wagon and shared by far the greater majority of sheetmetal components. New tooling was limited to an abbreviated turret top, rear window area, inner bed paneling and a few inexpensive odds and ends.

1. This is not a staged photo! When Motor Trend Magazine tested the El Camino for 1959, crew ran out of gas. More was summoned and, lo and behold, attendant arrived in a '57 Ranchero. In a way, this seems to have downgraded the Chevy right from the start.

2. Nearly everything from the cowl aft on the '59 El Camino required special tooling, except the lower door panels. This made unit cost high in relation to the Ranchero which borrowed much from 2-door station wagons, which Chevy didn't have for the 1959 model year.

3. El Camino windshield was borrowed from the station wagon, the tallest of three windshields used for '59. Upper door frames were unique to the car/truck, as was rear glass, top, etc.

4. The El Camino stood on a 119-in. wheelbase, 3 ins. more than Ranchero. Pickups beds, however, were almost identical in size. Chevy sported a styling trend that was almost outlandish in relation to more conservative Ford. For the first time since 1937, Ford took sales lead over rival.

1

2

3

4

5

6

7

8

of the cowl on the El Camino was special, with the exception of the tailgate (from a 4-door wagon). It was almost a totally unique, orphan vehicle with a potentially frightful tooling amortization cost per unit. Chevy hoped to produce them by the tens of thousands, but the really bad news was yet to come.

What it all amounted to was that while Ford brought out the Ranchero at a reasonable production cost, then skimmed the cream off the narrow but virgin market for this specialty vehicle, Chevy was left with the short end of the stick and found few takers for their more expensively-produced El Camino. It isn't recorded how many potential El Camino buyers were dismayed to learn that many states required they purchase commercial license tags (usually far more expensive than car tags) whether they hauled commercial goods or not, nor if any were ready to deal financially with the GMC Truck and Coach Division, although the vehicle was marketed through Chevy passenger car dealerships. But, these might have had at least a small effect on the numbers eventually sold.

Piling injury on top of insult, the whole Chevy line took a sales dive in '59, no doubt thanks in part to whoever OK'd that year's unfortunate big-finned styling, and after years of playing just a supporting role, Ford gained the sales edge with their more conservative styling for the first time since 1937.

In the final analysis, Chevy garnered only 32,000 buyers for the '59 version of the El Camino and exactly half that for '60. Such numbers were too small for the industrial behemoth to fool with (only the virtually hand-built, fiberglass Corvettes could be turned out in these limited quantities and survive), and when it came time to re-tool for the '61 model year, the El Camino was unceremoniously scrubbed.

Chevy, to its utter consternation, had been too late after investing too much. ☠

5. The '60 El Camino sported almost complete sheetmetal change, but all inner structures were the same. For this year, only 16,000 El Caminos were sold, too few for Chevy to keep producing the model. But even today both the '59's and '60's are popular, as this one with fat tires and wheels.

6. First of the Rancheros, the '57, was pieced together from 2-door station wagon parts with little special tooling required to get it into production. Initial year's sales amounted to 21,695 copies.

7. The trend to fins, garish styling had started in '58 and the Ranchero didn't escape use of the car's panels. This is the rarest one today, as only 9950 units were produced.

8. Last of the early "big" Rancheros was in '59, the year Chevy introduced the El Camino. Ford unloaded 14,169 of this model, the 3-year total of 45,814 Rancheros taking away much of Chevy's sales potential. In the final analysis, though, El Camino production was 48,000 in 2 years, but this still wasn't enough for GM to fool with, and when the restyled '61's appeared, the "El" was gone.

But when Chevy admitted to itself that Ford had a good thing going, and began to tool up for the El Camino, their lineup for '59 offered no 2-door wagon from which panels could be borrowed. The stylists had done the production people dirt, too, since little could be borrowed from the cars or wagons even though

many of the bits and pieces appear alike. In addition, then, to the relatively few parts that Ford had to produce specifically for their truck, Chevy also had to tailor special quarter panels, upper door frames, bed flooring and inner paneling, that huge wraparound rear window, and so forth. Nearly everything aft

FORD RANCHERO 6 UTILITY CAR (XA)

TEST HIGHLIGHTS

- Longer, lower and wider than earlier models
- Increased wheelbase and track for stability
- Firm load-carrier, comfortable conveyance
- Strong coachwork, but pillarless windows
- Verdict: Modern, capable and versatile . . .

Ford's popular Ranchero utility car has undergone a radical change in appearance in becoming the XA model for 1973. Its former smart and chunky lines have given way to a more aerodynamic form, about four inches longer than before, two inches wider and an inch lower.

In addition, the load-body sides have been raised and both windscreen and rear window rake greatly increased. Cab space and load area are increased, and the drop tailgate has been revised to open through 180 degrees as well as the usual 90 degrees.

Functionally, the new design has many improvements, but aesthetically, we preferred the earlier models. In profile, the new model seems to be all bonnet and load area, with a tiny little cab somewhere near the middle. Cab occupants are exposed to a lot of sun, and rearward vision is reduced by the higher load walls and lower seat.

WIDER WHEEL TRACK

Much of this impression is illusory, though: inside, the cab is as spacious as ever; forward vision is perfectly sound, and the exterior mirror on the driver door augments interior rear view.

There are solid advantages in the new design: wheelbase is increased substantially, and both front and rear track are extended considerably to improve handling and balance. Important features are that the load area is increased, and the loading sill lowered to 58 cm (23 inches).

Payload capacity remains at two-thirds of a metric ton (698 kg), and the flowing new styling would probab-

ly lend itself to a well-designed canopy, better than did earlier models.

BIG-SIX ENGINE

Since our original test of the Falcon-based Australian Ranchero 6 in September, 1969, engine capacity has been increased from 3,6 to 4,1 by using a longer stroke. This gives a big boost to the torque output, at the expense of some engine range. To counter this, a very good 3,23 to 1 final drive ratio is used to give the Ranchero sound all-round ability.

It is also available, of course, with 5-litre V8 engine with manual or automatic transmissions, but there is nothing wrong with the 4,1-litre "six" — it gives real workhorse capability (notably in developing torque at very low speed) and is both smooth and reasonably quiet-running.

SPARSE EQUIPMENT

The fascia is similar to that of the new Fairlane, with "droop" instrument panel, and equipment is sparse. A functional plastic moulded mat covers the floor, and the bench seat is only semi-resilient, so that occupants are not bounced too much.

There is good Aeroflow ventilation, but no heater/demister and nothing in the way of luxury. The seat has high-backed head restraints, and the spare wheel is in a locked drop-tray under the tailgate.

The unitary coachwork is solid and firm, with rope hooks all round the load body, and ground clearance is good. The suspension is robust without being too harsh, and the leaf springs at rear are two-stage, with two "donkey blades" coming into play when any serious load is carried.

PILLARLESS WINDOWS

Our single complaint about design practicality is that the door windows are pillarless, in coupé style. They are well bedded in rubber beads, but are likely to start wobbling and developing rattles later in the vehicle's life.

The windows seal against rubber cushions, and seemed to provide a

KEY FIGURES

Accel. 0−100 km/h	.14,0 seconds
Maximum speed	. 154,6 km/h
Optimum cruising speed	. 149 km/h
Cruising fuel range (120)	. 495 km
Engine revs per km	. . 1 565
National list price	. . R2 595

IMPERIAL DATA

Major performance features of this Road Test are summarised below in Imperial measures, for comparative purposes:

ACCELERATION FROM REST:

	(seconds)
0−60	. 13,4
¼ mile	.18,7

MAXIMUM SPEED (mph):

True speed . . .	.96,1

FUEL ECONOMY (mpg):

60 mph	.23,4
75 mph	.18,8

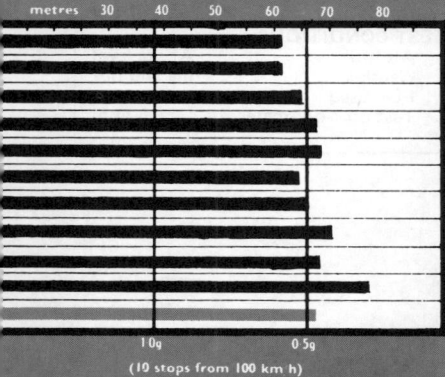

400m

Top

2nd

1st

MAXIMUM SPEED	**154,6**

k m / h

Time in seconds

BRAKING DISTANCES

metres   30   40   50   60   70   80

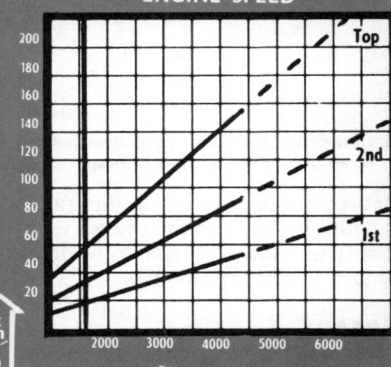

1 0g   0 5g

(10 stops from 100 km/h)

ENGINE SPEED

Top

2nd

1st

k m / h

Revs. per minute

GRADIENT ABILITY

MAX. TORQUE 1600 RPM

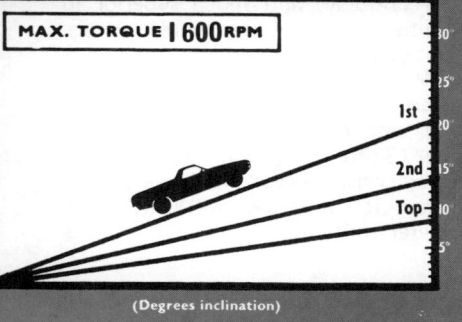

1st

2nd

Top

(Degrees inclination)

MAKE AND MODEL:
Make . . . . Ford
Model . XA Ranchero 6 (4,1 litre)

INTERIOR NOISE LEVELS:

	Mech.	Wind	Road
Idling	49,0	—	—
60	68,5	—	—
80	74,5	—	—
100	79,5	—	—
120	84,0	87,5	89,0

Full throttle . . . . See graph
Average dBA at 120 86,8
(Measured in decibels, "A" weighting, averaging runs both ways on a level road; "Mechanical" with car closed; "Wind" with one window fully open; "Road" on a coarse road surface.)

ACCELERATION FROM REST:
0—60 5,8
0—80 8,9
0—100. 14,0
0—120. 21,8
400 m sprint 18,7

OVERTAKING ACCELERATION:

	3rd	Top
40—60	2,4	3,9
60—80	3,3	4,9
80—100	—	5,4
100—120	—	7,6

(Measured in seconds, to true speeds, averaging runs both ways on a level road, car carrying test crew of two and standard test equipment).

MAXIMUM SPEED:
True speed 154,6
Speedo reading 155
Calibration:

Indicated:	60	80	100	120
True speed:	63	82	101	120

FUEL ECONOMY (km/l):
60 11,2
85 9,7
100 8,1
120 6,8
Full throttle . . . . See graph
(Measured in kilometres per litre, averaging runs both ways on a level road.)

FUEL CONSUMPTION (litres/100 km):
60 8,9
80 10,3
100 12,3
120 14,7
(Staged in litres per 100 kilometres, based on fuel economy figures recorded at true speeds.)

BRAKING TEST:
From 100 km/h:
First stop 4,1
Tenth stop 5,5
Average 4,59
(Measured in sec. with stops from true speeds at 3-second intervals on a good bitumenised surface.)

GRADIENTS IN GEARS:
Low gear . . . . . .1 in 2,7
2nd gear . . . . . .1 in 4,1
Top gear . . . . . .1 in 6,8
(Tabulated from Tapley (x gravity) readings, car carrying test crew of two and standard test equipment.)

GEARED SPEEDS (km/h):
Low gear 53,2
2nd gear 92,8
Top gear 156,5
(Calculated at engine peak rpm — 4 400.)

MECHANICAL NOISE

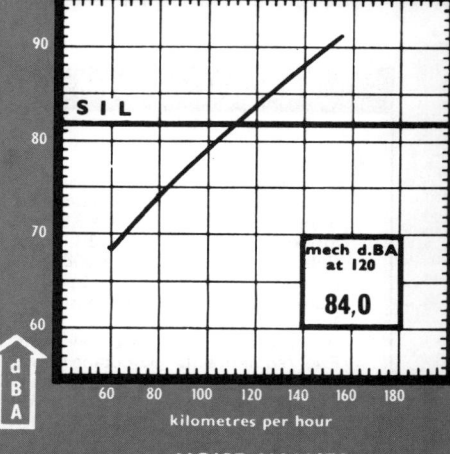

S I L

mech d.BA at 120
84,0

dBA

kilometres per hour

NOISE VALUES

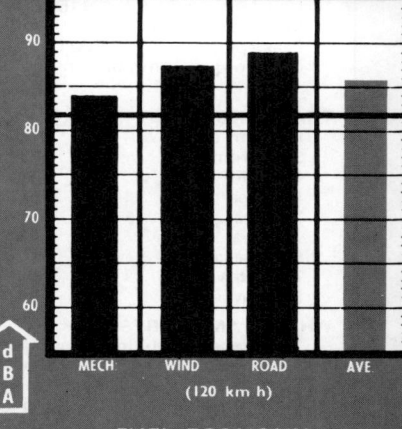

dBA

MECH.   WIND   ROAD   AVE.

(120 km h)

FUEL ECONOMY

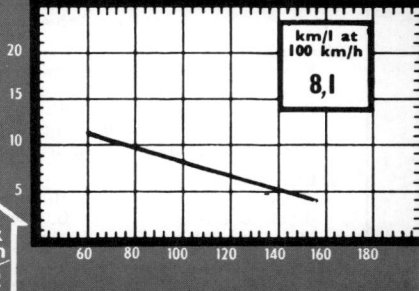

km/l at 100 km/h
8,1

k m / l

FUEL CONSUMPTION
(litres 100 km)

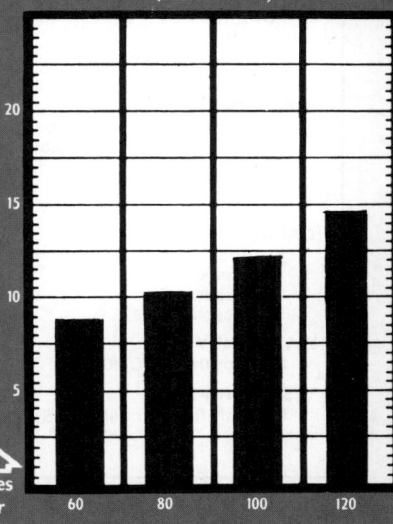

litres per 100 km

kilometres per hour

SPECIFICATIONS

ENGINE:

Cylinders	6 in line
Carburettor	single-choke
Bore	93,5 mm
Stroke	99,3 mm
Cubic capacity	4 098 cm³
Compression ratio	9,1 to 1
Valve gear	ohv, pushrods
Main bearings	seven
Aircleaner	paper element
Fuel requirement	97-octane Coast
	92-octane Reef
Cooling	water
Electrics	12-volt AC/DC

ENGINE OUTPUT:

Max. power SAE (kW)	115,5
	(155 b.h.p.)
Max. power net (kW)	98,5
Peak rpm	4 000 (see text)
Max. torque (N.m.) at rpm	324
	at 1 600

TRANSMISSION:

Forward speeds	three
Synchromesh	all
Gearshift	Column
Low gear	2,95 to 1
2nd gear	1,68 to 1
Top gear	Direct
Reverse gear	3,67 to 1
Final drive	3,23 to 1
Drive wheels	rear

WHEELS AND TYRES:

Road wheels	14 inch pressed steel
Rim width	6 inch JJ
Type of tyre	6-ply light commercial
Tyre size	7,75 x 14
Tyre pressures (front)	180 to 200
	kPa (26 to 28 lb.)
Tyre pressures (rear)	180 to 280
	kPa (26 to 40 lb.)

BRAKES:

Front	286 mm discs
Rear	254 mm TLS drums
Pressure regulation	dual system
Boosting	vacuum servo
Handbrake position	under dash

STEERING:

Type	recirculating ball
Lock to lock	5,0 turns
Turning circle	12,6 metres

MEASUREMENTS:

Length overall	4,862 m
Width overall	1,919 m
Height overall	1,450 m
Wheelbase	2,946 m
Front track	1,537 m
Rear track	1,524 m
Ground clearance	0,195 m
Licensing mass	1 400 kg

SUSPENSION:

Front	independent
Type	coils and stabiliser bar
Rear	live axle
Type	leaf springs, auxiliary load blades.

CAPACITIES:

Seating	three
Fuel tank	73 litres
Load space	3,2 m²
Load capacity	698 kg

WARRANTY:

Six months or 10 000 km.

TEST CAR FROM:

Ford Motor Company of S.A., Port Elizabeth.

CRUISING AT 120

Mech. noise level	84,0 dBA
0—120 through gears	21,8 seconds
km/litre at 120	6,8
litres/100 km	14,7
Braking from 120	4,6 seconds
Maximum gradient (top)	1 in 13,2
Speedometer error	nil
Speedo at true 120	120 km/h
Engine rpm (top)	3 372

good weather seal — at least on a new vehicle.

One other small eccentricity concerns the ignition switch: apparently as an anti-theft measure, the key cannot be removed unless reverse is engaged. The switch also proved a bit sticky to operate at times.

PERFORMANCE

The whole emphasis in this Ranchero with its long-stroke motor is on torque. The gearbox is three-speed, with synchromesh throughout, but rather slow on the cross-gate shift into second.

A racing-type start from rest produces a burst of wheelspin and a leap away from rest, but the cross-gate shift has to be made at 50 km/h, and the shift into top at 90 km/h, owing to restricted engine range. (The specifications give engine peak as 4 000 rpm, but the Ranchero goes to 4 400 a bit roughly — and in fact, pulls these revs in top on a level road.) The speedometer becomes fully-accurate at speed.

Top-gear flexibility is tremendous: it pulls away from 40 km/h easily in top, so not much gearshifting is needed once on the move. Gradient ability is strong for the same reason, suggesting that this car is almost the equal of the V8 in load and towing ability.

BRAKING AND HANDLING

With big discs at front and finned drums at rear, braking is quite well-balanced and the tendency towards rear-wheel locking not severe. Trying to get a fast stop from 120 produced a bit of drama in terms of broadsiding tendencies, and the 10-stop test from 100 showed up some fade towards the end. This started with a "cooking-linings" smell early on, developing into smoking and a lifeless pedal towards the end. (See graph.)

The Ranchero handles very well — a feature which makes it more car than pick-up. It is firm and stable, and the recirculating ball steering is light, shock-free and accurate. The steering is low-geared, requiring five turns from lock to lock, and the longer wheelbase and wider track have increased the turning circle to a poor 12,6 metres.

TECHNICAL

PERFORMANCE FACTORS:

Power/mass (W/kg) net	70,4
Frontal area (m²)	2,78
km/h/1 000 rpm (top)	35,6

(Calculated on licensing mass, gross frontal area, gearing and net power output.)

SERVICE REQUIREMENTS:

Sump capacity	4,4 litres
Change interval	5 000 km
Oil filter capacity	1,0 litres
Change interval	10 000 km
Gearbox capacity	1,5 litres
Change interval	nil
Diff capacity	1,3 litres
Change interval	nil
Air filter change	Up to 10 000 km
Greasing points	nil

(These basic service recommendations are given for guidance only, and may vary according to operating conditions. Inquiries should be addressed to authorised dealerships.)

STANDARD EQUIPMENT:

Boosted brakes, disc at front, on dual-line system, exterior rear view mirror, windscreen washers, Aeroflow ventilation.)

TEST CONDITIONS:

Altitude	At sea level
Weather	fine and hot
Fuel used	98-octane
Test car's odometer	1 150 km

Side view shows how the cab is dwarfed by the overall body dimensions and shape.

It becomes bouncy over rough stuff, but not to the point where it is difficult to control. It should respond very well to a moderate load.

SUMMARY

This new Ranchero is a stylish and road-capable workhorse, able to turn to anything from caravan towing to fast open-road cruising. It is simple and un-fussy, and much superior in comfort and handling to the average light commercial vehicle.

It is at its best at middle speeds, when it runs silently and strongly, and with quite reasonable economy. The 73-litre (16-gallon) tank gives it a fine cruising range, and its versatility makes it an attractive vehicle for general utility use. ■

Ranchero Spotter's Quiz

Can you identify the model year?

I f you're a Ford fan—and statistics show that many of you are—you should be able to identify the various Rancheros in this conglomerate of years. Remember that all Rancheros use the same front fenders, hood and grille as the same-year passenger cars, if that's any help. Turn the page for the answers, but don't call on us to settle any arguments. ❦

1

2

3

4

5

6

7

Ranchero Spotter's Quiz

8

9

10

11

12

13

14

15

16

17

18

19

20

21

stylish hauler

by Michael Lamm
PHOTOS BY THE AUTHOR

A nationwide
survey based
on 1,300,000
owner-driven
miles.

'Does most everything a real
pickup will do, but rides
and handles like a luxury
car and looks great.'

There's a boom in pickups right now—large ones,
small ones, and in between. While the Japanese imports battle it out in the mini range, and while there's
no end of rugged full-sized standard pickups to choose
from, only two automakers offer contenders in what we
might call the "coupe pickup" class: Ford and Chevrolet.

It's easy to see why people buy these vehicles. Ford's
Ranchero combines the riding qualities and appearance
of a coupe with the workhorse stamina and versatility
of a true pickup. So, too, does the El Camino.

The Ford/Chevrolet feud has raged for decades, so
the choice of a Ranchero over an El Camino (or vice-

versa) becomes largely a matter of emotion. Dimensions, load capacity, and prices
fall within fractions of each other. The
Ranchero offers a Six and El Camino
doesn't, but hardly anyone buys one of
these vehicles with a six-cylinder engine
anyway, so it's almost academic. The
Ranchero's heritage is strictly Torino; the
El Camino's pure Chevelle.

Here are some typical answers to our
why-did-you-buy-a-Ranchero question: A
Florida steelworker said, "I'd already used
up six Rancheros since the first one came
out in 1957, so why not another?" An Illinois construction superintendent: "I
bought mine for work and camping, and
I think it looks better than an El Camino."
An Ohio oiler: "Needed something the wife
would drive and could use as a second car."
"I need it to do light hauling, and it rides
and drives like an auto," wrote a Tennessee
industrial foreman. Many of our respondents mentioned that they particularly
liked the Ranchero's appearance. "It's just
a good-looking car," affirmed an Indiana
factory worker.

Here are some specific praises owners
had for their Rancheros: "Does most everything a real pickup will do, but rides
and handles like a luxury car and looks
great." "Am especially happy with the riding qualities." "Appearance seems to catch
the eye of others as well as myself." "My
wife would rather drive the Ranchero than
our LTD." "Holds the road better than
most medium-sized cars." "It's the best-handling American car I've driven—feels
more like a sports car than a pickup."

How about complaints? As with most
newer U.S. cars, poor gas mileage headed
the list of grumbles. A Missouri computer
technician sums it up for many owners by
saying, "I have an opinion about the anti-pollution equipment on *all* 1973 cars. I previously owned a 1969 Ranchero with the
identical engine and options and got 15-
17 mpg (as against 10-12 for this one). It
seems to me that I'm now burning 67 percent more gas, defeating the intended purpose of the smog equipment by burning up
the earth's energy supply more quickly,
plus costing me more money."

What changes would Ranchero owners

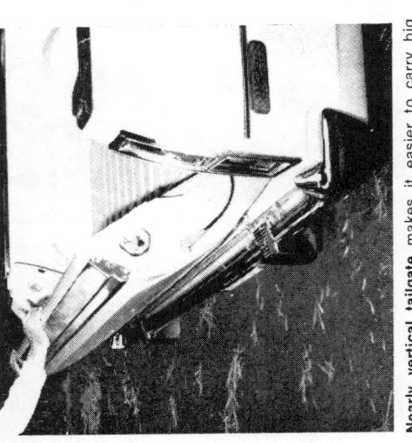

Nearly vertical tailgate makes it easier to carry big
boxes and camper shells. Some owners grumbled about
poor vision to rear sides but liked hold-downs inside
bed. A few suggested incorporating two-way tailgate.

Versatility and good looks rank
highest as reasons for buying
both the Ranchero and El Camino.
Ranchero offers six-cylinder engine,

use pickups of this type exclusively for business: contractors, welders, salesmen of various sorts, and so on. More normally, the owner tends to have a bit of acreage somewhere or a business that lends itself to occasional light hauling—filling-station owners, repairmen, painters, and at least one horseshoer in New Jersey.

Quite a number of owners mentioned hauling recreational equipment—not so much campers but skis, snowmobiles, motorcycles, bikes, hunting and fishing gear, boats, small trailers and surfboards. One Air Force captain says he uses his Ranchero to carry his flying and parachuting paraphernalia.

Owners rated the Ranchero's quality of workmanship quite high, and several of them praised such small touches as tie-downs in the bed and the nearly vertical tailgate.

Asked whether they'd buy another, 83.5 percent said yes, and a West Virginia coal miner notes, "If everyone owned a Ranchero they would never want any other kind of pickup truck."

★ ★ ★

'I am a horseshoer; find the Ranchero most convenient.'

Ranchero and El Camino both make front disc brakes standard, backed by finned rear drums for greater fade resistance. Discs are much less affected by water; thus make sense for soggy service on ranches and farms.

Summary of 1973 Ford Ranchero Owners Reports*

Total miles driven 1,292,081

Engines:
250-cu.-in. Six	0.4%
302-cu.-in. V8	35.2
351-cu.-in. V8	57.8
400-cu.-in. V8	3.3
429-cu.-in. V8	3.3

Transmissions:
Automatic	98.5%
Three-speed manual	0.7
Four-speed manual	0.7

Series:
Ranchero 500	51.2%
Ranchero GT	36.5
Ranchero Squire	12.3

Average miles per gallon:
250-cu.-in. Six, not enough replies	
302-cu.-in. V8: local driving	11.0
302-cu.-in. V8: long trips	13.3
351-cu.-in. V8, not enough replies	
400-cu.-in. V8: local driving	10.4
400-cu.-in. V8: long trips	12.5
429-cu.-in. V8, not enough replies	

Why the Ranchero?
Pickup feature	48.1%
Styling	32.8
Owned one before	11.6
Comfort	7.1

Specific likes:
Handling	46.5%
Styling	43.3
Comfort	32.2

Ride	31.8
Power	13.5
Hauling ability	10.2

Specific dislikes:
Poor gas mileage	26.0%
Emission control devices	9.9
Poor rear vision	6.5
Poor workmanship	5.0

Types of work used for:
Hauling	26.9%
Construction	14.4
Farming	9.3
Commuting	7.4
On-the-road selling	6.0

Types of recreation used for:
Fishing	32.3%
Traveling	26.0
Hunting	24.0
Camping	22.9
Boating	10.4

Number of vehicles owned:
Ranchero only	19.4%
Two vehicles	58.1
Three vehicles	15.8
Four or more vehicles	6.9

Other makes of vehicles owned:
Ford	23.7%
Chevrolet	10.3
Buick	10.3
Oldsmobile	9.4
Mercury	8.7
Ford truck	7.1

Comfort opinion:
Good to excellent	92.4%
Average to poor	7.6

Workmanship opinion:
Good to excellent	70.6%
Average to poor	29.4

Had any mechanical trouble?
No	58.5%
Yes	41.5

What type of trouble?
Carburetor	17.5%
Transmission	12.3
Hard starting	7.0

Did you repair it yourself?
No	91.2%
Yes	8.8

Dealer repairs satisfactory?
Yes	59.4%
No	40.6

What changes would you like?
Better rear vision	15.5%
Better gas mileage	8.8
Different styling	7.1
Seatback angle	6.7
Remove smog equipment	5.0

Age distribution of owners:
15-29 years	19.9%
30-49 years	42.6
50-plus	37.4

Would you buy another Ranchero?
Yes	83.5%
No	16.5

*Percentages might not equal 100% due to rounding or insufficient data.

'I have to let smoke out by opening the side window, and that's noisy and lets the rain in.'

Ranchero's spare and jack bolt behind passenger's seat, leaving not enough lockable storage space, say some. Seatback angle also didn't please everyone, but there was no agreement whether it's too steep or too recumbent. Ranchero offers choice of five engine displacements. Poor gas mileage loomed as a major complaint, as with all 1973 cars, and a high percentage of owners blamed antismog equipment for sluggish performance plus gas guzzling.

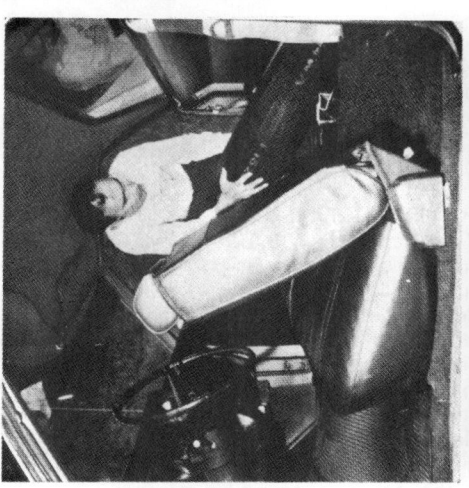

suggest? "Move the spare to give more luggage space." "Spare makes seat too upright." "If they'd make the rear pillars thinner, it would be easier to see out the back window." "Improve the ventilation or add a vent wing, because as it is now, I have to let smoke out by opening the side window, and that's noisy and lets the rain in." "Needs built-in hooks behind seat to accommodate clothes rod." "The front bumper sticks out too far."

How do owners rate comfort? "Very comfortable, and I especially like the air-conditioning." "No complaints from passengers, but I think the seatback leans too far back, and there's no adjustment." "Fresh air should feed through the heater without having to turn on the blower." "After owning a rough-riding Mach I Mustang, the Ranchero is very comfortable." "I'm glad I picked the Ranchero over standard pickups—much less noise, and it rides like a car." "Very comfortable, but the windows don't seal properly, and to prevent them from rattling, you have to roll them all the way down before you roll them up again."

Not surprisingly, both Ranchero and El Camino owners put their pickups to nearly the same uses: work, recreation and simply driving them as another car. On the average, most owners use their Rancheros more for recreation and simple driving than for work. Certain types of professionals can

Ford Ranchero 500 A/T

This rugged V8 Automatic car/truck is great motoring value.

There is no doubt that one of the best motoring "buys" available in South Africa is the V8 utility car. For a price not much above R3 000, the motorist gets a rugged 5-litre V8 engine, three-speed automatic transmission, and a pretty high standard of equipment.

Add a ventilated and styled glass-fibre canopy, and that strong and attractive utility becomes a quite exceptional multi-purpose vehicle.

Ford's contender in this field is the Ranchero 500, introduced in XA form in the middle of 1973 as part of Ford's rationalisation programme:

the 500 replaces earlier Ranchero V8 manual and automatic models. So Ford in South Africa now has only two Ranchero's: 4,1 litre manual, and 500 (V8) Automatic.

UPRATED EQUIPMENT

The Ranchero 500 has extensive equipment and luxury trim: there is a heater/demister, courtesy light switch on both doors, a cigar lighter, and armrest-pullhandles inside the doors. Seats are individually tailored, with high backrests, and exceedingly comfortable for this class of vehicle.

Main distinguishing feature is the full wheel trims used on the 500, and the tonneau cover is standard equipment. Special badges and drip rail mouldings are used.

It is a smoothly-styled vehicle with not much to criticise — though it feels very big from the driving seat because of its high coachwork, and we dislike the frameless door windows, which seem out of place on a working vehicle.

EXCITING PERFORMANCE

The five litres of Cleveland Mustang V8 engine guarantees something well above the ordinary in performance: this Ranchero tears away from rest with a burst of wheelspin to reach 100 km/h in 10,2 seconds and 120

before 15 seconds comes up. It will go on to a straight-line maximum of 180 k's.

But what is more important to the average owner is that the soft-growling V8 does not make the interior noisy, and that fuel economy is pretty reasonable under the influence of a long-legged 2,92 to 1 final drive — it should return something like 22 mpg overall — 13 litres/100 km in terms of consumption. The V8 Automatic is actually faster and more economical than the 4,1 litre "six" with manual shift (see CAR Road Test, April 1973).

It is mildly heavy-handling, but stable at speed, with 7,75 six-ply tyres on 6 JJ rims, and pressures ranging from 160 to 250 kPa, depending on load and speed.

SUMMARY

This V8 utility, with its strong suspension, is rated for a payload of 768 kg (three-quarter ton) and has many virtues. In this de luxe form it has a high standard of general comfort (subject to a somewhat harsh ride when light), it can cruise as quietly and effortlessly as a big V8 sedan, and it makes a wonderful towing vehicle.

It could best be described as a car with truck capabilities, and as such is great motoring value. ∎

KEY FIGURES

Accel. 0–100 km/h .10,2 seconds
Maximum speed . . 180,2 km/h
Cruising speed (4 200) .176 km/h
Cruising fuel range (120) . 505
Engine revs per km . . . 1 425
National list price . . . R3 260

SPECIFICATIONS

ENGINE:
Cylinders . . . . V8, crossflow
Carburettors . twin-choke Autolite (Ford)
Bore . . . . . . 101,6 mm
Stroke. . . . . . 76,2 mm
Cubic capacity . . 4 950 cm^3
Compression ratio . .9,8 to 1
Valve gear. . . ohv, pushrods
Main bearings. . . . . . five
Aircleaner. . . . .paper element
Fuel requirement 98-octane Coast, 93-octane Reef
Cooling . . water; 14,7 litres
Electrics . . . . .12-volt AC
ENGINE OUTPUT:
Max.power SAE (kW) . . 171,6 (230 bhp)
Max. power net (kW) . . 146,0
Peak rpm 4 400
Max. torque (N.m) at rpm . 406,8 at 2 600
TRANSMISSION:
Forward speeds . . . . three, Cruise-O-Matic
Selector . . . steering column
Low gear . . . . 2,46 to 1
2nd gear . . . . 1,46 to 1
Top gear . . . . . direct
Reverse gear . . . 2,20 to 1
Final drive . . . . 2,92 to 1
Drive wheels . . . . . . rear
WARRANTY:
Six months or 10 000 km.
TEST CAR FROM:
Ford Motor Company of S.A., Port Elizabeth.

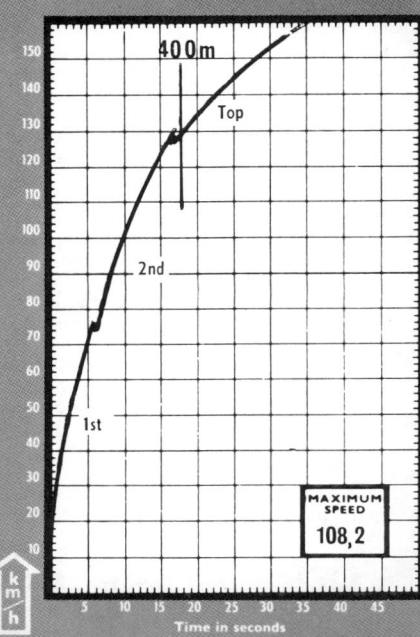

400m

Top

2nd

1st

MAXIMUM SPEED
108,2

km/h

Time in seconds

BRAKING DISTANCES

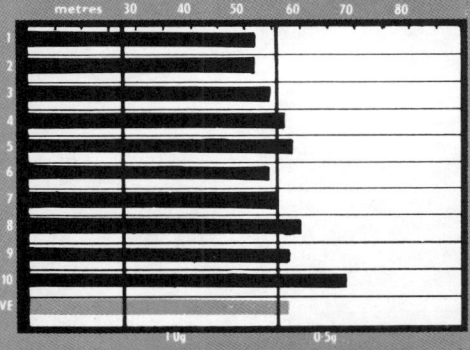

metres 30 40 50 60 70 80

1
2
3
4
5
6
7
8
9
10
AVE

1,0g 0,5g

(10 stops from 100 km/h)

ENGINE SPEED

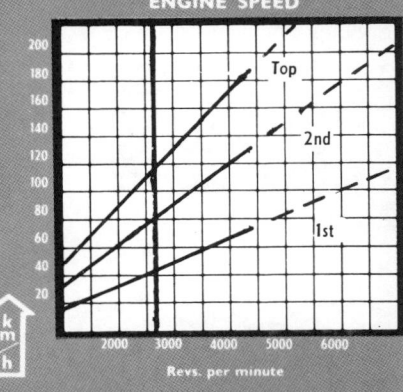

Top

2nd

1st

km/h

Revs. per minute

GRADIENT ABILITY

MAX. TORQUE 2 600 RPM

1st
2nd
Top

(Degrees inclination)

PERFORMANCE

MAKE AND MODEL:

Make	Ford
Model	Ranchero 500

INTERIOR NOISE LEVELS:

	Mech.	Wind	Road
Idling	45,0	—	—
60	65,5	—	—
80	70,5	—	—
100	74,5	—	—
120	78,5	88,0	89,0
Full throttle	see graph		
Average dBA at 120	85,2		

ACCELERATION FROM REST:

0—60	4,5
0—80	6,5
0—100	10,2
0—120	14,5
400 m sprint	17,3

IMPERIAL DATA

ACCELERATION FROM REST:

	(seconds)
0—60	9,7
¼ mile	17,3

MAXIMUM SPEED (mph):

True speed	112,0

FUEL ECONOMY (mpg):

60 mph	24,1
75 mph	19,4

PERFORMANCE FACTORS:

Power/mass (W/kg) net	96,6
Frontal area (m2)	2,78
km/h/1 000 rpm (top)	42,1

(Calculated on licensing mass, gross frontal area, gearing and net power output.)

OVERTAKING ACCELERATION:

(A/T):

40—60	1,8
60—80	2,2
80—100	3,5
100—120	4,3

MAXIMUM SPEED:

True speed	180,2
Speedo reading	177

Calibration:

Indicated:	60	80	100	120
True speed:	60	80	100	120

FUEL ECONOMY:

(km/l — litres/100 km in brackets)

60	10,5 (9,6)
85	9,6 (10,4)
100	8,3 (12,2)
120	6,9 (14,4)
Full throttle	see graph

ECONOMY DATA

Fuel tank capacity	72,7 litres
Litres/100 km at 80	10,4
Fuel range at 80	698 km

BRAKING TEST:

From 100 km/h:

First stop	4,1
Tenth stop	5,5
Average	4,59

GRADIENTS IN GEARS:

Low gear	1 in 2,7
2nd gear	1 in 4,1
Top gear	1 in 6,6

GEARED SPEEDS:

Low gear	75,2
2nd gear	128,7
Top gear	185,2

(Calculated at engine peak rpm — 4 400.)

MECHANICAL NOISE

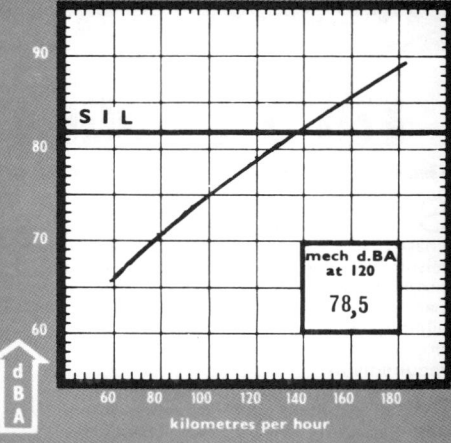

SIL

mech d.BA at 120
78,5

dBA

kilometres per hour

NOISE VALUES

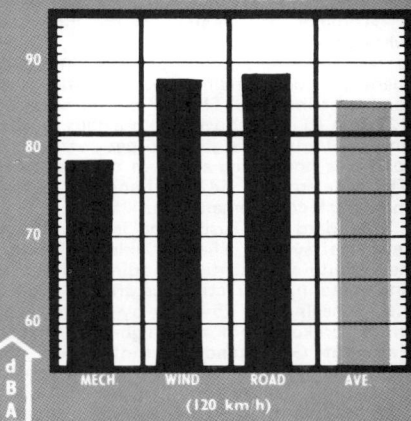

dBA

MECH   WIND   ROAD   AVE.

(120 km/h)

FUEL ECONOMY

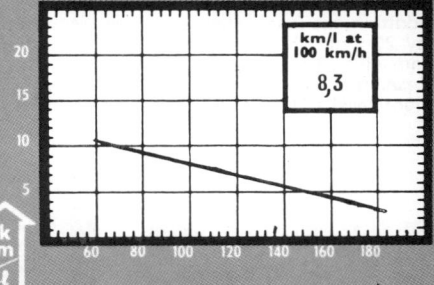

km/l at 100 km/h
8,3

km/l

FUEL CONSUMPTION

(litres 100 km)

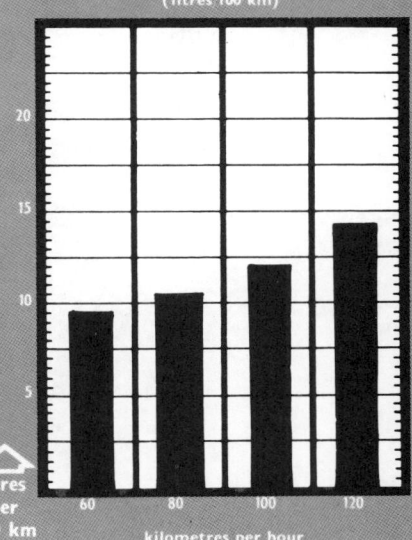

litres per 100 km

kilometres per hour

Ford Ranchero 6 and V8

Since its introduction in 1968, 14 880 Ford Ranchero units have been purchased in South Africa as second cars, leisure vehicles and as workhorses for businessmen, farmers and construction companies. This utility, available in six and eight-cylinder versions, has established a broad character and one that suits many requirements.

Now Ford has introduced the new, restyled Ranchero which combines durability and versatility with good looks. It also offers improved comfort in ride, seating, handling and safety, the company claims.

A major new feature is the increased wheelbase, 2 946 mm (116 inches), which is said to bring about substantial improvement in ride, handling characteristics and load distribution. This is an increase of 129 mm (5 inches) over the previous model, and results in more than 55 per cent of the load area now being ahead of the rear axle. The wide front (1 537 mm) and rear (1 524 mm) track complement this.

Standard rear suspension is a two-stage, seven-leaf system. The rear axle is of extra-heavy-duty specification. Adding to the ride and handling characteristics are the big 6J steel wheels with 254 mm by 57 mm rear drum brakes from the high-performance Fairmont GT. Standard front brakes are 282 mm diameter ventilated, turbo-cooled discs.

The pick-up box has also been greatly improved: the tailgate opens to 90 and 180 degrees, allowing heavy articles to be loaded without damaging the tailgate stays. In addition, the loading height has been reduced by 23 mm, while the tailgate opening is 133 mm wider. The pick-up box dimensions have been improved by an increase of 69 mm at floor level in length, 66 mm extra width at the top and 15 mm more between the wheel arches.

CLEVELAND V8 ENGINE

Engine capacities remain the same as for the previous model with a six cylinder at 4 098 cm^3 (250 CID) and the V8 at 4 949 cm^3 (302 CID). However, the V8 has been redesigned, adopting the proven Cleveland design parameters resulting in greater durability, more power and better economy.

Coupled with this is a new large 73-litre (16 gallon) fuel tank which gives a significant improvement in touring range.

The long, low lines of the new Ranchero,

besides taking maximum advantage of the long wheelbase, will appeal particularly to those wanting the vehicle for recreational and leisure use. Wide-opening doors improve accessibility to the passenger area. The interior itself is designed to provide comfort and safety for three. The driver sits on high-back seats behind an oval steering wheel facing a cockpit-styled instrument/control panel with safety rocker switches, surrounded with a deeply padded dash. Within fingertip reach are the Aeroflow flow-through ventilation controls, the two speed windshield washer and wiper controls, light switch, panel dimmer and ashtray.

Safety features are the collapsible steering column, impact-absorbing steering wheel with full width padded hub, double-sided safety wheel rims, non-lift, non-reflecting wiper blades and the dual line braking system.

Prices are: six-cylinder R2 545; V8 Manual R2 791; V8 A/T R3 031. ●

Ford Ranchero 1967/8

FORD RANCHERO VS. CHEVROLET EL CAMINO

PV4 COMPARISON TEST

WE DIDN'T EXPECT MUCH AND WE WERE QUITE SURPRISED

The Ford Ranchero makes a pretty picture in this woodland setting. Front end treatment of Ford's personal pickup is outstanding. The handling off the pavement was much better than we anticipated. The option list was seemingly endless.

WE HAVE NOT normally thought of the Chevrolet El Camino and the Ford Ranchero as our kind of vehicles here at PV4. They did not seem to really meet the definition of a pickup. After giving it some more thought, however, we concluded that perhaps we were being a bit shortsighted and should do an evaluation of them as they are actually pickups in that they do have a bed behind the cab. So we decided to compare them.

Well, we got quite a surprise. These are exceptionally nice vehicles with good handling and gobs of comfort. The styling is a matter of preference in choosing between the two, of course, but generally we think the Ranchero lines are better.

Under the hood, both manufacturers offer a wide range of engines: Chevrolet sells the El Camino with a 350-cu-in. 2-bbl V-8 as standard equipment. Then the optional engines are a 4-barrel 350, a 2- or 4-barrel 400 V-8 or the 4-barrel 454 V-8. In the Ford Ranchero, the basic engine is the trusty 302-cu-in. V-8 and the options are the 351, 400 and 460 V-8s.

The transmission offerings from Chevrolet include the standard manual 3-speed and optional 4-speed manual or 3-speed Turbo Hydra-Matic. Ford offers either the 3-speed manual or 3-speed automatic but no 4-speed manual. As far as final drive ratios, Chevy has available a 2.73, 3.08 or 3.42:1 while Ford offers the 3.00, 3.25 or 3.50:1 ratios.

Both the Ranchero and El Camino are equipped with disc brakes in front as standard equipment along with drums at the rear. Both also have recirculating ball steering and a wide variety of wheel and tire options.

The suspension systems of the two pickups are also quite similar with independent A-arms, coil springs and tube shocks at the front, while at the rear the El Camino has coil springs on a live axle with tube shocks and the Ranchero has semi-elliptic leaf springs on a live axle with tube shocks. Both Ford and Chevrolet offer special packages for improved handling and additional carrying capacity.

The standard seat is a bench in both vehicles with optional bucket seats available if you care to spend the extra money. As far as interior dimensions, there is not a whole lot of

Dash of Ranchero is very stylish and complete with all the gauges, including a tachometer, and all were easy to read.

The 460-cu-in. V-8 is Ford's largest engine—and best. Power made it very difficult to stay within the posted speed limits.

El Camino has simpler lines than Ranchero but front end treatment doesn't come off quite as well. Radial tires and the tuned suspension gave the Chevrolet the best highway handling of any pickup we've ever tested.

The instrument panel of El Camino has classic look. Center console is nice touch and blends into the decor well.

Engine compartment is full of horsepower in the Chevy. The 454-powered El Camino was quickest we've ever tested.

difference between them and some of our staff members preferred the Ranchero while others opted for the El Camino. The Ranchero gave a feel of more room for the larger staffers (over 6-ft).

Outside, the Chevrolet has a slightly larger overall bed size and tailgate in some dimensions while the Ranchero is larger in others. Both vehicles weighed in at slightly more than 4400 pounds as tested and they both offer a variety of Gross Vehicle Weight Ratings.

Other measurements confirmed the similarities between the two, the Ranchero having a 118-in. wheelbase while the Chevy's is 116 in. Overall length, height and width dimensions are also within a couple inches of each other.

TEST & IMPRESSIONS

As you no doubt have noted by now, there is not a great deal of difference between the Ranchero and El Camino. Our test models were both equipped with all the fancy bells and whistles. We had the largest engines, automatic transmissions, bucket seats, power this and power that, including power windows and door locks in the El Camino. The West Coast list price of the Ranchero as we tested it was $5756 and the Chevrolet listed at $5738. Again, not much difference between them.

Both the Ranchero and El Camino were exciting performers at Orange County International Raceway. Unfortunately, it was impossible to test them on the same day and the track conditions were not ideal the day we tested the Ranchero. Nevertheless, the performance of both vehicles is quite good, certainly the best we have experienced in the world of PV4s. The El Camino accelerated from 0-60 mph in just 9.2 seconds while the Ranchero performed the same feat in 9.9 seconds. In our standing-start quarter-mile tests, the Ranchero completed the distance in 17 seconds at a speed of 78 mph while the El Camino went through the traps in 16.4 seconds at 84 mph.

In braking performance, there was also quite a bit of similarity. Both vehicles were able to come to a safe and steady stop in less than 180 feet from 60 mph and the percent

FORD RANCHERO

PRICES

Basic list, FOB Detroit
Ranchero 500 .... $3029
Ranchero GT $3264

Standard equipment: 302-cu.-in. V-8, 3-spd manual transmission, heater/defroster, 2-spd electric wiper/washers, cargo tiedowns, backup lights, chrome bumpers (front energy absorbing), chrome hub caps, front disc brakes, E78 x 14B tires

ENGINES

Standard 302-cu.-in. V-8
Bore x stroke, in. .... 4.00 x 3.00
Compression ratio 8.0:1
Net horsepower @ rpm ..... 140 @ 3800
Net torque @ rpm, lb-ft .... 230 @ 2600
Type fuel required .... 91 octane

Optional 351-cu.-in. V-8 .... $44
Bore x stroke, in. .... 4.00 x 3.50
Compression ratio .... nk
Net horsepower @ rpm ..... 162 @ 4000
Net torque @ rpm, lb-ft .... 275 @ 2200
Type fuel required .... 91 octane

Optional 400-cu.-in. V-8 .... $135
Bore x stroke, in. .... 4.00 x 4.00
Compression ratio 8.4:1
Net horsepower @ rpm .... nk
Net torque @ rpm, lb-ft .... nk
Type fuel required .... 91 octane

Optional 460-cu.-in. V-8 .... $274
Bore x stroke, in. .... 4.36 x 3.85
Compression ratio 8.0:1
Net horsepower @ rpm ..... 195 @ 3800
Net torque @ rpm, lb-ft .... 355 @ 2600
Type fuel required .... 91 octane

DRIVE TRAIN

Standard transmission .... 3-spd manual
Clutch dia., in. .... 10 & 11
Transmission ratios: 3rd 1.00:1
2nd 1.75:1
1st 2.99:1
Synchromesh .... all forward gears

Optional 3-spd automatic $244

Transmission ratios: 3rd 1.00:1
2nd 1.46:1
1st 2.46:1

Rear axle type .... semi-floating hypoid
Final drive ratios . 3.00:1, 3.25:1, 3.50:1
Overdrive .... none
Limited slip differential $46

CHASSIS & BODY

Body/frame: ladder-type frame with separate steel body

Brakes (std): front, 10.72-in. dia disc; rear, 10 x 2.5-in. drums
Brake swept area, sq in. 373
Swept area/ton (max load) 131
Power brakes $48

Steering type (std) .... recirculating ball
Steering ratio .... nk
Turns, lock to lock .... nk
Power steering $112
Power steering ratio .... nk
Turning circle, ft .... nk

Wheel size (std) .... 14 x 5.5JJ
Optional wheel sizes .... 14 x 6.0JJ
Tire size (std) .... E78 x 14B
Optional tire sizes: F78 x 14B, G78 x 14B, HR78 x 14B

SUSPENSION

Front suspension: independent A-arms with coil springs and tube shocks
Front axle capacity, lb 2855
Optional .... none

Rear suspension: semi-elliptic leaf springs on live axle and tube shocks
Rear axle capacity, lb 3020
Optional .... none

Additional suspension options: HD shock absorbers front and rear, HD springs front and rear, HD front stabilizer bar, $47

ACCOMMODATION

Standard seats: full width bench with head restraint and split back

Optional bucket seats $146

Headroom, in. 34.0
Pedal to seatback, max 41.8
Steering wheel to seatback, max .. 17.5
Seat to ground 19.5
Floor to ground 10.3

Heater & defroster .... std
Tinted glass $42
Air conditioning .... standard $424
temp control $487

Unobstructed load space (length x width x height) in. .... 77.7 x 48.5 x 16
Tailgate (width x height) ..... 59 x 16.5

INSTRUMENTATION

Instruments: 0-120-mph speedometer, 99,999.9-mi. odometer, fuel gauge
Warning lights: ammeter, water temp, oil pressure, brake system warning, hazard warning
Optional: instrument cluster (tachometer, clock, ammeter, water temp, oil pressure, trip odometer) $94

GENERAL

Curb weight, lb (test model) 4445
GVW (max. laden weight) 5367
Optional GVWs ... from 4725 to 5685

Wheelbase, in. 118.0
Track, front/rear 63.4/63.5
Overall length 215.7
Overall height 53.1
Overall width 79.0
Overhang, front/rear 38/51

Approach angle, degrees 20
Departure angle 17

Ground clearances (test model):
Front axle 6.8
Rear axle 7.3
Oil pan 10.0
Fuel tank 15.0
Exhaust system (lowest point) 6.5

Fuel tank capacity (U.S. gal) 22.5
Auxiliary tank .... none

PERFORMANCE DATA

TEST MODEL

Ranchero GT, 460-cu.-in. engine, automatic transmission, air conditioning, bucket seats, conv. group, appearance group, power steering, tilt steering wheel, power brakes, AM/FM stereo radio, instrument cluster, light group, tinted glass, mag wheels, 3.00 ratio Traction-Lok rear axle, H78 x 14B tires
West Coast list price $5756

ACCELERATION

Time to speed, sec:
0-30 mph 3.9
0-45 mph 6.1
0-60 mph 9.9
0-70 mph 13.9
Standing start, 1/4-mile, sec 17.0
Speed at end, mph 78

SPEED IN GEARS

High
3rd (3500 rpm) 89
2nd (4000 rpm) 78
1st (4000 rpm) 47

BRAKE TESTS

Pedal pressure required for ½-g deceleration rate from 60 mph, lb 30
Stopping distance from 60 mph, ft 173.5
Fade: Percent increase in pedal pressure for 6 stops from 60 mph 80
Overall brake rating .... good

INTERIOR NOISE

Idle in neutral, dBA 52
Maximum during acceleration 72
At steady 70-mph cruising speed 75

OFF PAVEMENT

Hillclimbing ability .... fair
Maneuverability .... very good
Turnaround capability .... good
Handling .... very good
Ride .... excellent

GENERAL

Heater rating .... excellent
Defroster effectiveness .... excellent
Wiper coverage .... very good

FUEL CONSUMPTION

Normal driving, mpg 11.5
Off pavement 8.6
Range, normal driving, miles 258
Range, off pavement 193

CHEVROLET EL CAMINO

PRICES

Basic list, FOB Detroit
El Camino $3139
El Camino classic $3277

Standard Equipment: 350-cu-in. V-8 engine, 3-spd manual transmission, chrome front and rear bumpers, backup lights, 2-spd electric wipers/washers, heater/defroster

ENGINES

Standard 350-cu-in. V-8
Bore x stroke, in ....4.00 x 3.48
Compression ratio 8.5:1
Net horsepower @ rpm ..... 145 @ 3800
Net torque @ rpm, lb-ft ..... 250 @ 2200
Type fuel required .... 91 octane

Optional 400-cu-in. V-8 ....$51
Bore x stroke, in ....4.126 x 3.76
Compression ratio 8.5:1
Net horsepower @ rpm ..... 150 @ 3200
Net torque @ rpm, lb-ft ..... 290 @ 2000
Type fuel required .... 91 octane

Optional 454-cu-in. V-8 ....$209
Bore x stroke, in ....4.25 x 4.00
Compression ratio 8.25:1
Net horsepower @ rpm ..... 235 @ 4000
Net torque @ rpm, lb-ft ..... 360 @ 2800
Type fuel required .... 91 octane

DRIVE TRAIN

Standard transmission ..... 3-spd manual
Clutch dia., in 10
Transmission ratios: 3rd 1.00:1
2nd.....................1.68:1
1st 2.85:1
Synchromesh ....all forward gears

Optional 4-spd manual $190
Transmission ratios: 4th 1.00:1
3rd 1.27:1
2nd 1.64:1
1st 2.20:1
Synchromesh ....all forward gears

Optional 3-spd automatic $237

CHASSIS & BODY

Transmission ratios: 3rd 1.00:1
2nd 1.52:1
1st 2.52:1

Rear axle type ..... semi-floating hypoid
Final drive ratios 2.73, 3.08, 3.42
Overdrive ....none

Limited slip differential $45

Body/frame: ladder-type frame with separate steel body
Brakes (std): front 11-in. dia. disc, rear 9.5 x 2-in. drums
Brake swept area, sq in 337
Swept area/ton (max load) 117
Power brakes....................$46

Steering type (std) ..... recirculating ball
Steering ratio 28.0:1
Turns, lock to lock 6.6
Power steering....................$117
Power steering ratio .... variable 16/13:1
Turning circle, ft 39

Wheel size (std) ....14 x 6JJ
Optional wheel sizes ...14 x 7JJ, 15 x 7JJ
Tire size (std) .... G78 x 14B
Optional tire sizes: H78 x 14B, GR78 x 15B, GR70 x 15B, HR70 x 15B

SUSPENSION

Front suspension: independent A-arms with coil springs and tube shocks
Front axle capacity, lb 2900
Optional ....none

Rear suspension: coil springs on live axle and tube shocks
Rear axle capacity, lb 2950
Optional ....none

Additional suspension options: HD front and rear springs and shock absorbers, $17

ACCOMMODATION

Standard seats .... full-width bench
Optional bucket seats $133

Headroom, in 34.0
Pedal to seatback, max 45.5
Steering wheel to seatback, max 17.2
Seat to ground 22
Floor to ground 12

Heater & defroster .... std
Tinted glass $42
Air conditioning $397

Unobstructed load space (length x width x height, in.) 79.0 x 45.2 x 13.7

Tailgate (width x height) ..... 62 x 13.7

INSTRUMENTATION

Instruments: 0-120-mph speedometer, 99,999.9-mi. odometer, fuel gauge
Warning lights: alternator, oil pressure, water temp, brake system warning, hazard warning
Optional: instrument cluster includes: clock, tachometer, ammeter and temp gauge $88

GENERAL

Curb weight, lb (test model) 4415
GVW (max. laden weight) 5555
Optional GVWs ....5200 to 5750

Wheelbase, in 116.0
Track, front/rear 61.5/60.7
Overall length 216.2
Overall height 54.0
Overall width 76.7
Overhang, front/rear 33/50

Approach angle, degrees 21
Departure angle 18

Ground clearances (test model):
Front axle 6.5
Rear axle 8.0
Oil pan 7.0
Fuel tank 12.2
Exhaust system (lowest point) 7.5

Fuel tank capacity (U.S. gal) 26
Auxiliary tank ....none

PERFORMANCE DATA

TEST MODEL

El Camino Classic, 454-cu-in. V-8, automatic transmission, bucket seats and console, tinted glass, air conditioning, power steering, power brakes, power windows, Conquista option, tilt steering wheel, AM/FM radio, HD radiator, HR70 x 15B tires, 2.73 rear axle, Positraction, power door locks, 2-tone paint, rally wheels
West Coast list price $5738

ACCELERATION

Time to speed, sec:
0-30 mph 3.7
0-45 mph 6.1
0-60 mph 9.2
0-70 mph 11.5
Standing start, ¼-mile, sec 16.5
Speed at end, mph 84

SPEED IN GEARS

High
3rd (3500 rpm) 100
2nd (4000 rpm) 81
1st (4000 rpm) 48

BRAKE TESTS

Pedal pressure required for ½-g deceleration rate from 60 mph, lb 32
Stopping distance from 60 mph, ft . 176.5
Fade: Percent increase in pedal pressure for 6 stops from 60 mph 56
Overall brake rating ....good

INTERIOR NOISE

Idle in neutral, dBA 53
Maximum during acceleration 74
At steady 70-mph cruising speed 73

OFF PAVEMENT

Hillclimbing ability .... fair
Maneuverability .... very good
Turnaround capability ....very good
Handling ....very good
Ride ....excellent

GENERAL

Heater rating ....excellent
Defroster effectiveness ....excellent
Wiper coverage .... very good

FUEL CONSUMPTION

Normal driving, mpg 10.8
Off pavement 8.4
Range, normal driving, miles 280
Range, off pavement 211

of fade in the six consecutive stops from 60 was not excessive in either vehicle. We were also pleased to note that both are among the quietest vehicles we have tested.

We were amazed, frankly, at how they both handled off the pavement. First of all, we were reluctant to even leave the asphalt with them as they look so much like cars, and a bit fragile at that. However, you can go off into the dirt and as long as you keep in mind the limited ground clearances, you can have a more pleasant time than you imagined. The ride, with the more sophisticated suspension systems and better wheel travel, is superior to any normal pickup, van or 4wd and bumps, dips and holes are taken with relative ease. Both do have a tendency to drag the tail a bit when climbing hills but then there is quite a bit of overhang at the rear.

Getting into other points that we noticed that are worthy of mention, the Ranchero seems to be easier to get in and out of although the El Camino is equipped with a swivel seat. However, in our opinion, the swivel mechanism is more trouble than it's worth. Both vehicles came with AM-FM stereo radios and one staff member commented that the one in the Ford Ranchero has a better sound than his component system at home. It was truly outstanding and everyone who drove or rode in the Ranchero noticed the quality of the stereo immediately. The interior appointments of both vehicles are in the superior class, with seemingly more attention to detail than in most PV4 vehicles. Both the Chevrolet and the Ford have room behind the seats for stowing smaller objects and the Ranchero has a compartment behind the driver's seat which extends a couple feet under the bed for putting things away. It is covered by a vinyl flap.

We found the quality of the handling to be high with both vehicles although the El Camino exhibited a bit more wallow in sudden maneuvers, probably because it was not equipped with the heavy-duty suspension components. Both vehicles are quite responsive and a lot of fun to drive.

All in all, we learned a good lesson from testing these two pickups. While they are not strictly trucks, they do have the capability for carrying cargo loads in the bed, especially camping gear and motorcycles and things like that. They are comfortable, responsive, well built and will get you there

The Ranchero can handle this type of off-pavement travel even with its limited ground clearance. Ride is very smooth.

quickly as long as "there" does not involve getting too far away from civilization. We like them both. We should mention that neither of them was economical with fuel although we were surprised that the Ranchero delivered better than 11 mpg with the 460 V-8 which is not that bad. But, as we said, we like them and we won't turn our noses up at them in the future. ●

The Chevrolet El Camino is one of the nicest vehicles we have tested in quite some time. While it may not fit the usual PV4 image, it does have the ability to carry a payload in the bed and can even be driven off the pavement with some care.

FORD RANCHERO SIX AUTOMATIC

The Ford Motor Company's six cylinder Ranchero adopts an automatic transmission option for 1975. This model, fitted with the 3-speed Cruise-O-Matic gearbox — similar to that of the Fairlane — joins the six-cylinder manual and the eight-cylinder Ranchero 500, and is the latest addition to the company's utility range.

As a utility vehicle, the Ranchero has acquitted itself well in many applications — be they light industrial, agriculture or leisure, Ford reports.

The Ranchero "6" range has a number of refinements and changes for 1975. It has a redesigned front end with a honey-combed grille and a new raking bonnet. The changes include a wrap-around front light cluster, which is now protected by an over-hanging bumper.

Inside, the safety steering column now incorporates a stalk control, allowing finger-tip operation for the horn, high and low beam lights and the direction indicators.

Like the manual version, the new unit is powered by a 4,1 litre engine with an output of 89 kW at 3 800 r/min, and torque of 293 N.m at 1 600 r/min.

The gear ratios for the automatic are as follows:

    1st: 2,393 to 1.
    2nd: 1,45 to 1.
    Top: 1,00 to 1.
    Reverse: 2,094 to 1.
    Rear Axle: 3,23 to 1.

In either the manual or automatic versions, the Ranchero "6" at full GVM, has a trailer mass of 1 200 kg — more than sufficient to tow most family caravans, the manufacturer claims. ●

RANCHERO

The new Ranchero has a new look. Stacked rectangular headlamps and a new grille design are the most noticeable in that department. The truck comes as a 500, Squire or GT. Each is basically equipped with a 302 V-8, except for good old California, which gets the 351. A 400 V-8 is available. The 500 can be ordered with two-tone paint, if that's your thing. The Squire, of course, has simulated wood sides, and the GT gets a tape stripe treatment.

ACCELERATION

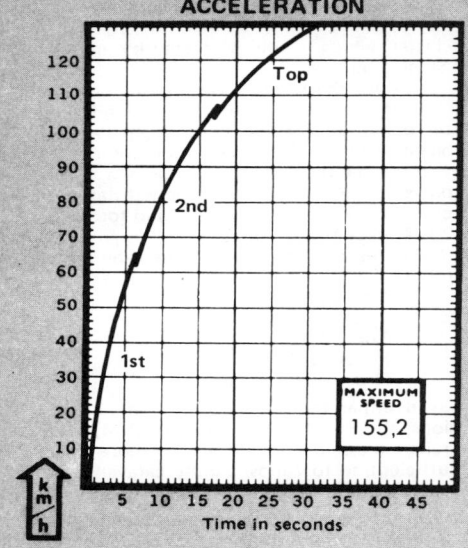

Top

2nd

1st

MAXIMUM SPEED
155,2

km/h — Time in seconds

BRAKING DISTANCES

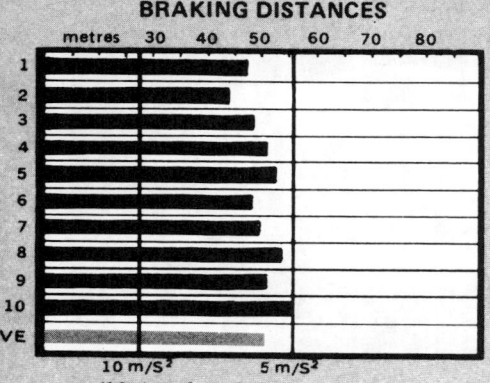

metres 30 40 50 60 70 80

10 m/S²   5 m/S²
(10 stops from 100 km/h)

ENGINE SPEED

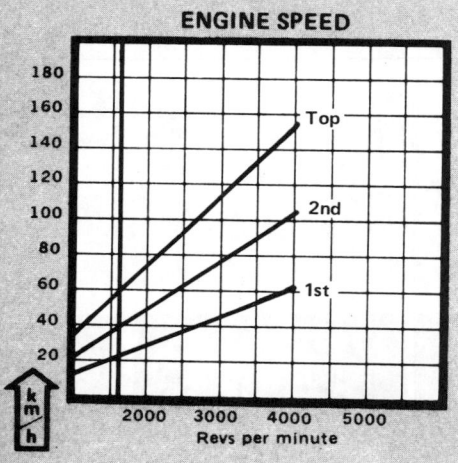

Top
2nd
1st

km/h

2000 3000 4000 5000
Revs per minute

GRADIENT ABILITY

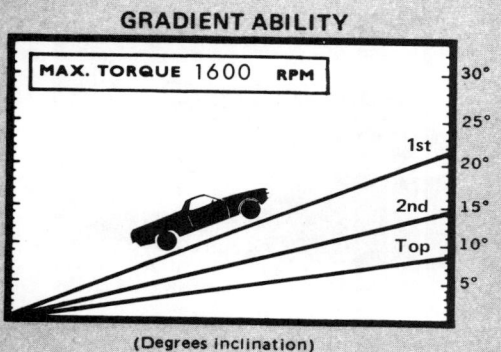

MAX. TORQUE 1600 RPM

30°
25°
1st
20°
2nd
15°
Top
10°
5°

(Degrees inclination)

PERFORMANCE

MAKE AND MODEL:
Make . . . . Ford
Model. Ranchero 6 Automatic (4100)

INTERIOR NOISE LEVELS:

	Mech	Wind	Road
Idling	.47,0	—	—
60	.67,5	—	—
80	.72,5	—	—
100	.77,0	81,0	83,0
Average dBA at 100			.80,3

ACCELERATION FROM REST:
0-60 5,2
0-80 8,7
0-100 14,0
400 m sprint 7,6
1 km sprint 35,3

CRUISING AT 80

Mech. noise level . . . . 72,5 dBA
0-80 through gears . . . . . 8,7 seconds
km/litre at 80 10,2
litres/100 km 9,8
Braking from 80 . . . . 3,0 seconds
Maximum gradient (top) . . . . 1 in 9,0
Speedometer error . . . . . 2,5% over
Speedo at true 80 . . . . .82 km/h
Engine r/min. (top) 2 105

OVERTAKING ACCELERATION:
(A/T)

40-60 2,5
60-80 3,4
80-100 5,3

MAXIMUM SPEED:
True speed 155,2
Speedo reading 155
Calibration:

Indicated:	60	80	100
True speed:	56	77	98

IMPERIAL DATA

Major performance features of this
Road Test are summarised below in
Imperial measures, for comparative pur-
poses:

ACCELERATION FROM REST
(seconds):
0-50: 8,9
0-60: 13,1
MAXIMUM SPEED (mph):
True speed 96,4
FUEL ECONOMY (mpg):
40 mph 34,0
50 mph 28,7
60 mph 24,4

GEARED SPEEDS: (km/h)
Low gear 63,6
2nd gear 105,0
Top gear 154,2
(Calculated at engine peak r/min.
– 4 000.)

FUEL CONSUMPTION (litres/100 km):
60 8,0
80 9,8
100 12,1

BRAKING TEST:
From 100 km/h:
First stop 3,8
Tenth stop 4,5
Average 4,03

GRADIENTS IN GEARS:
Low gear . . . . 1 in 2,7
2nd gear . . . . 1 in 4,0
Top gear . . . . 1 in 6,6
(Tabulated from Tapley (x gravity)
readings, car carrying test crew of two
and standard test equipment).

NOISE VALUES

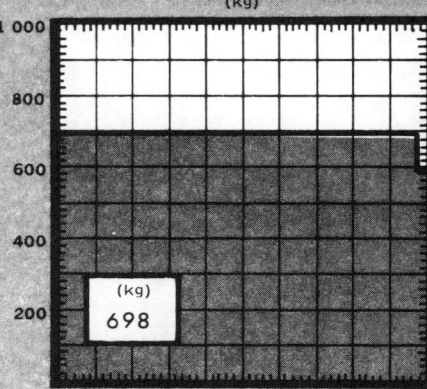

90
85
80
S.I.L. 75
70
65

dBA

MECH. WIND ROAD AVE.
(at 100 km/h)

LOAD CAPACITY
(kg)

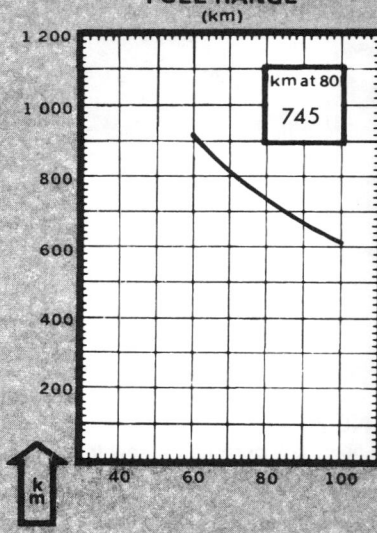

1 000
800
600
400
200

(kg)
698

FUEL RANGE
(km)

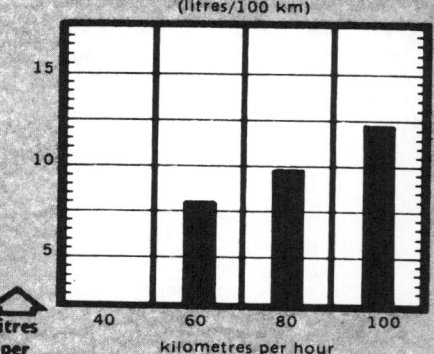

1 200
1 000
800
600
400
200

km at 80
745

km

40 60 80 100

FUEL CONSUMPTION
(litres/100 km)

15
10
5

litres per 100 km

40 60 80 100
kilometres per hour

FORD RANCHERO 4100 A/T

CAR test

The Ford Ranchero range in South Africa was expanded for the 1975 model year with the introduction of a six-cylinder Automatic, to join the six-cylinder manual and Ranchero V8 Automatic (500).

At the same time, all three models introduced some revision of styling and equipment: the flowing, aerodynamic lines introduced in 1973 have a new front end this year, with raked bonnet line and honeycomb grille, and wrap-round front indicators protected by bumper overhang.

At the interior, a stalk switch incorporates control of direction indicators, headlight dipping and hooter.

STRONG ON TORQUE

The long-stroke six-cylinder engine of 4,1 litres is developed from the earlier 3,6 litre unit by using a longer stroke, and while this limits engine range, it gives strong torque characteristics which are well suited to the utility-car role.

The big-six engine sounds a bit like a V8 — throaty and deliberate — and it gives a strong spread of performance capability. For instance, Ford rates the towing capacity of the Ranchero Six at 1 200 kg at full load (full GVM) — and we would estimate that there is abundant strength for caravan-towing.

For normal purposes, engine range is limited to about 4 000 r/min. (the full-throttle change points were exactly at this level on the test car) but the 3,23 final drive ratio ensures long-legged cruising ability, as well. (Overall gearing works out to 38,0 km/h per 1 000 revs in top)

BIG LOAD AREA

The Ranchero is derived from the Falcon XA range in Australia, and is the biggest Ranchero of them all — longer, wider and slightly lower than previous models. The cab looks rather small in relation to bonnet and load deck, but this is largely an optical illusion created by the high load body sides: the cab is actually more spacious than on earlier models.

The load area is bigger than before, as well, and the higher load body sides will be useful in many applications. This Ranchero also has a wider track, a lower loading sill, and the tailgate can now be dropped through a full 180 degrees.

KEY FIGURES

100 metres sprint	7,6 seconds
Terminal speed	74,0 km/h
1 km sprint	34,8 seconds
Terminal speed	142,5 km/h
Fuel tank capacity	73 litres
litres/100 km at 80	9,8
Fuel range at 80	745 km
litres/100 km at 90	10,8
Fuel range at 90	672
Engine revs per km	1 580
National list price	R3 925

It might have been a failing on the test car only, but we found the Ranchero 6 Automatic a somewhat reluctant cold starter — the engine tended to flood easily. But once running it was smooth and stall-free, and yielded very sound performance.

The Ranchero pulled away from rest quickly, but without developing wheelspin, to reach 60 km/h in 5,2 seconds — it is actually quicker off the mark than the manual-shift model (CAR Road Test, April 1973). It reaches 100 in 14 seconds — level with the manual-shift model — and goes on to a maximum-speed capability of 155 km/h — again, exactly on its geared peak of 4 000 revs. It is interesting that the speedometer becomes increasingly accurate as speed rises.

This big, smooth utility car is notably good on gradient ability, and will climb a 1-in-7 in top, for instance.

FUEL ECONOMY

This Automatic seemed to have been better-tuned than the manual-shift model used in the original test, and returned quite fair economy when driven at steady speeds: at 80 km/h it required 9,8 litres/100 km (a yield of just under 29 mpg) and this increased to 10,8 litres/100 km (26 mpg) at full statutory cruising speed of 90 km/h.

The XA model has always had a big 73-litre fuel tank — even before the fuel crisis — and it is capable of notching 600-700 km between refills in open-road running. (At 90, our test produced a theoretical range of 672 km).

BRAKING AND NOISE

This test car outbraked the one tested in 1973, by a fair margin — an average of nearly 0,6 seconds in stops from 100 km/h. The brakes took sharply, and in maximum-effort stops the front wheels locked before the rears when riding light, and the engine tended to stall.

Mechanical noise levels were very low — even during performance tests — but both wind and road noise were high enough to spoil the car's averages.

SUMMARY

The driver sits comparatively low and, with much high-bodied car round him, the Ranchero seems even bigger than it is. This effect is heightened by low-geared (but light) steering which needs five turns from lock to lock, and a big turning circle. But it is actually an easy-handling car, well-balanced, and pleasant to drive — particularly as an automatic. The suspension is well-rated, capable of taking the three-quarter-ton load well, yet not riding too harshly when light.

This smooth-lined new Ranchero really needs a glassfibre canopy to give it a "finished" look — to make it an attractive and serviceable all-rounder. ∎

Fascia has the downward-facing aspect peculiar to Australian Fords. (Seen here on the manual-shift model).

The load space measures 3,2 m², and the Ranchero is rated for a three-quarter-ton load.

The big-six engine has a deep, throbbing note and produces abundant power.

Guilt Complex:
RANCHERO GT
Ford's blend of temperature control, tape deck and brute horsepower...

PV4 TEST

It's not often that a **PICKUP, VAN & 4WD** test crewman experiences a twinge of guilt during an evaluation of a vehicle. However, it's not every day that staffers have the opportunity to test a vehicle as smooth, plush, comfortable and eye-appealing as the '77 Ford Ranchero GT.

A short stint behind the brushed aluminum, leather-trimmed steering wheel while seated on a downy-soft fabric Flight bench seat, gazing upon a luxurious Sports Instrument Panel that would do justice to a Learjet, will, indeed, cause pangs of guilt. The guilt feelings continue as the test crewman dials the automatic temperature controlled air conditioner to the perfect setting to maintain the just-pressed-look of his new leisure suit and inserts Olivia Newton-John's latest tape into the AM/FM stereo radio/tape deck.

The twitch is prolonged as the power windows are lowered slightly to expel the pungent aroma of the staffer's cheap cigar. A glance into the dual color-keyed racing mirrors alerts the driver that all is clear for a burst of brute horsepower from the 400-cu-in. V-8 housed in that long, sweeping hood, accented forward by four vertically-stacked, rectangular headlights. The rakish look of the dark brown GT side stripes is hardly discernible from the dark red basic body color as the Ranchero flashes by.

Wrestling the keys from the first crewman was about as easy as winning approval of an expense report without a luncheon receipt.

On a serious side for a moment, the Ranchero is not the answer for the hard-core off roader. However, in its basic form the Ranchero can be a valuable utility vehicle that will satisfy a segment of people that needs pickup truck capability, but wants passenger car comfort and handling. The degree of comfort and convenience is limited only by the buyer's bank account.

The basic Ranchero is designated the 500 and is by no means spartan. Standard equipment includes 302 V-8, automatic transmission, power steering and brakes, chromed front and rear energy absorbing bumpers, and interior carpeting. Base price of the 500 is $4618, FOB, Detroit.

Next in line is the Squire. This model features all the 500's equipment, plus vinyl-clad moldings and simulated wood grain paneling on the sides and tailgate, deluxe wheel covers, wood tone instrument panel, electric clock and black vinyl flaps which cover behind-seat stowage compartment. The Squire is priced at $4971.

Top of the line is the slick Ranchero GT. In addition to, or alternative to, features not included in the 500 package, the GT is assembled with paint/tape stripes for the body sides and tailgate, remote-control racing mirrors on each side, wheel trim rings with hubcaps and Flight bench seat with folding center armrest. Also included is an instrumentation group comprised of tachometer, trip odometer, electric clock, and oil, alternator and temperature gauges, plus "engine turned" cluster applique and deluxe steering wheel. The GT also includes the black vinyl flap for the stowage compartment. The spare tire is located in this area on all models. Price of the GT, at a list figure of $4984, is only slightly higher than that of the Squire. A quick price comparison indicates the Ranchero 500 to be about $200 less expensive than a comparably equipped F-100 pickup.

In addition to the equipment items listed previously, the test Ranchero GT was equipped with a convenience group, light group, protection group, tinted glass, cornering lamps, wheel lip moldings, Mag 500 wheels, locking rear differential, H70 x 14B raised white letter tires, and a trailer towing package that includes heavy-duty handling components, high capacity cooling system, wiring harness and 3.00:1 axle ratio. Price of the total package, as delivered on the West Coast, is $7049, which includes freight charges of $383.

It's worth relating that the handling package includes heavy-duty rear springs and rear stabilizer bar. The package increases payload capacity from 750 lb to 1250 lb.

A couple of items not found on the majority of light-duty trucks are an illuminated entry system and front cornering lamps. The added illumination system makes nighttime entry to the vehicle easier by lighting the outside door lock and vehicle interior when the outside door handle is pulled up. Both the interior light and door lock light remain switched on for approximately 20 sec, then automatically switch off. This affords ample time to insert the key in the door lock, open the door, buckle up and start the vehicle before the lights go off automatically.

The front cornering lamps are not only great for city driving, but also are of service while off-roading at night. The large side lamps are designed to illuminate the side of the road into which a turn is being made. The cornering lamps are activated by the regular turn signal lever. Test crewmen found the lights to be valuable during the off-pavement portion of the vehicle evaluation. At night, the lamps could be turned on to help chart the way through boulders and debris during slow crawling maneuvers.

The Ranchero features coil springs, front and rear. The front coils are mounted on long lower A-arms and attached by upper mounting brackets to the frame. The upper A-arms are shorter than the lower arms to control scrubbing contact with the road surface. Drag struts are attached to the lower arms and anchored with rubber bushings to the frame. A front stabilizer bar is also utilized.

The rear suspension system is made up of four longitudinal arms which control the position of the axle assembly and absorb braking and acceleration forces. An optional heavy-duty handling/suspension package with rear stabilizer bar and heavy-duty springs also is available.

Ford uses a unique method to arrive at a GVWR (Gross Vehicle Weight Rating) for the Ranchero. The Ford truck data book lists the maximum GVWR for a Ranchero at 5759 lb. However, the test Ranchero carried a GVWR of 6061 lb, which could actually qualify this particular vehicle for heavy-duty, rather than light-duty, exhaust emission standards. On pickup trucks, such as the F-100, Ford sets a maximum GVWR of, say, 5650 lb. If the curb weight of the vehicle happens to be 4650 lb, then the payload for that vehicle is 1000 lb. However, if the vehicle weighs 5000 lb instead of 4650, because of added equipment, then the payload is reduced to 650 lb.

The Ranchero GVWR is computed differently. With the heavy-duty handling suspension package, the rated payload is 1250 lb. The payload remains 1250 lb, regardless of whether the Ranchero is a bare bones model or loaded with heavy optional equipment, such as air conditioning, large V-8, etc. The test Ranchero was fully loaded,

RANCHERO

which necessitated a GVWR of 6061 lb to accommodate a payload of 1250 lb. Got that?

Another unusual aspect of the Ranchero is engine availability. The 302 V-8 is standard, with 351 V-8s as options. There's nothing unusual about that—except that two 351 V-8s are being offered. One is the 351W. This, basically, is the engine that is being used in Ford vans. The other engine is the 351M, similar to the one used in Ford's pickup line. Confusing the issue is the fact that a prospective buyer is not able to specify which 351 he would rather purchase. He pays his money but he gets no choice. The vehicle might be delivered with either 351 V-8.

There's a slight difference in horsepower ratings for the two 351s. The 351W is rated at 149 hp at 3200 rpm, whereas the 351M delivers 161 hp at a higher 3600 rpm. However, because of a higher compression ratio (8.3 for the 351W, 8.0 for the 351M) the 351W offers greater torque at a lower engine rpm—291 lb-ft at 1600 rpm as compared with 285 lb-ft at 1800 for the 351M.

Two axle ratios are offered, 2.50:1 and 3.00:1. Traction-Lok can be specified only with the 3.00:1 ratio. However, residents of California cannot order the 3.00 ratio—which means no locking differential for those folk.

The Ranchero is a pleasure to drive, either in heavy city traffic or in freeway commuting. There's plenty of leg and headroom, and the steering wheel is positioned at a comfortable angle to body and arms. Visibility is good, although the hood is quite long. Caution should be exercised when pulling the Ranchero into a parking spot. The front bumper extends a considerable distance forward of the grille because of the energy absorbing feature. It's very easy to misjudge the clearance between the bumper and a parked car in front. Test crewmen used the energy absorbing feature several times before finally becoming accustomed to the extended bumper.

The Ranchero GT's ride can be classified as "firm" on asphalt because of the stiffness of the heavy-duty handling package. Off pavement, the ride was comfortable—very acceptable altogether. Limited wheel travel resulted in the Ranchero bottoming-out on the rougher sections, but the effect was not objectionable. Of critical concern, however, was the limited ground clearance, both at the differential and at certain body areas. Front and rear overhang distances are almost a complete deterrent to any sort of enthusiastic off-road travel, especially so because the vehicle is so low-slung. Extreme care was required to avoid bashing an undercarriage component on an oversize boulder. In dropping down an incline or climbing a small rise, the front or rear bumper would almost always drag because of the Ranchero's extreme overhang dimensions.

Discounting the clearance problems, the Ranchero is an excellent off-roader. The vehicle can be run at speed while delivering excellent handling characteristics. The rear end not once skated out of shape, even on soft sandy berms while negotiating sweeping turns. The locking differential and abundant horsepower of the 400 V-8 simply powered the Ranchero in a slight drift with minimal steering wheel corrections. There's all this—and comfort, too.

Performance at the raceway was very respectable. The Ranchero accelerated from zero to 60 mph in just over 10 sec, with a standing-start quarter-mile time of 18 sec flat at 78 mph.

The Ranchero's overall brake rating was excellent. The vehicle was brought to an arrow-straight stop from 60 mph with no wheel lockup, in only 152 ft. This is especially impressive because the cargo box was empty.

Fuel economy was reasonable, considering the large displacement engine. As monitored with electronic fuel flow equipment, the Ranchero delivered an acceptable 14.7 mpg in the city/freeway driving cycle.

As a family car, occasional utility vehicle or bike hauler, the Ranchero is a highly capable vehicle. As a serious off-roader, it displays several shortcomings, notably minimal ground clearance and wheel travel. In the coming weeks, test crewmen will be working in conjunction with long-time off-roader Bill Stroppe to modify the Ranchero by raising the body a few inches and fitting new shock absorbers, wheels and tires, plus other off-pavement accessory equipment.

The intent is not to build an off-road racer, but is rather to make the Ranchero less susceptible to off-road hazards. Coverage of this exciting project will appear in these pages—soon. ●

Rectangular headlights, cornering lamps, mark GT's front design. GT instrument package includes engine-turned panel.

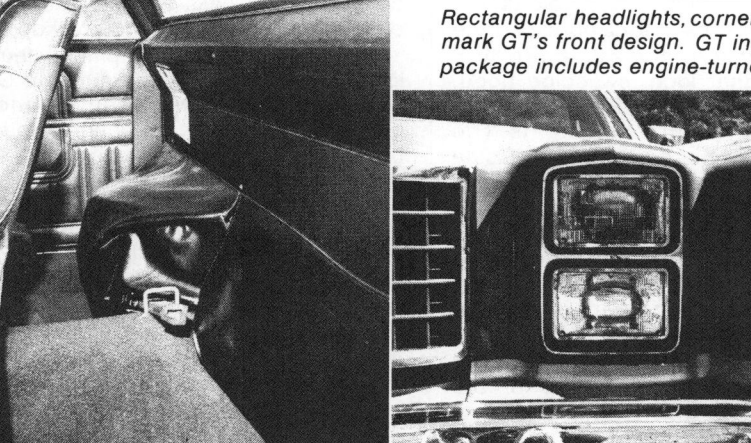

Vinyl flap covers spare, tools, right. Flight bench, below, is easy on the Ranchero driver's body.

FORD RANCHERO
SPECIFICATIONS AND PERFORMANCE

PRICES
Basic list, FOB Detroit
Ranchero 500 ....$4618
Ranchero Squire $4971
Ranchero GT $4984

Standard Equipment...............302-cu-in. V-8 engine, automatic transmission, chrome front and rear energy absorbing bumpers, power steering, power front disc brakes, 2-spd electric wiper/washers, heater/defroster, carpeting, driver remote control mirror, four cargo tie-downs, G78 x 14B tires

GENERAL
Curb weight, lb (test model)...................4215
Weight distribution, %, front/rear 58/42
GVWR (test model)............................6061
Optional GVWRs.....................5220, 5759

Wheelbase, in. 118.0
Track, front/rear 63.6/63.5
Overall length....................................220.1
Overall height...................................53.5
Overall width....................................79.6
Overhang, front/rear.....................47.6/54.5

Approach angle, degrees......................14
Departure angle, degrees......................15

Ground clearances (test model):
Front axle 6.8
Rear axle 7.0
Oil pan 7.9
Fuel tank 15.8
Exhaust system (lowest point)............7.5

Fuel tank capacity (U.S. gal.).....................26
Auxiliary ....none

ACCOMMODATION
Standard seats ....full-width bench
Optional seats ....full-width Flight bench, $24; bucket seats, $83; Brougham split bench (includes door trim and carpeting), $187
Headroom, in. 32.3
Accelerator pedal to seatback, max.........44.7
Steering wheel to seatback, max..........17.2
Seat to ground 23.8
Floor to ground 11.3

Unobstructed load space (length x width x height) ....78.4 x 48.9 x 16.0
Tailgate (width x height)..............53.4 x 16.0

INSTRUMENTATION
Instruments ....speedometer, odometer, fuel gauge
Warning lights.............oil pressure, alternator, water temp, brake system warning, hazard warning
Optional.....................Sports instrumentation cluster (includes tachometer, ammeter, oil pressure gauge, clock, trip odometer, luxury steering wheel), $130

ENGINES
Standard 302-cu-in. V-8
Bore x stroke, in...................4.00 x 3.00
Compression ratio 8.4:1
Net horsepower @ rpm ....130 @ 3400
Net torque @ rpm, lb-ft ....243 @ 1800
Type fuel required ....unleaded

Optional 351-cu-in. V-8, $93
Bore x stroke, in...................4.00 x 3.50
Compression ratio 8.3:1
Net horsepower @ rpm ....149 @ 3200*
Net torque @ rpm, lb-ft ....291 @ 1600*
Type fuel required ....unleaded
*Rating listed is for 351W engine. See text for rating of 351M engine which is also available.

Optional 400-cu-in. V-8, $156
Bore x stroke, in...................4.00 x 4.00
Compression ratio 8.0:1

Net horsepower @ rpm ....173 @ 3800
Net torque @ rpm, lb-ft ....326 @ 1600
Type fuel required ....unleaded

DRIVETRAIN
Standard transmission ....3-spd automatic
Transmission ratios: 3rd 1.00:1
2nd 1.46:1
1st 2.46:1

Optional ....none

Rear axle type ....semi-floating hypoid
Final drive ratios 2.50:1, 3.00
Overdrive...none
Limited slip differential $54*
*Available only with 3.00:1 ratio. Not available in Calif.

CHASSIS & BODY
Body/frame ....ladder-type frame with separate steel body
Brakes (std)................front, 10.7-in. dia. disc; rear, 11 x 2.25-in. drum
Brake swept area, sq in. 368
Swept area/ton (max load)....................139
Power brakes ....std
Steering type (std) ....recirculating ball
Power steering ....std
Power steering ratio 21.9:1
Turning circle, ft.................................43.0
Wheel size (std) ....14 x 5.5JJ
Optional wheel sizes ....14 x 6JJ, 14 x 7
Tire size (std)......................G78 x 14B
Optional tire sizes..........................H78 x 14B, G70 x 14B, H70 x 14B, HR78 x 14B

SUSPENSION
Front suspension............independent A-arms (short upper arm, longer lower arm) with drag struts, coil springs, front stabilizer bar and tube shocks
Front axle capacity, lb 2875
Optional..none
Rear suspension ....coil spring on live axle with four longitudinal control arms and tube shocks
Rear axle capacity, lb 2850
Optional..none

Additional suspension options ....handling suspension package (includes heavy-duty rear springs and rear stabilizer bar), $33

TEST MODEL
Ranchero GT, 400-cu-in. engine, automatic

transmission, convenience group, light group, protection group, trailer tow package, automatic air conditioner, tinted glass, cornering lamps, wheel lip moldings, AM/FM stereo tape radio, sport steering wheel, power windows, power steering and brakes, mag 500 wheels, 3.00:1 locking rear axle, H70 x 14B tires
West Coast list price ....(includes $383 freight) $7049

ACCELERATION
Time to speed, sec:
0-30 mph 3.9
0-45 mph 6.8
0-60 mph 10.7
0-70 mph 14.5
Standing start, ¼-mile, sec...............18.0
Speed at end, mph 78

SPEED IN GEARS
High range, 3rd (3700 rpm) 94
2nd (4000 rpm) 72
1st (4000 rpm) 43
Engine rpm @ 55 mph 2150

BRAKE TESTS
Pedal pressure required for ½-g deceleration rate from 60 mph, lb 29
Stopping distance from 60 mph, ft 152
Fade: Percent increase in pedal pressure for 6 stops from 60 mph 100
Overall brake rating ....excellent

INTERIOR NOISE
Idle in neutral, dbA 47.5
Maximum during acceleration 72.0
At steady 60 mph cruising speed............69.5

OFF PAVEMENT
Hillclimbing ability ....fair
Maneuverability ....excellent
Turnaround capability ....very good
Driver visibility ....fair
Handling ....very good
Ride...very good

ON PAVEMENT
Handling ....excellent
Ride ....excellent
Driver comfort ....excellent
Engine response ....excellent

FUEL CONSUMPTION
City/freeway driving, mpg 14.7
Off pavement 10.3
Range, city/freeway driving, miles...........382
Range, off pavement................................268

RITZY RANCHERO

IT WOULD TAKE A LONG, HARD HUNT TO FIND A RANCHO THAT EQUALS THIS

The basic concept behind the Ford Ranchero is the combination of a nice looking, smooth riding vehicle with the convenience and practicality of a pickup truck. The Ranchero provides that compromise by integrating good looks, a comfortable ride and plenty of room.

But, try as they may, the factory design people cannot seem to satisfy everyone as far as styling is concerned. One of the first things to do when improving a car's original appearance is to remove all excess chrome. As evidenced by Ron Hunt's 1972 Ranchero, the removal of the chrome trim simplifies the basic body lines.

Another change that helps individualize the styling of a truck is the paint job, and the paint on this truck is a tribute to the applier's ability. The two-tone pearl yellows, blended with orange from the bottom up, along with two shades of candy blue along the bottom, draw admiring looks from anyone within view.

The clean and simple appearance of the truck is enhanced by four Fenton aluminum wheels and blackwall Pro-Trac tires. Inside the cab of the Ranchero is a completely redone interior by Tooter and Frank Weaver, Mesa, Arizona. Utilizing orange cloth and brown vinyl, the carpets, headliner, seats, dash and door panels have been transformed into something unique, setting it apart from the run-of-the-mill Ranchero.

A beautiful truck like this would cost a lot of money to put together if much of the work were not done by the owner. If a friend can be sold on the relative merits of the project, so much the better. In the case of this Rancho, owner Ron persuaded Squeege Jerger to help with everything except the interior, and he saved additional dollars by doing the paint job himself rather than sending it to a custom shop. Of course the fact that Ron is a custom painter by profession could have had something to do with his decision.

A well executed custom vehicle is a joy to behold. Whether a '29 Ford or a '72, the time and effort spent making it look right is always well worthwhile. In this particular case, most of us would be happy to spend twice the time to achieve half the joy this Ranchero must have brought its owner. ●

1. The overall styling of Ron's Ranchero is greatly enhanced by basic dechroming and the blended yellow and orange paint scheme. Grille is blacked out.

2. If this view doesn't make your heart beat faster, nothing will. Orange pearl panels, black rocker panel stripes and the Fenton/Pro-Trac combo is pure class.

3. Although the dash is your basic Ford, the upholstery is all new, emphasizing the exterior and adding much class.

4. One of several tasteful custom touches is the sunken and molded electric antenna mounted on the Ranchero's front fender.

5. Custom stitched door panels show the tasteful combination of brilliant orange fabric and rich, heavy-grain brown Naugahyde.

Coils and Shocks:

OFF~ROAD RANCHERO

Preparing a personal pickup for improved performance in the outback . . .

BY DON E. BROWN

FORD RANCHEROS, and Chevy El Caminos, are not noted for being highly effective vehicles for rough off-roading. As delivered from the factory, the "personal" pickups from Ford and Chevy are softly sprung, sit low to the ground and handle as well on pavement as many so-called luxury cars. Indeed, as reported earlier in this magazine, a Ranchero with all the convenience and comfort options is a luxury vehicle in every sense of the word (PV4, May, '77).

Of course, the Ranchero is car-like because it shares body and chassis components with the Ford LTD II 4-door passenger car. As pointed out in the Ranchero test report, the luxury pickup was not only a pavement runner of the first water, but turned in a creditable performance off pavement, considering the limited ground clearance of body and chassis components. A run through a rock-strewn stretch of California desert produced a bent front license plate, a scraped engine crossmember and a tweaked rear bumper. The rear bumper actually was warped while the Ranchero was heading down a steep sand dune. The vehicle's extreme rear overhang caused the rear bumper to dig-in and pull several yards of sand ahead of it as the Ranchero's front wheels reached level terrain.

The obvious cure for the Ranchero's shortcomings for rough-terrain off-roading was to raise the body, which in turn allowed fitting taller tires and wheels.

The problem was discussed with Bill Stroppe and Son of Long Beach, Calif. The Ranchero could have been modified with extensive front end rebuilding and major body surgery. However, the project required that all modifications be kept as simple as possible so that readers who wish to improve the off-roading capabilities of their own Ford Rancheros can do so.

A search through parts catalogs indicated that the front springs on a Lincoln Continental could probably be substituted for the stock Ranchero coils. The Lincoln coils are slightly taller, with a stiffer spring rate, but are of the same outside diameter as the stock coils.

Fitting of the Lincoln springs (Part No. D6AZ5310F) simply meant removal of the stock coils and bolting in the new units. In stock configuration, the Ranchero sat low at the front. Installation of the Lincoln springs brought the Ranchero to a level attitude when viewed from the side.

The next step, of course, was to fit the heavy-duty shock absorbers. A check with Monroe brought the suggestion that a set of the company's new Handler series shocks would be correct for street use as well as for heavy off-roading. On arrival, the front shocks (Part No. HP-4854) were discovered to be too short to allow full travel of the front suspension because of the taller front coil springs. Another check with Monroe engineers brought the sad news that the firm's inventory didn't contain shocks of proper length with end fittings to match Ranchero mounting brackets. However, to avoid use of shock extenders, the Monroe folk supplied two front shocks with extended shafts of the correct length required. The rear Monroe Handlers (Part No. HP-4967) were an exactly perfect fit.

Raising the front suspension altered factory camber settings slightly and, while the test Ranchero's handling characteristics remained excellent without realignment, it is recommended that the vehicle be set to factory specs following any front suspension modifications.

The taller springs raised the Ranchero's body sufficiently to allow fitting of larger tires and wheels. The original stock tires, as tested, were H70 x 14s, rather short for adequate chassis ground clearance.

Starting with a 10 x 15 tire to check for front wheelwell clearance, it was determined that the 10 x 15 could not be used without major trimming of the rear portion of the fenderwell. The 10 x 15s would be acceptable for street running with only

minor cutting, but for heavy-duty off-roading, more than a mere slice with a hacksaw would be required.

A set of L60 x 15 Formula I Super Stock tires had recently arrived at the editorial office for a future tire test. The L60s were mounted on four new Emco Wildcat aluminum alloy mag-style wheels. The combination of the wide, raised white letter Super Stocks and the finned aluminum Wildcat wheels presented an outstanding custom appearance. Mounting the wheels on the Ranchero showed no tire-to-fenderwell contact with the vehicle in the static position. However, turning the steering wheel lock-to-lock indicated it would be necessary to trim the rear portion of the front wheelwell to prevent tire contact in rough terrain. This was accomplished in under five minutes with a hacksaw, and would require very close inspection to reveal that the fenderwell had been trimmed.

A roll bar was scheduled to be installed for reasons of safety and cosmetics. The thought was to make the Ranchero more off-roadable, and to look the part as well. A quick check revealed that roll bars for late-model Rancheros (especially '77s) were as scarce as hen's teeth. Several phone

Right, specially built roll bar bolts through cargo deck and bed's inner wall. Below, Ranchero heads off-road.

PHOTOS BY DON E. BROWN AND GLENN HAMAGUCHI

RANCHERO

Stock, the Ford Ranchero's pronounced front and rear overhang dimensions prevent any sort of off-pavement activity. Fitting of new front coils and shocks all-around enabled the vehicle to go off road.

calls later, Tom Smith at Smittybilt agreed to custom build a roll bar for the Ranchero. Because of the limited demand for Ranchero roll bars and the unique installation procedure required, Smittybilt does not plan to offer a kit for this vehicle. Any roll bar shop can custom fabricate a bar in fairly short order. Smittybilt tied the roll bar into the cargo bed floor and plated

Photo left, Ranchero fenderwell top height stock is 28.25 in. Photo right shows 31-in. height after installation of springs, shocks, wheels and L60 x 15 tires.

Front shocks, top, had to be specially fabricated by Monroe. Rear shocks, above, were off-the-shelf equipment.

it on the underside in the spare tire cavity inside the cab. The bar was also bolted to the side of the cargo box at the front.

Light tabs were welded to the top bar to accommodate a pair of KC Hi-Lite quartz halogen lights.

The tendency here would be to not stop now, but to add other components and make additional modifications. However, as was stated in the original Ranchero test, "The intent is not to build an off-road racer, but is rather to make the Ranchero less susceptible to off-road hazards." With the modifications performed, that goal has been achieved.

Putting a tape to the Ranchero tells the story. Measurements taken before the project was started were: front bumper height, 13.5 in.; front wheelwell at tire centerline, 28.1 in.; rear wheelwell, 29.5 in.; and rear bumper, 15.0 in. Modifications resulted in height increases in the first three measurements and a decrease in the last one. The front bumper was now 17.3 in.; front wheelwell, 31.5 in.; rear wheelwell, 30.2 in.; and the rear bumper dropping to 14.2 in. The drop at the rear resulted from significantly raising the front. The rear differential ground clearance, stock, was 7 in. and 7.5 in. after modification.

The modified Ranchero's ride is firm when compared with the stock ride. Driving on city streets was not that much different from stock. However, traversing drainage dips and encountering expansion strips on concrete freeways resulted in a

noticeable increase in spring rate. The ride on pavement must be considered a little harsh, but only when compared to the stock Ranchero. A fair comparison would be to equate the modified Ranchero's ride to that of a heavy-duty 1/2-ton pickup.

Stability, both on and off the pavement, improved perceptively. A level roll attitude was retained easily in sweeping turns, no matter the speed. The Monroe Handlers effectively snubbed wheel rebounds from pavement irregularities, resulting in a firm but acceptable ride.

The Ranchero was taken to a remote mountain area for off-pavement evaluation. Here the terrain varies from smooth fire roads to erosion-rutted forest roads to rocky side trails. The fire roads were duck soup for the Ranchero. Winding roads were handled by simply applying more throttle and powering through the turns. The Formula Super Stocks are certainly more at home on asphalt than they are in the outback. The tread is very wide, putting a great deal of rubber to the ground. However, the finely grooved street tread breaks traction any time the throttle is pressed aggressively. Of course, the Super Stocks were not designed for serious off-roading. The tires will be mounted on another vehicle and tested in the environment for which they were intended.

Driving the Ranchero slowly in rough terrain produced a lot of pitching and lurching. But increasing the speed produced a much more acceptable ride. In

stock form, the Ranchero would have bottomed-out and dragged its undercarriage. Not once in the off-road portion of the test did the Ranchero bottom-out or scrape its underside. The front suspension did top-out against the rubber snubbers a couple of times when the front wheels bounced off the ground—nothing to be concerned about in everyday off-roading.

Smaller rocks could now be straddled without fear of leaving the front crossmember attached permanently to a hunk of granite. Previously it had been necessary to drive around rocks of any size.

Reworking the Ranchero's front suspension gives the already excellent vehicle another dimension, that of an effective off-pavement runner. The Ranchero still is not a Bronco, but with these simple modifications a personal pickup owner can go a little farther into the outback, drive a little harder, make it back to pavement and ride in comfort on the way home. However, the owner shouldn't attempt to climb hills or drive down steep slopes. The Ranchero's approach and departure angles just won't allow these maneuvers. But then, few vehicles are perfect. ●

FORDS

To Stay No. 1 in Trucks, Ford Is Offering Sporty Packages and New Powertrain Combinations

Quick! What's the best-selling vehicle in America? A truck, you say? That's right. Ford's F-series pickups, which range in size from 117-in. wheelbase and a GVWR of 4800 lbs., on up to 155-ins. and 8500 lbs. There are four sizes; the other two are 113-ins. and 139 ins., with GVWRs starting, respectively, at 4800 and 5200 lbs. This great variety is probably what contributes to its popularity.

New for '79 are rectangular headlights, "sporty options" (tapes, stripes, paint, blackout treatments), a tilt steering wheel with 4-speed manual, a super-cooling package for all engines, a catalytic converter for all trucks rated under 8500 lbs. and a pickup-box cover.

Four-wheel-drive has been added to the F-350 (the largest pickup, now making that available on all but the smallest (F-100) model. Engines include the 300-cid six and 351-cid V8 as standard, 302-cid V8, 400-cid 2V V8 and 460-cid 4V V8 optional.

RANCHERO

Not a truck, not a car, but a combination of a pickup with its utility and the comfort, luxury and styling of a passenger car, the Ranchero is available in 3 models. Each is on a 118-in. wheelbase (the LTD II chassis) and has various stages of trim and seats (all bench).

The pickup box is large enough to carry a 4x8 ft. sheet of plywood (the industry's standard for wagons for many years). Not being a truck, it has no GVWR, but weighs 3901 lbs.

Selling only about one-half as many Rancheros as Chevy does El Camino in a small market (about 75,000 total), it's unlikely Ford will continue this model after it retools its LTD II for 1980. Might be a good investment.

CONTINUED FROM PAGE 49

ting, '66 T-Bird unit got the nod (Part No. C6SW 4200-H). Right now you are probably asking yourselves why, out of all the possible heavy-duty-cum-high-performance choices a person might have in the FoMoCo parts box, a relatively plush bucket like the 'Bird might have the hot tip on rear ends. Well, to begin with, the T-Bird is a nice heavy machine, so it gets a nice heavy axle. OK? Then, as a bonus, it has those ultra-hard, 31-spline axles that they use in competition, not to mention a 9⅜-inch ring gear (biggest in the Ford passenger line) and an Equal-Loc limited slip. You better believe this Skelton guy is all business when it comes to knowing the parts book.

Alright. When Ed put the rear end in he'd already relocated the heavy-duty leaf springs 1-inch behind stock position because the truck could use a little more wheelbase for ride and besides, this way the wheels would be centered in the well. A set of Air-Lifts in conjunction with Monroe 500 shocks finished off the area nicely. (Springing in front is by a set of 1980-pound coils). Bridging the gap between the transmission and the rear axle is a stock, uncut, unrebalanced 390 Fairlane station wagon driveshaft (Part No. C60Z 4602-S) that just happened to fit.

With all this power pounding the bricks, and with a trailer to worry about, Ed thought it was time for a little upgraded anchor action. There's no argument that the giant economy-sized, finned T-Bird drums would do their share on the rear but up front, something that offered a mite more security was in order. Well, what about trying a set of Mustang factory funny car discs that have identical bearing area to the Falcon and will bolt on? Fine and dandy.

There were a few more items like a stereo tape that fits sleekly into the dash instead of being hung on underneath, Fairlane wagon blinkers, and a couple gallons of Night Mist Blue paint. The critical thing chassis-wise though, is that Ed Skelton had what amounted to a 427-street Fairlane months before the factory announced theirs (reported on in our July issue). Doubtless the people in Dearborn had a prototype along these lines a while back too, but when you're a Ford fan you can't always wait for the next model run.

Style-wise the quality of Ed's creation is belied by the fact the casual observer thinks the thing is the genuine article. Further, our agents in Detroit say that the '67 Ranchero may look nearly identical to the truck on these pages. Should this be true, Ed Skelton will have had the unique distinction of owning an ultra hot luxury version of next year's model before the factory built it. ■ ■

ALL-NEW RANCHERO BY FORD

Long, low, lively luxury!

Not just new. But completely, excitingly, *all-over* new! That's the '68 Ranchero, Ford's better idea in pickup luxury. The look is longer, lower, leaner! Inside you can have every luxury, every option you could ask: color-coordinated styling, crush-grained vinyl trim, bucket seats, full carpeting, AM/FM stereo radio, SelectAire conditioning. And Ranchero has the go to go with it! Six or V-8 power up to 325 lively horses. 3- or 4-speed manual transmission. Or SelectShift Cruise-O-Matic that operates manually or automatically. Three spirited models, including a racy new GT. At your Ford Dealer's.

FORD ...has a better idea.

Meanwhile,

back at the Ranchero...

**Mike Preston's
'57 Ford Ranchero custom
is not your regular sled but the story
of its building is a classic hot rod tale.**
Words and pictures by Dave Fetherston.

Mike Preston went through the custom builder's handbook and ticked off tuck 'n' roll upholstery, Appleton spots, foot-shaped gas pedal, pool ball shifter...

Flying pumpkin? Glovebox cartoon by Ralph Finney mixes the influences of hot rodding's two greatest pinstripers, Roth and Von Dutch.

The original Y-block 312ci motor has been dressed up with period gear including a rare Edelbrock six-pack manifold with Holley two-barrel carbs.

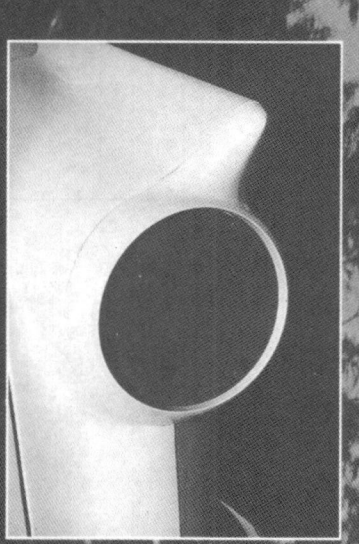

The fins and taillight surrounds are trimless and smoothed out and the taillight lenses replaced with smooth, Lexan items.

'y dad had one of those,' said Mike to his friend on spying a '57 Ranchero trundling about his neighbourhood street. 'I should buy it,' he joked and they both laughed.

Three months later Mike was standing in his driveway assessing the condition of his new toy. For the last 17 years of its life the truck had been in the same family and was in pretty good shape. 'I'll just give it a tidy-up,' thought Mike.

Going down

Mike dug the rust out and blew some primer over the fresh metal, then he chopped the coils 1¼in at the front and slung 3in lowering blocks under the back axle. Apparently, the truck's previous owner was not overly impressed when he saw it running about dropped and primered. 'It'll be great when I'm done,' explained Mike.

The Ranchero had come with a number of spare parts which included a pair of fender skirts which had never been on a car. Mike fitted these up and started thinking about adding further custom touches. For reference, he delved into *How To Customise Cars and Rods* by George Barris and Wayne

The Ranchero rolls on 14in chrome reverse steels shod with 205/70R14 whitewall radials.

Thoms where he discovered '56 Ford pick-up headlamp trims would go onto his '57 and give the appearance of frenched headlamps.

Mike continued the trad tricks theme with a tube grille at the front and smooth, Lexan taillight lenses at the rear.

Cosmetic surgery

Although Mike loaded his Ranchero with traditional custom features (Lake pipes, Appleton spots, chrome reverse steels, tuck 'n' roll) he was conservative with the body modifications. Tom O'Connell at Bensen's Body Shop in Vallejo, California, cherried the sheet metal and shaved off the door handles and smaller trim pieces. Tom also applied the Persimmon Orange and Wimbledon White and Mike added the pinstripes on the hood and the tailgate.

Mike retained the original drivetrain comprising a 312ci Y-block Ford mill and two-speed Ford-O-Matic slushbox. Everything was freshened up with a rebuild and the big-block dressed with a pair of Offenhauser finned rocker covers and an Edelbrock six-pack manifold topped with three 200cfm Holley two-barrel carbs.

There's something kinda sneaky about Mike's Ranchero. We're not quite sure what it is but we suspect that it's something to do with the fact Mike has created a lovely and instantly recognisable custom without getting into the complex business of chopping roofs or pancaking hoods. ●

The pick-up bed sports an upholstered hard tonneau and the rear window a Von Dutch flying eyeball.

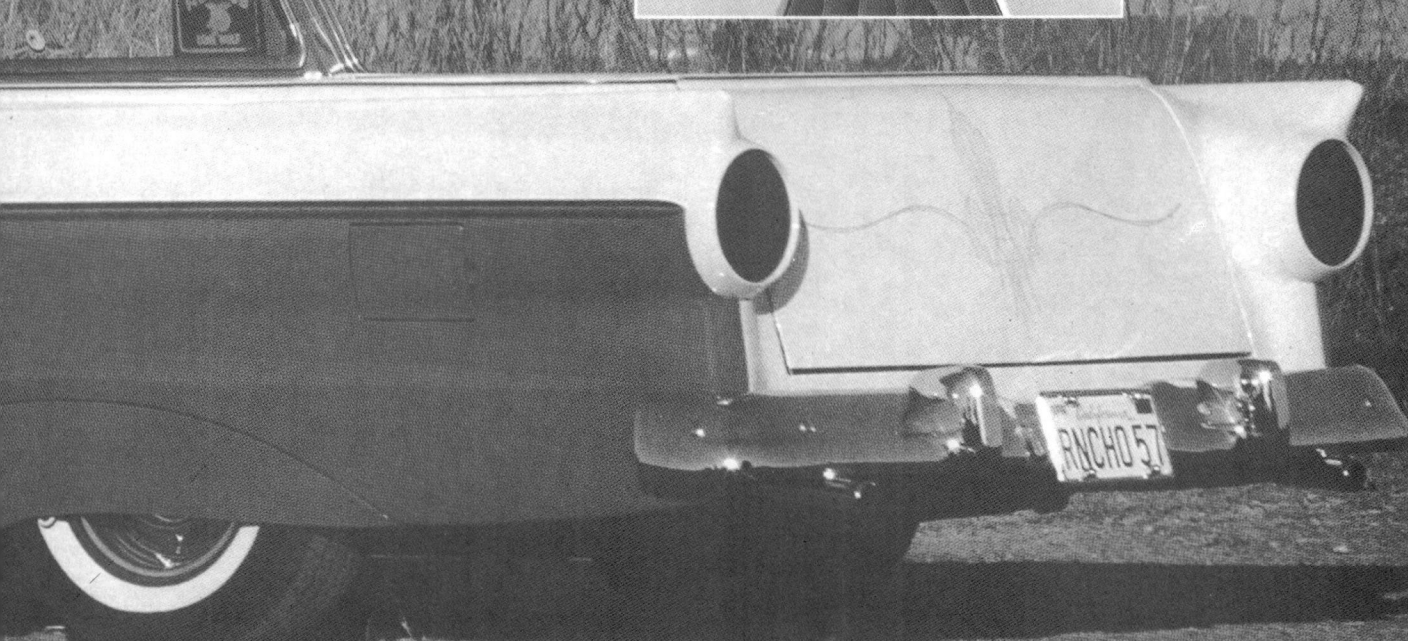

TANGERINE (& White) DREAM

Bo Bertilsson falls head over heels for a '57 Ranchero pickup that's mildly custom but heavy on rock 'n roll

Mike Preston lives in Vallejo, California, and after seeing this '57 Ford Ranchero sitting outside one of his neighbours' houses for sometime, he decided to try and buy it. Just as you or I would. The car (or truck, if you prefer …) was in a pretty good and stock shape, but needed to be restored. It was still worth at least the $2500 he paid for it, and he could even drive it home. Mike had dreamed about having a '50s style cruiser for a long time, and *this* was going to be it.

He started to look things over, and found that the motor and trans didn't have many miles on it, so the stock 312in Y-block motor and the Fordomatic transmission were left alone for now. A cruiser has to 'sit right', so the front suspension was taken apart and the front coils cut 11/8 coil, and *everything* was cleaned and painted. While the front end was apart he also took a look at the front brakes, and got that handled. The 9-inch rear end is stock with 3.56:1 gears, and with the help of a set of 3- inch lowering blocks, the cruiser was now 'sittin' pretty' in the rear too.

When Mike told his neighbour that he was going to customise the Ranchero, he was a little reserved about it, but when he saw the work done he was impressed with the result. Sometimes small modifications can be just the right medicine, like 'frenching' the headlights and cleaning off all the handles and emblems, and that's just what Mike did too. The front bumper was cleaned off its bumperhorns and rechromed together with the grill. The

TANGERINE (& White) DREAM

making the inside as pretty as the outside, and stitched up a '50s style tuck and roll in a matching orange and white. Matching carpets in orange made the interior look just right, but a cruiser has to have some 'tunes' too … so Mike installed a hidden 100watt stereo system with a CD player and speakers behind the seat.

To finish off his new cruiser, Mike installed a set of new chromed reversed 14x6 wheels with whitewall tyres, a set of lake pipes and a pair of repro Appleton bullet lights. We met Mike at the West Coast Kustoms yearly meeting in Paso Robles, California about four or five months after he bought the Ranchero, and Mike was cruisin' to some good time rock 'n roll in a pickup that's *pure* rock 'n roll itself. ∎

Fenderskirts and a 3-inch lowering job plus a set of chromed reversed wheels with whitewalls can make any '50s American car look just right. Mike also installed a set of lake-pipes and a pair of repro Appleton bullet lights. Bedcover in matching colour makes a difference too.
The headlights were 'frenched' and a new chrome rim made it look a lot better. The front bumper was stripped of the bumperettes and rechromed together with the grill.

hood goes 'the wrong way' on the '57s but that didn't stop Mike from taking it to a local hot rod shop for six rows of louvres – to let the hot air out of the engine compartment during those sizzling hot California summer days (most of the year, that is). When the bodywork basics were all done, Mike took it over to Bensen's Body & Paint, in his home town, for the finishing work and paint. The colours he wanted were orange and white, so when they looked through all the samples they came up with Persimion orange and Wimbledon white. Tom O'Connell did the spraying after they had spent plenty of hours getting the body really smooth. A '50s cruiser should have some pinstripping too, so Ralph Finley was called to do a little artistic work in orange.

The interior was stripped out of the truck before the paint, so everything got a coat of the bright orange finish inside too. Precision Auto Interiors in Vallejo took care of

Follow the fun in a Falcon Pickup

Fiberglass body lifts lightly on or off, provides sleeping room for two or more. Made expressly for the Falcon Ranchero, it takes vacation gear or business loads with equal ease.

New way to vacation...Great way to save!

**A BEAUTY FOR BUSINESS, TOO...
CAN DELIVER UP TO 30 MILES PER GALLON!**
Sends your hauling costs tumbling in every direction! Priced as much as $231* below leading conventional pickups! Can deliver up to 30 mpg! Saves up to 15% on insurance! Aluminized muffler lasts up to 3 times as long as ordinary types! See it now at your Ford Dealer's!

Add a low-cost camper body to a Ford Falcon Ranchero and you're all set. Set to head for the hills—or the beach, lake or park—on a half-hour's notice. And it's more play, less pay all the way! No reservations to make, no schedule to keep, no tickets to buy, no motel bills to pay. Any questions? Your Ford Dealer has the answers—complete information on the many sport/camper bodies now available for Ford pickups . . . and on the Falcon Ranchero, America's sportiest and savingest pickup truck!

FORD DIVISION, *Ford Motor Company*,

*Based on a comparison of latest available **manufacturers'** suggested retail delivered prices*

FOR FULL INFORMATION ABOUT TRUCK AND CAMPER-BODY MODELS . . . SEE YOUR FORD DEALER

FORD TRUCKS COST LESS

1957 RANCHERO

FORD WITH A BED IN THE BACK

by Tim Howley
photos by the author

AS time goes by, '57 Fords just look better and better to car collectors. Like the '36 and '40, the '57 has a certain something that defies time and change. Ford had 20 bodies that year, all attractive, with clean, advanced no-nonsense styling that the industry (and Ford itself) should have followed. When the year was over Ford had nearly outsold Chevrolet. Not counted in this figure was the trendsetting Ranchero sedan pickup which was turned over to the Ford Truck Division for sales. This light-duty hauler, using a 116-inch chassis and Ranch Wagon body cut down in the rear, brought about some far reaching changes in the pickup truck business.

The Ford Ranchero was a pickup in a Sunday suit. It was a sporty wagon with its top off. It was quite a departure from the simple, backroad pickups of the past, and it foretold a whole new trend in personal transportation. Not surprisingly, the Ranchero was an immediate sales success; the name and concept would last into the seventies. Now, the farmers "down east" didn't think much of its low-slung frame. This was no rig for the muddy spring roads of Vermont. Midwestern corn growers were divided in their vote. But westerners really went for it. Whether you grew peaches up in Oregon, raised grapes in California's valleys, or were retired to the desert, you could easily see yourself behind the deep-dish wheel of Ford's happy new Ranchero. Pat Boone drove one in the 1957 movie, "April Love," crooning to a giddy Shirley Jones while riding through the Kentucky bluegrass country. The Ranchero's appeal was fifties country western romantic, and the concept was as old as a Jordan Playboy with a pickup bed in the back.

During the twenties it was commonplace to cut down the rear sections of sedans for hauling, and pickup beds were frequently added to coupes and roadsters. This was nearly always done on a custom basis. To a great degree, the Ranchero was derived from the Australian Ford "Ute," short for Utility, introduced in 1932, and the earlier Model A roadster pickup (see sidebar, page 55). Between 1936 and 1948, Hudson, Terraplane, Nash and Studebaker all offered smartly styled pickups using passenger car bodies. For 1937, Chevrolet had the Expeditor coupe with a pickup box in place of a trunk. A few late thirties Buick sedans had their rear sections cut off and custom pickup beds added. Probably the most famous of these cars is the 1938 Buick Century sedan that San Francisco Buick dealer C.S. Howard had made into a smart pickup. The vehicle was used to pull the trailer of the famous race horse Seabiscuit.

Beginning in 1949, the industry turned away from pickups using passenger car bodies. In the early fifties,

gangly pickup trucks slugged along with outdated engines, solid front axles and a minimum of options. Meanwhile, cars became more stylish, powerful and comfortable, and offered an increasing list of options. The first sporty truck was the 1955-56 Chevrolet Cameo (see *SIA #43*). Still, with all its fancy trim, two-tone paint and passenger-car appointments, the Cameo remained a tall, boxy Chevrolet half-ton pickup at heart.

The true motivation behind the 1957 Ford Ranchero was the 1949 Plymouth Suburban all-steel two-door station wagon (see *SIA #72*). Up until this time, station wagons had wooden bodies and they were the most expensive cars in the line. Ford was the undisputed leader in wooden station wagon construction and sales. But production never got much beyond 30,000 due to the high initial cost and high wood-body maintenance. The low-cost 1949 Plymouth Suburban tapped into a whole new market previously unrecognized by Detroit. So successful was the Plymouth

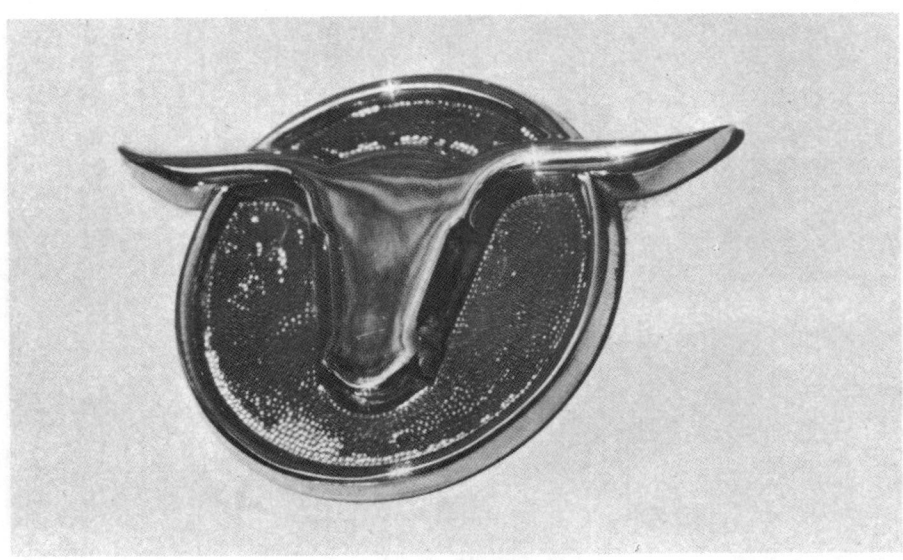

Above: Stylized steer's-head emblem appears on tailgate. Right: Wheel covers are same as '57 passenger cars. Below: Ranchero script appears at ends of rear fenders.

1957 RANCHERO

Suburban that in its first year 19,222 units were produced, nearly double that of Chevrolet. In addition, Plymouth produced 3,443 wooden-bodied wagons. Chevrolet produced 6,006 with steel body and 3,342 with wood and steel body. Plymouth enjoyed a 400 percent increase over 1948 wagon sales. 1950 Plymouth Suburban production was 34,457. In the years 1949-54, Plymouth would sell ten times as many wagons as it had sold in all the years previous to 1949. The *SIA* Plymouth Suburban report points out that by 1950 Plymouth was producing 59 percent more

station wagons than Ford, with Chevrolet coming in a poor third. This would not go unnoticed by Ford.

In 1949, Ford introduced an all-new two-door wagon as part of the 1949 Ford passenger car line. It had a steel top and steel inner body panels. Only the outer body panels and lower tailgate section were wood. It was essentially like a Plymouth Suburban with deluxe appointments and a few concessions left to the days of wood and romance. At $2,119 it was the highest priced car in the Ford line, whereas the Suburban at $1,840 was not cheap, but was perceived as being much more affordable. To complicate matters, the 1949-51 Ford wagon had the worst resale of any car in the Ford line. Ford wagon builders had to retrench.

In about 1950 Ford management had designer Gordon Buehrig working on a whole new line of all-steel wagons. Using a styling studio 1952 sedan with two doors on one side and four doors on the other, Gordon designed the 1952 wagons. The idea was to offer three different series of wagons using maximum interchangeability of parts with sedans. Buehrig came up with the two-door Ranch Wagon for the Mainline Series. This was essentially a Ford sedan delivery with a large window in each side panel. His Country Sedan was a four-door station wagon in the Customline Series. Finally, his Country Squire was an imitation woody in the Crestline Series. Like the other two, it had an all-steel body. But it had some real wood trim on the outside plus decals. Inside, it had a good old-fashioned woody look and aroma, but no wood! IN addition to these three, Buehrig designed a Ranchero type of vehicle inspired by the Australian Utes which Ford had been selling successfully down under for nearly 20 years. So Ford now had a plan to blanket the station market and dominate sales once again. Only the Ute type vehicle was delayed pending the success of the other three.

In 1952 Ford fielded the widest choice of all steel station wagons in the industry. This was a Korean War year, so production of all cars was curtailed. In 1953 Ford wagon sales leaped up to well over 100,000. 1953 production was 116,000. 1954 production was nearly 142,000. About half that figure was the Ranch Wagon, proving the popularity of that model. While the 1951 Ford wagon had the lowest resale of any car in the Ford line, the Ranch Wagon now had the highest. Ford could now clearly see a growing market for wagons in all price ranges. By appealing to this broad market, Ford became America's wagon master. Neither Plymouth or Chevrolet could keep pace with Ford wagon sales. In 1955 Chevrolet finally introduced a two-door Handyman at the low end and a fancy Nomad at the high end. Still, their 1955 wagon production dragged behind Ford by some 47,000 units. It was all of this wagon success which ultimately led to the Ranchero. Ford management viewed its introduction as one more way of penetrating deeper into the burgeoning wagon market, though, oddly enough, they turned Ranchero sales over to the Ford Truck Division.

In the 1957 Ford passenger car lineup there were 20 different models on two separate wheelbases. At the top end was the show-stopping Skyliner retractable hardtop introduced later in the model year. In the station wagon camp there were now five different models. The newest was the fancy two-door Del Rio, Ford's answer to Chevrolet's Nomad. All wagons, including the Country Squire,

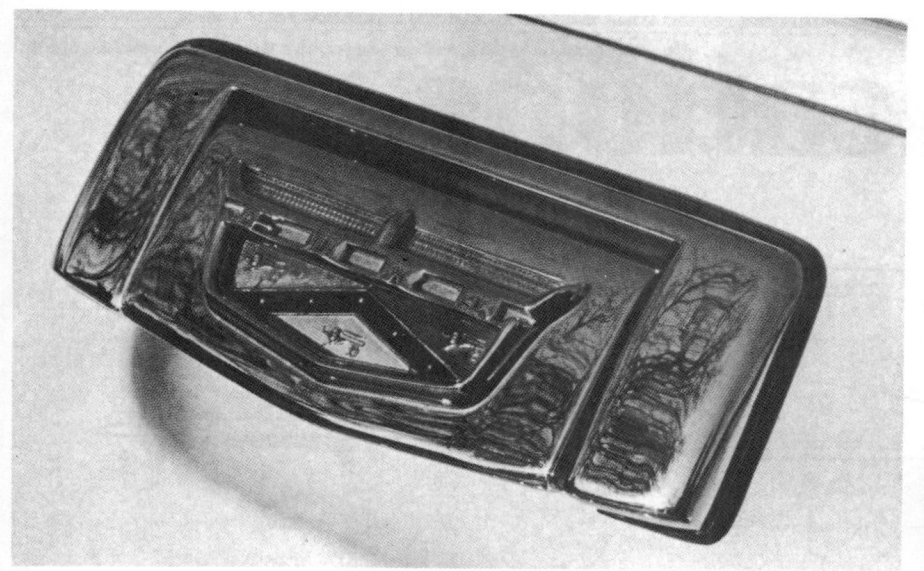

were on the shorter 116-inch wheelbase. The Ranchero, too, would be on that wheelbase. Simply stated, it would be a Ford Ranch Wagon with the roof cut off in back of the driver's compartment and a bed floor placed above the standard station wagon floor.

The 1957 Ford chassis was all new. Frame side rails were flared out in the passenger area between the front and rear wheels. This allowed for recessed wheels and a lower silhouette without sacrificing interior room. The chassis design permitted lowering the car two inches, while 14-inch wheels lowered it another two inches. This quest for a lower silhouette necessitated a change in driveshaft and rear-axle design. In addition, side rail kickup for rear axle clearance was much sharper than in the past. Kickup started 12 inches further back than in 1956, so there was a longer level section of the frame and rear seat room could be improved. Heavier stock for the frames along with tubular crossmembers made 1957 frames about 27 percent more rigid than they were in 1956. Both the 118-inch wheelbase and 116-inch wheelbase frames were nearly identical except that the 118-inch wheelbase frame was a little stronger and was five inches longer in back of the kickup.

A unique and simple variable-rate rear suspension was developed with the springs mounted almost completely outboard of the frame side rails. The semi-elliptic rear springs were lengthened from 53 to 55 inches, with most of the extra length going ahead of the rear axle. This made the section in front of the axle much stiffer than the rear section — cutting rear-end "squat" under acceleration and reducing nose-dives in hard stops. Also, special rubber bumpers were added to the frame side rails midway between the front supports for the rear spring and axle. This limited spring deflection under heavy load and rough road conditions; in effect, this reduced spring length and stiffened the spring action — thus producing a variable rate characteristic. The station wagons and Ranchero differed from the standard rear suspension only in that they had five spring leaves instead of four.

A redesigned ball-joint front suspension had single-unit upper and lower arm construction. Hinged with live rubber bushings, these arms were swept back in a modified trailing arm manner. Wheel motion was directed upward and rearward which, in effect, caused the wheel to be pulled rather than pushed over a bump.

All of the 1957 engines had increased horsepower from a higher compression ratio and improved manifold and valve design. The intake manifolds on the

Ford Utes: Dinkum Aussie Workhorse

The "Ute" is the granddaddy of the Ranchero, and was introduced by Ford in Australia in 1932. The economy of Australia in the thirties was as harsh as the land. Few farmers could afford an automobile and a truck, therefore a combination of both had a special economic appeal. The first "Ute," short for "Utility," was a 1932 Australian Ford roadster with the body section removed just behind the doors. It was replaced with a steel utility box set flush with the doors. According to the story, an Australian farmer inspired the Ute when he suggested to the Ford plant at Geelong that they build a vehicle which would have the front of a coupe and the back of a truck.

So successful were Ute sales during that Depression year that Ford added a coupe Ute in 1933. The coupe looked rather like a five-window Ford coupe of the era except that the rear quarter windows were a little smaller. While the coupe was not nearly as stylish as the roadster, it was a darn sight more practical under the searing outback sun. Both versions carried an optional leatherette tonneau cover that snapped on the box top edges. The spare was carried outboard on the left side just below the rear quarter window 1935-39 and behind the front seat from 1940 on. The smartest looking Utes are the 1932-34 models with the spare carried in the left front fender well.

The roadster was carried through 1938 only, but the coupe version was continued through 1956, those postwar years being rather stylish in their own special way. The Ford Utes were not without competition. Both Chevrolet and Dodge offered Australian market coupe Utes beginning in 1936, but the Fords were always the most popular. Beginning with the 1957 model, the Utes became merely right-wheel-drive versions of the Rancheros, but they were still called Utes through 1959. The Australian Utes lived a rugged life, and very few survive today. Those that have survived are highly prized by Australian collectors and are even more prized in the United States. Probably the rarest is the 1937 roadster.

specifications

Illustrations by Russell von Sauers, The Graphic Automobile Studio

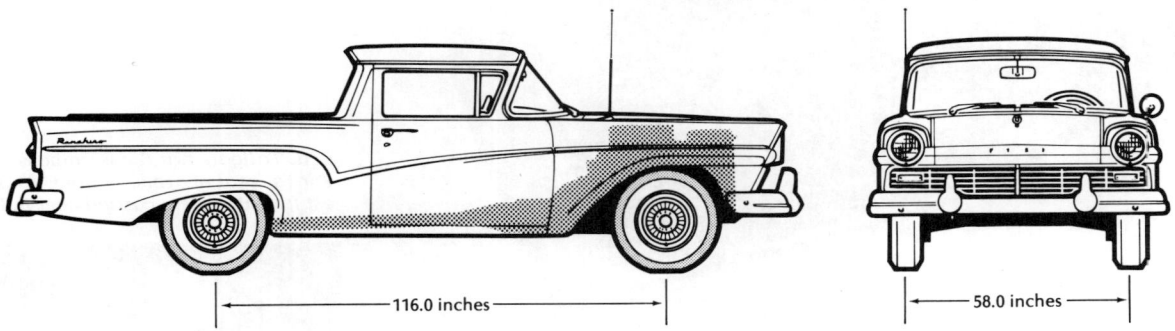

116.0 inches   58.0 inches

1957 Ford Custom Ranchero

Price	$1,920 f.o.b.
Options	Fordomatic transmission, radio

ENGINE

Type	Ohv V-8
Bore & stroke	3.75 x 3.30 inches
Displacement	292 cubic inches
Max bhp @ rpm	212 @ 4,500
Max torque @ rpm	297 @ 2,400
Compression ratio	9.1:1
Induction system	2-barrel carburetor
Exhaust system	Cast iron manifolds, dual exhausts
Electrical system	12-volt battery/coil

TRANSMISSION

Type	Fordomatic 2-speed automatic planetary torque converter

DIFFERENTIAL

Type	Hypoid, semi-floating
Ratio	3.10:1
Drive axles	Hotchkiss drive with outboard mounted leaf springs

STEERING

Type	Worm and triple-tooth gear
Turns lock to lock	4.5
Ratio	27:1
Turn circle	40 feet

BRAKES

Type	4-wheel hydraulic drum
Drum diameter	11 inches
Total swept area	191 square inches

CHASSIS & BODY

Frame	Flared box section side rails; 5 crossmembers, 3 are tubular
Body construction	All steel
Body style	Ranchero

SUSPENSION

Front	Independent ball-joint with stabilizer bar and airplane-type shock absorbers
Rear	Five-leaf semi-elliptic springs with diagonally mounted shock absorbers
Tires	8.00 x 14
Wheels	5.50 x 14 stamped steel, 5-bolt

WEIGHTS AND MEASURES

Wheelbase	116 inches
Overall length	202 inches
Overall height	57.2 inches
Overall width	77 inches
Front tread	58 inches
Rear tread	58 inches
Ground clearance	7.5 inches

CAPACITIES

Crankcase	5.0 quarts
Cooling system	21.0 quarts
Fuel tank	18.5 gallons

FUEL CONSUMPTION

Best	18 mpg
Average	14 mpg

Marque Club Address
Fabulous Fifties Ford Club of America
Box 286
Riverside, California 92502

Rancheros could be ordered with anything from a 144-horse six to a 245-horse V-8; driveReport Ranchero is powered by popular 292 V-8.

1957 RANCHERO

V-8s were opened up in true competition style. The valve area was increased considerably and the camshaft was redesigned for higher valve lift. The air cleaner went from an oil bath to an air filter type, and its new silhouette design cut restriction in half for better breathing. Carburetors were also a new low silhouette design. A new two-barrel carburetor had more venturi area than the '56 four-barrels and theoretically gave better fuel atomization and distribution. New distributors had a combined centrifugal-vacuum mechanism in place of the former full-vacuum, another boost for performance.

The engines offered were an ohv six at 144 horsepower, the 272 ohv V-8 now at 190 horsepower, and the 292 V-8 now

*Above: With tailgate down, Ranchero has over 32 feet of hauling area. **Left:** With 'gate closed rearend styling is tidy. **Below:** Gas filler cap lives behind door in left fender.*

at 212 horsepower. Both the V-8s had the new two-barrel carburetor. The big Thunderbird 312 V-8 had four barrels and was rated at 245 horsepower. On the 272 and 292, the familiar crossover pipe of previous years was dropped in favor of a Y-type system. In this design the pipes run from the rear of both exhaust manifolds and join just ahead of the muffler. The 312 had a dual exhaust system as standard equipment. Any Ford engine could be chosen for the Ranchero. These engines could be combined with three-speed forward manual transmission with or without optional overdrive or the dependable but jerky two-speed Fordomatic. 1957 Fordomatics were water-cooled for the first time. Cruis-O-Matic would not be available until 1958.

From a design standpoint the '57 Fords were rather spectacular for their time, and the Ranchero is as handsome as any of them. (For the complete 1957 Ford story see *SIA #64*) With the '57 model, Ford originated a long-term styling theme that can be traced all the way to 1964. Those primarily respon-

sible for designing the '57 were Bill Boyer, Damon Woods, Frank Hershey, Bob McGuire, Chuck Mashigan, A.J. Middlestead and L. David Ash. Pulling the '57 together ultimately became a $200 million project keynoted by the longest, lowest Fords to date and the biggest Ford change between 1949 and 1965. These cars sacrificed no interior room and achieved new highs in style and luxury previously unavailable in the Ford price range.

The '57 Ford's sculptured styling was made possible by technological advances in body stamping. Until that time, automakers were unable to stamp sharp edges or creases in large panels of sheet metal without having them break. As beautiful as the '57 was, its body sculpturing problems were never completely solved, and this led to early rust-out. It would be another couple of years before the industry could really sculpt body panels on a mass production basis without a high rejection rate or panel weaknesses which showed up later. Being essentially a '57 Ford wagon, the

Ranchero shared all the '57 Ford's weaknesses and strengths.

The Ranchero was offered in two series — Standard and Custom. The Standard was quite Spartan. But the Custom carried a chrome side spear, dual sun visors, horn ring, full custom door panels and seat and wheel covers. The reflective side trim often seen on 1957 Rancheros today was never applied at the factory. This was a dealer item until 1958. The Custom had bright metal trim framing the rear window and sweeping down at both sides to con-

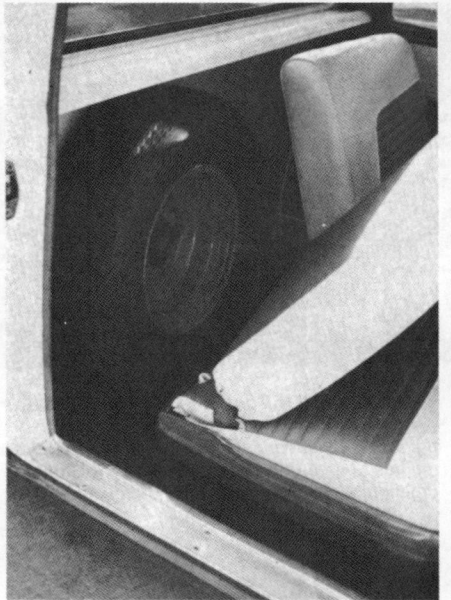

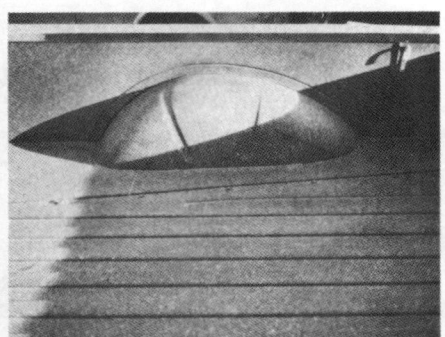

1957 RANCHERO

tinue around the upper edge of the bed. After market equipment makers were quick to fashion chrome guardrails for the bed and tonneau covers for security.

The Ranchero's spare tire was mounted in the area behind the seat, although many owners later put it in the rear where it was placed in the wagons. The entire Ranchero subfloor was a station wagon floor covered by the bed floor. This bed floor was bolted down so it could be easily removed for subfloor access. By hinging part of this floor the owner could put the spare in the rear where it belonged and have some luggage room in back of the seat.

The Ranchero had 32.4 feet of hauling area, not even as much as today's small pickup longbeds. The tailgate was simply the lower section of a '57 wagon tailgate. It had a latch containing the Ford logo and below this is a chrome steer's head, the Ranchero emblem.

The Ranchero did not come out with the entire Ford line in October 1957. It made its debut at the National Automobile Show which opened at the New York Coliseum on December 8, and it caused a great deal of excitement in the trade. The competition simply was unprepared for such a Ford offering. By mid-1957 the Dodge Truck Division cobbled

station wagon rear fenders onto a Model 100 pickup and called it the "Sweptside 100." In 1959 Chevrolet gave pursuit with their El Camino (see *SIA* #82). But for 1957 and 1958 the Ranchero had its corner of the market all to itself.

The 1958 Ranchero shared the ugly duckling 1958 Ford facelift which so unsuccessfully copied the Thunderbird. In 1959 the Standard Ranchero was dropped and only the Custom remained. Like all 1959 Fords it was offered on a 118-inch wheelbase only. For 1960 the Ranchero was moved over into the Falcon line where it continued to be a sales success. After 1966 it became a part of the intermediate-sized Fairlane Series and grew increasingly luxurious and powerful with XL and GT variations. By the end of the decade, sales for all pickups of this type were on the decline. There was now increasing competition from sporty Japanese pickups, vans and four-wheel-drives and a resulting decline in the market for wagons and pickups based on sedan bodies.

Driving Impressions

Our driveReport car is a '57 Custom Ranchero owned by Gene Hoerner of Tustin, California. This is a solid, 115,000-mile car which has been given a complete restoration and looks and drives like factory new. It has a 292 V-8 with Fordomatic, but lacks power steering and power brakes. Hoerner points out that while Rancheros are fairly easy

to find, good ones are not. Most of them, he says, are either rusted out or otherwise worn out beyond restoration. This particular one was a car worth restoring, he says.

We found the Ranchero rode nearly as soft as any '57 Ford despite its stiffer wagon springing. The ride is quiet and comfortable with body noises very effectively dampened by the extensive use of live rubber mounts. Having owned both the 116-inch and 118-inch wheelbase models in the past, I have found there is a noticeable difference. The smaller model rides every bit as well as the bigger model but handles better and parks easier.

On any '57, you will really notice the four-inch-lower center of gravity over the older Fords. Tom McCahill wrote of his 1957 Fairlane 500 test in *Mechanix Illustrated*, "I found the '57 cornering as flat as a mailman's feet and in real competition style. The front wheels bit and seemed to make a furrow for the rear wheels to follow, without the slightest trace of breakaway, even when I came close to rolling it a few times." But he complained about the low road clearance and was especially critical of the 14-inch wheels. To quote Uncle Tom, "Driving these super underslungs over farm paths or secondary roads with high crowns will cause more oil to be spilled than the torpedoing of an Esso tanker. Besides, worms are a very important part of farming, and worms stand to be decapitated by the millions this year." It seems that old Tom's cryptic comments would be especially applicable to the Ranchero.

Motor Trend's Walt Woron had this to say about a '57 Ford Ranchero tested on a weekend trip between Los Angeles and Apple Valley, near Victorville in the Mojave Desert: "In city driving, you'll have better vision than in most cars, though not as good as in ordinary pickups because of the advantage the latter have in their greater height. With the back of the cab close to you, and the large rear window to see out of, it's almost as if you could touch everything behind you.

"Over the road you can cruise as quickly and easily as in any car. Bad dips on desert roads that come up unexpectedly won't make the Ranchero misbehave. When encountering sudden bends in the road or when driving continuously through winding, hilly country, you won't have to back off for fear of leaving the road; its attitude in turns, including the small amount of body lean, is remarkably good. It seems a shame though that it takes almost five turns lock to lock, less turns would mean less work and a more positive feel.

"On the way back from the Apple Valley Inn, where I guested for the weekend, I stopped for some firewood and a trial of the Ranchero with a load. Up to just slightly over the side rails made about one-third cord, or some 700 pounds of extra weight. From the wood yard I drove over roads where asphalt was chewed out in big bitefuls, over dirt washboards that would shake out any loose fittings, and over other roads that are reminiscent of a roller coaster. On all of these roads the Ranchero's behavior was better than when it was unloaded. With the added weight it hugged the road closer and took some of the float out of the ride. Over washboard it stayed in line; empty at speeds above 30 mph, the rear end would begin to come around."

We did not feel that the rear end felt light at all, even with the bed completely empty. Nor did the rear end tend to slide in panic stops. The vehicle seemed to always be under strong, positive control. Wish we could say the same for Granadas. We found the steering quite effortless despite lack of power assist. But we heartily agree with Woron that it takes too many turns lock to lock. What

really amazed us is how well the Ranchero stays glued to the road. Body lean is very modest. There is some oversteer, but it is not bothersome. For a 28-year-old pickup this one stacks up remarkably well against today's imports.

We did not try the 0-60 test. Here's what McCahill found in 1957: "The performance of this 292 (Fairlane hardtop with Fordomatic) two barrel job was certainly adequate though not much more exciting than a good reproduction of Whistler's Mother." Zero to 60 mph averaged 12.1 seconds. The lighter weight Ranchero should easily be able to crack 10 seconds with a stick, and in proper tune should run up to a top speed of about 110 mph.

The Things They Said
1957 Ford Ranchero

Hot Rod Magazine, July 1957
"One interesting comparison between the Ranchero and the ½-ton pickup is that with station wagon springs, the Ranchero is sprung slightly heavier both front and rear than the pickup. In other words, the Ranchero is equipped to handle a heavier load than the F-100 pickup."

Compiled by R. Perry Zavitz

Below: Seating is low and wide, with plenty of room to slide around on vinyl upholstery. **Bottom:** *Nicely balanced instrument panel with sweep-arc speedometer.*

The '57 Ford has been justly criticized for poor workmanship. It was one of Ford's all time rustbuckets, especially up around the headlights. Rarely will you see a rusty '57 in California, and in ensuing years we can think of a lot of others that have been just as prone to rust. This particular '57 was solid, tight and appeared extremely well constructed. We can only conclude that the poor quality complaint many '57 owners had originally was in the fit and finish. This fine restoration only testifies to the basic soundness of the car's design and construction. Ford's problems in '57 had to be getting quality from the drawing boards and onto the assembly lines on Monday mornings and Friday afternoons. Basically, the '57 is a hard Ford to fault.

Twenty-eight years ago Tom McCahill summed it up this way: "The '57 Ford is a great new car and as rugged as an Irish riot in a Russian saloon. It's as sound an investment as an 'E' bond, and Ford won't be sending your money to Southeast Lapvania. If you like it, buy it — you won't go wrong." Good words of advice for a collector, even today. □

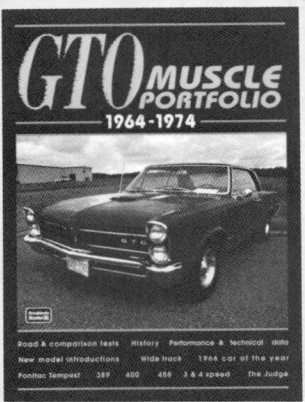
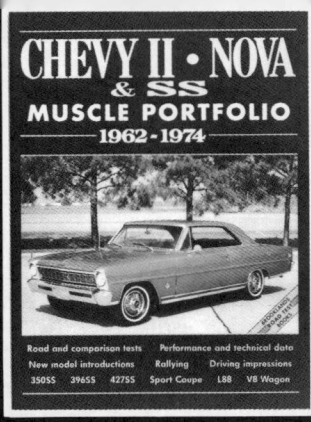
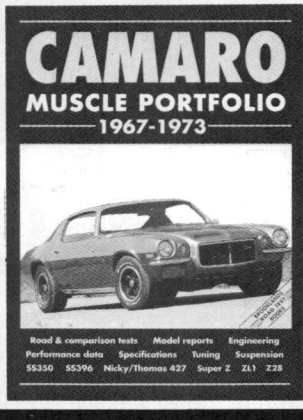
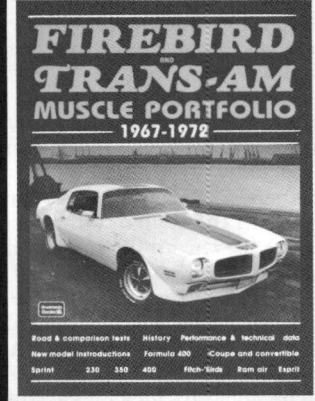
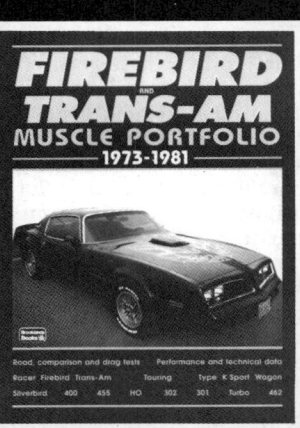

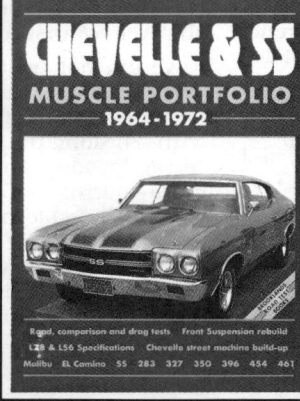
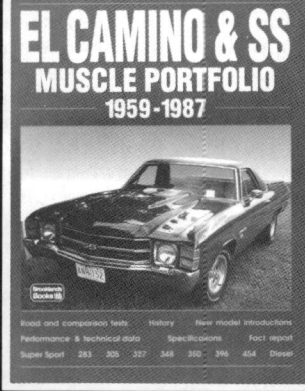
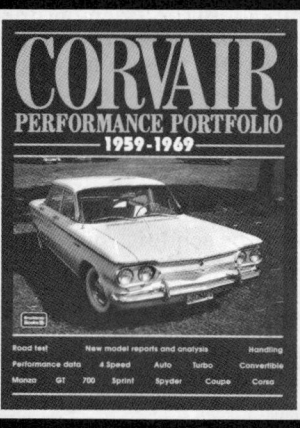

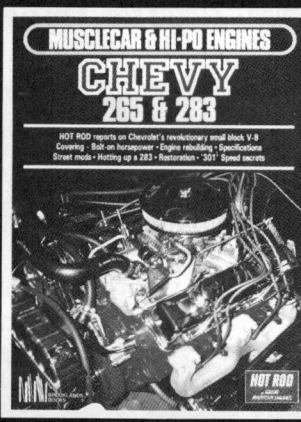

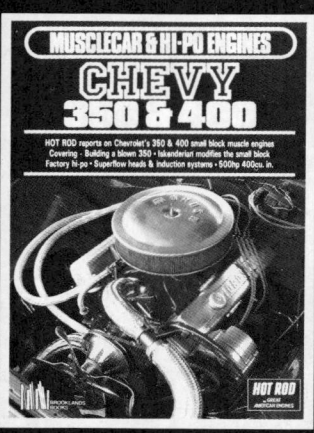